The Constitutional Origins of the American Revolution

Using the British Empire as a case study, this succinct study argues that the establishment of overseas settlements in America created a problem of constitutional organization that elicited deep and persistent tensions within the empire during the colonial era and that the failure to resolve it was the principal element in the decision of thirteen continental colonies to secede from the empire in 1776. Challenging those historians who have assumed that the British had the law on their side during the debates that led to the American Revolution, this volume argues that the empire had long exhibited a high degree of constitutional multiplicity, with each colony having its own discrete constitution and the empire as a whole having an uncodified working customary constitution that determined the way authority was distributed within the empire. Contending that these constitutions cannot be conflated with the metropolitan British constitution, it argues that British refusal to accept the legitimacy of colonial understandings of the sanctity of the many colonial constitutions and the imperial constitution was the critical element leading to the American Revolution.

Jack P. Greene taught at Michigan State University, Western Reserve University, and the University of Michigan before he moved in 1966 to Johns Hopkins University, where he was a member of the Department of History for thirty-nine years, except for two years spent at the University of California, Irvine in 1990–2. A specialist in the history of Colonial British and Revolutionary American history, he has published and edited many books, chapters in books, articles, and reviews. Perhaps his best-known works are *The Quest for Power: The Lower Houses of Assembly in the Southern Royal Colonies, 1689–1776* (1963), *Peripheries and Center: Constitutional Development in the Extended Polities of the British Empire and the United States, 1607–1789* (1986), *Pursuits of Happiness: The Social Development of the Early Modern British Colonies and the Formation of American Culture* (1988), and *The Intellectual Construction of America: Exceptionalism and Identity from 1492 to 1800* (1993).

New Histories of American Law

Series Editors

Michael Grossberg, *Indiana University*
Christopher L. Tomlins, *University of California–Irvine*

New Histories of American Law is a series of bold, synthetic, and path-breaking interpretive books that will address the key topics in the field of American legal history, written by the leaders of the field and designed for scholars and students throughout universities, colleges, and law schools.

Other Books in the Series:

Barbara Young Welke, *Law and the Borders of Belonging in the Long Nineteenth Century United States*

The Constitutional Origins
of the American Revolution

JACK P. GREENE
Johns Hopkins University

CAMBRIDGE
UNIVERSITY PRESS

CAMBRIDGE UNIVERSITY PRESS
Cambridge, New York, Melbourne, Madrid, Cape Town,
Singapore, São Paulo, Delhi, Mexico City

Cambridge University Press
32 Avenue of the Americas, New York, NY 10013-2473, USA

www.cambridge.org
Information on this title: www.cambridge.org/9780521132305

First published 2011
Reprinted 2011 (twice), 2012

A catalog record for this publication is available from the British Library.

Library of Congress Cataloging in Publication Data

Greene, Jack P.
The Constitutional Origins of the American
Revolution / Jack P. Greene.
    p.   cm. – (New histories of American law)
Includes index.
ISBN 978-0-521-76093-5 (hardback)
ISBN 978-0-521-13230-5 (pbk.)
  1. Constitutional history – United States – States.   2. Constitutional
history – Great Britain – Colonies.   3. Constitutional history – Great
Britain.   4. United States – History – Revolution, 1775–1783.
5. United States – Politics and government – To 1775.
6. United States – Politics and government – 1775–1783.
7. Great Britain – Colonies – America – History.   I. Title.
II. Series.
KF4541.G743   2010
342.7302′9–dc22   2010030377

ISBN 978-0-521-76093-5 Hardback
ISBN 978-0-521-13230-5 Paperback

CONTENTS

PREFACE

As the title announces, this is a book about the constitutional origins of the American Revolution as they were reflected in the unfolding debate over the distribution of authority within the British Empire during the late colonial era and the years of imperial crisis from 1764 to 1776. This subject has been of recurrent interest to me for almost sixty years. Through most of the 1950s and early 1960s, I was hard at work trying to sort out the institutional, constitutional, and theoretical dimensions of the development of representative government in four early modern British American colonies between the Glorious Revolution and the American Revolution. Among other things, I was endeavoring to understand the bearing of that development on the controversy that produced the American Revolution. Briefly put, the argument I developed about the Revolution had two main points. The first was that the new British taxation and coercive measures after 1748, some emanating from the Crown and some from Parliament, represented a formidable challenge both to the customary constitutions that the colonies, severally, had been working out for themselves over the previous century or longer and to the thoroughly English rights and principles that those constitutions had been constructed to preserve. The second was that colonial responses to that challenge, responses that drew heavily on the colonists' own customary constitutions, articulated a conception of the imperial constitution that diverged sharply from the one held at the imperial center, and that this disagreement over the nature of the imperial constitution had an important causal bearing on the American Revolution.

When I finally began to publish this work in the late 1950s and early 1960s,[1] few scholars of the origins of the Revolution paid much attention to this particular argument. Concerned principally with showing the many deficiencies of the Progressive interpretation of the Revolution as the product of internal conflict, a view that had enjoyed a brief vogue in the 1930s and 1940s, most students of the Revolution focused on analyzing the *ostensible* issues that divided metropolitans and colonials between 1763 and 1776 and manifested little concern with exploring the political and constitutional traditions or the patterns of assumptions that underlay and informed that division. When, in the late 1960s, Bernard Bailyn and others did begin to explore those traditions and assumptions in depth, they assigned little causative weight to the specifically constitutional dimensions of the conflict. In Bailyn's *ideological* interpretation of the Revolution, neither the early modern English jurisprudential tradition of political writing nor the related liberal and Whig traditions that had been largely constructed on that jurisprudential tradition received much emphasis, especially not in comparison with the fears of corruption and ministerial power that, for Bailyn, principally informed colonial protests of the pre-Revolutionary era.[2] The force of my protest that throughout the era before 1763 colonial legislators and polemicists had been infinitely more concerned about limiting prerogative than about preventing corruption was, it seemed to me, mostly lost on a historical community that was rushing to absorb and work out the implications of Bailyn's ideological interpretation.[3]

When I returned to the subject in the early 1980s, I discovered that over the previous decade few scholars had

---

[1] Summarized in Jack P. Greene, *The Quest for Power: The Lower Houses of Assembly in the Southern Royal Colonies, 1689–1776* (Chapel Hill: University of North Carolina Press, 1963).

[2] Bernard Bailyn, *The Ideological Origins of the American Revolution* (Cambridge, Mass.: Harvard University Press, 1967).

[3] Jack P. Greene, "Political Mimesis: A Consideration of the Historical and Cultural Roots of Legislative Behavior in the British Colonies in the Eighteenth Century," *American Historical Review*, 75 (1969): 337–67.

concerned themselves with the classic question of the causes of the American Revolution or with the years leading up to the War for Independence. Evidently, the Bailyn paradigm had closed off serious discussion in that direction. Beginning in the early 1970s, interest in the Revolution among historians and, increasingly, political theorists had turned to the years *after* independence and to the problem of working out the powerful contentions of John Pocock,[4] built mainly on his reading of Bailyn and Gordon Wood,[5] about the vitality of civic humanist political traditions and the limited relevance of Lockean liberalism among post-independence American political cultures.

Indeed, insofar as I could tell, when I did a survey of the literature in 1983 and 1984, only three scholars had sought to reopen for serious scholarly discussion the question of the origins of the American Revolution. Two of them were the political scientists Robert W. Tucker and David C. Hendrickson, whose 1982 book, *The Fall of the First British Empire: Origins of the American War for Independence*, offered a high Tory account that, in essence, saw the Revolution as the product of a drive for American nationalism.[6] The third was the lawyer John Phillip Reid, who had published three monographs and at least a dozen articles on the legal dimensions of the contest between metropolis and colonies between 1763 and 1776.[7] My reaction to these two sets of work, the one by Tucker

[4] J. G. A. Pocock, *The Machiavellian Moment: Florentine Political Thought and the Atlantic Republican Tradition* (Princeton: Princeton University Press, 1975).

[5] Gordon S. Wood, *The Creation of the American Republic 1776–1787* (Chapel Hill: University of North Carolina Press, 1969).

[6] Robert W. Tucker and David C. Hendrickson, *The Fall of the First British Empire: Origins of the American War for Independence* (Baltimore: Johns Hopkins University Press, 1982).

[7] The books by John Phillip Reid are *In a Defiant Stance: The Conditions of Law in Massachusetts Bay, the Irish Comparison, and the Coming of the American Revolution* (University Park: Pennsylvania State University Press, 1977); *In a Rebellious Spirit: The Argument of Facts, the Liberty Riot, and the Coming of the American Revolution* (University Park: Pennsylvania State University Press, 1979); and *In Defiance of the Law: The Standing-Army Controversy, the Two Constitutions, and the Coming of the American Revolution* (Chapel Hill: University of North Carolina Press, 1981).

and Hendrickson and the other by Reid, could scarcely have been more different. Whereas I found the former analytically impressive but largely unpersuasive, Reid's work struck me as being of fundamental importance. Never having accepted Bailyn's contention that the American Revolution's sufficient cause was colonial absorption of opposition ideology,[8] I found in Reid's work effective support for my long-standing contention that, to a very important degree, the American Revolution had derived out of a disagreement over the nature of the constitution of the British Empire.

To my surprise, a quick survey of the review sections of the major historical journals revealed little appreciation of the importance of Reid's work. Some journals that should have reviewed any work on the American Revolution had not reviewed his, and those that did review his work seem mostly to have assigned his books to people who, for whatever reasons – whether they were incapable of breaking out of the Bailyn paradigm, resented Reid's sometimes acerbic criticism of historians (which, as historians continued to ignore his work, became increasingly strident), or simply found his *legal* perspective uncongenial – failed to comprehend the salience of his findings. Both because I thought that Reid had an enormous amount to teach historians about the Revolution and because I myself needed to master his and other legal historians' work in connection with the book I was then writing on the constitutional development of the early modern British Empire, I wrote an article, entitled "From the Perspective of Law: Context and Legitimacy in the Origins of the American Revolution," published in 1986 in the *South Atlantic Quarterly*, in which I endeavored to translate for historians the works of Reid and other legal scholars, including Barbara Black, Thomas Grey, Hendrik Hartog, and William Nelson, on the origins of the American Revolution.[9]

---

[8] In Bernard Bailyn, *The Origins of American Politics* (New York: Alfred Knopf, 1968).

[9] Jack P. Greene, "From the Perspective of Law: Context and Legitimacy in the Origins of the American Revolution," *South Atlantic Quarterly*, 75 (1986): 56–77.

In this highly appreciative translation, I pointed to a whole series of insights that, in my view, both called into question the adequacy of the reigning paradigm and constituted a powerful reinterpretation of the pre-Revolutionary controversy. These insights included (1) the centrality of legal and constitutional concerns in the politics of pre-Revolutionary America; (2) the disputants' law-mindedness and constitution-mindedness and the legal and constitutional nature of the argument; (3) the anachronism during the Revolutionary era of considering law as nothing but the command of the sovereign; (4) the continuing vitality in Britain itself of the jurisprudential conception of English government as limited government and of the English (British) constitution as a constitution in which law confined the discretion or will of monarchs, ministers, judges, and legislators; (5) the consensual nature of law throughout the English-speaking world; (6) the contractual basis of English – and, of course, colonial – legal and constitutional thought; (7) the fundamental and continuing importance of the doctrine of usage in British legal and constitutional thought; (8) the bicentric character of law within the early modern British Empire, specifically the distinction between what Reid called imperial law and local law; (9) the relative weakness of imperial law in the colonies; (10) the strength of local law and of local control over that law, in that whichever settler groups controlled the colony controlled the law; (11) the indeterminancy of the imperial constitution; and (12) the legitimacy, that is, the quintessential Englishness, of American constitutional arguments in the pre-Revolutionary debates.

Not all of these points were new, but no one, it seemed to me, had explored them as fully or argued them as cogently as Reid and his fellow legal historians had, in the impressive and substantial body of literature that they produced during the decade after 1975, a literature that few historians seemed to read and even fewer to appreciate. For this historian, however, their findings were extraordinarily resonant and useful. They formed a parallel and much more legally informed literature that, explicitly or implicitly, supported, informed, and amplified six points that I wanted to make in my 1986 book *Peripheries and Center*, a study of the constitutional development of the early modern English or, after 1707, British Empire and the influence of that development on the federal system created for the new United States in 1787–8: (1) that, in operational terms, that empire was a consensual empire; (2) that authority within it was not concentrated at the center but dispersed among the center and the peripheries; (3) that authority did not flow downward or outward from the center but was negotiated among the center and the peripheries; (4) that effective authority in the peripheries was local; (5) that both the many colonial constitutions and the emerging imperial constitution rested on a customary base (i.e., that custom was the most accurate guide to what these constitutions were); and (6) that the American Revolution *principally* resulted from a dispute over the nature of the constitution of the British Empire, a dispute in which both sides had a legitimate case.[10]

Yet, *Peripheries and Center* also departed significantly from Reid's and his colleagues' work. Whereas Reid was content to characterize the argument as a debate over two competing views of the British constitution, an older view emphasizing customary restraints on political institutions and a newer Blackstonian view stressing the omnipotence of the Crown in Parliament, I carefully distinguished the metropolitan British constitution from the constitutions of each of the several colonial polities, on the one hand, and from an implicit emerging imperial constitution, on the other. Even though all these "British" constitutions drew on the same legal principles, I argued, neither the colonial constitutions nor the imperial constitution could be conflated with the constitution of the home island, or metropolis, as earlier historians had supposed.

And there were other significant differences between Reid's position and mine. In my view, Reid had made a false contrast between the colonies and Ireland; ignored the extent to which

[10] Jack P. Greene, *Peripheries and Center: Constitutional Development in the Extended Polities of the British Empire and the United States, 1607–1788* (Athens: University of Georgia Press, 1986).

nonrevolting British colonies in North America, the West Indies, and the Atlantic islands shared the constitutional ideas of the revolting colonies; and completely neglected the specifically colonial roots of colonial legal and constitutional arguments of the 1760s and 1770s. Peter N. Miller, in his book, *Defining the Common Good*,[11] may be right to suggest that metropolitan thinkers only began to think systematically about the nature and constitutional structure of the empire in the late 1740s and early 1750s, but colonists throughout the empire had been considering such matters almost from the first days of colonization, had produced a rich and extensive body of literature on the subject, and had built a solid and thoroughly internalized political tradition on which writers in the 1760s and 1770s could draw.[12] A consideration of the similarities of the constitutional and legal ideas of the Protestant ascendancy in Ireland, the earlier generations of colonists throughout the empire, and the spokesmen for nonrevolting colonies in the 1760s and 1770s, I argued in *Peripheries and Center*, considerably strengthened the broad general case I was trying to make.

Moreover, if, in its stress on the colonial emphasis on custom in formulating their constitutional arguments and the legitimacy of those arguments, *Peripheries and Center* reinforced and paralleled Reid's arguments as they had developed by the mid-1980s, it also moved beyond those arguments to make a number of important interpretive points that significantly challenged existing accounts of the origins of the Revolution. More specifically, the book emphasized Grenville's uncertainty over the constitutionality of the Stamp Act when he initially proposed it; the breadth of colonial opposition to the Stamp Act in 1764 and

---

[11] Peter N. Miller, *Defining the Common Good: Empire, Religion and Philosophy in Eighteenth-Century Britain* (Cambridge: Cambridge University Press, 1994), 195–213.

[12] Craig B. Yirush, "From the Perspective of Empire: The Common Law, Natural Rights and the Construction of American Political Culture, 1689–1774," unpublished doctoral dissertation, Johns Hopkins University, 2003, provides the fullest and most penetrating study of colonial British American political thought.

1765, which extended not just to taxation but to legislation relating to the internal polities of the colonies; the strength of the conciliatory thrust on both sides of the Atlantic during the quarrel over the Townshend Acts and its immediate aftermath; and the colonial resistance to defining the controversy in terms of metropolitan conceptions of sovereignty as indivisible.

Over the two decades since the publication of *Peripheries and Center*, few students of the American Revolution have revisited the question of the origins of the Revolution, the principal exceptions being Eliga H. Gould,[13] P. J. Marshall,[14] and Reid. Focusing on the broader European and imperial context over the entire period from 1750 to the end of the Revolution in 1783, both Gould and Marshall acutely place the intraimperial debate of the 1760s and 1770s in a larger international and imperial perspective, but neither of them is principally concerned with constitutional issues. By contrast, Reid has published nine further volumes on these issues: two on the concepts of liberty[15] and representation,[16] published by the University of Chicago Press in 1988 and 1989: four on the principal issues of rights,[17] taxation,[18] legislation,[19] and law,[20] published by the University of Wisconsin Press between 1986 and 1993 as

[13] Eliga H. Gould, *The Persistence of Empire: British Political Culture in the Age of the American Revolution* (Chapel Hill: University of North Carolina Press, 2000).

[14] P. J. Marshall, *The Making and Unmaking of Empires: Britain, India, and America c. 1750–1783* (Oxford: Oxford University Press, 2005).

[15] John Phillip Reid, *The Concept of Liberty in the Age of the American Revolution* (Chicago: University of Chicago Press, 1988).

[16] John Phillip Reid, *The Concept of Representation in the Age of the American Revolution* (Chicago: University of Chicago Press, 1989).

[17] John Phillip Reid, *Constitutional History of the American Revolution: The Authority of Rights* (Madison: University of Wisconsin Press, 1986).

[18] John Phillip Reid, *Constitutional History of the American Revolution: The Authority to Tax* (Madison: University of Wisconsin Press, 1987).

[19] John Phillip Reid, *Constitutional History of the American Revolution: The Authority to Legislate* (Madison: University of Wisconsin Press, 1991).

[20] John Phillip Reid, *Constitutional History of the American Revolution: The Authority of Law* (Madison: University of Wisconsin Press, 1993).

the *Constitutional History of the American Revolution,* with
a one-volume abridged version published by the same press in
1995,[21] and two on the English concepts of the rule of law[22]
and the ancient constitution,[23] published by the Northern
Illinois University Press in 2004 and 2005– all together more
than 2,500 pages of text and supporting materials!

This truly monumental body of post-1986 work makes
three general contributions to our understanding of the origins of the Revolution. First, as an aggressive advocate for
working out and paying close attention to the contemporary
meaning of words, Reid has thoroughly deconstructed key
concepts in late eighteenth-century British–American discourse: constitution, law, sovereignty, liberty, slavery, arbitrary rights, rule of law, custom, precedent, analogy, consent,
representation, property, and contract, among others. More
deeply than any previous scholar, this inveterate foe of anachronism has dissected such terms and convincingly elaborated
the ways they were understood by participants in the pre-
Revolutionary debates. This achievement alone makes Reid's
work fundamental to the understanding of the Revolutionary
era. No serious scholar of that era can possibly ignore this
aspect of his work.

Second, Reid richly elaborates on, expands, and gives
added cogency to many of the more significant points that
he made about the Revolution in his pre-1986 work. Thus,
he persuasively reiterates his observation about the extent to
which "the revolutionary controversy was conducted like a
common-law litigation even though there was no tribunal
to which the parties could appeal except the court of public opinion."[24] Considerably more fully and persuasively, he

[21] John Phillip Reid, *Constitutional History of the American Revolution: Abridged Edition* (Madison: University of Wisconsin Press, 1995).

[22] John Phillip Reid, *Rule of Law: The Jurisprudence of Liberty in the Seventeenth and Eighteenth Centuries* (DeKalb: Northern Illinois University Press, 2004).

[23] John Phillip Reid, *The Ancient Constitution and the Origins of Anglo-American Liberty* (DeKalb: Northern Illinois University Press, 2005).

[24] Reid, *Constitutional History of the American Revolution: Abridged Edition,* 34.

emphasizes the pervasiveness of a common culture of constitutionalism that made the entire transatlantic English-speaking
world into a single discursive community with a common
vocabulary, if not always a common definition of crucial concepts within that vocabulary. Similarly, he greatly adds to his
cases for (1) the centrality of rights and the rule of law in the
pre-Revolutionary controversy; (2) the legitimacy of the colonists' insistence that their rights as Britons dictated that they
not be governed by laws without their consent and, moreover, of their demand for restraints on Parliamentary power
(as Reid puts it, in the colonists' view Parliamentary supremacy over the Crown did not mean Parliamentary sovereignty
over law and the constitution); (3) the continuing authority of
custom and precedent in British *and* colonial constitutional
thought; (4) the relative unimportance of natural law theory
for the colonial case; and (5) the extraordinary consistency of
and lack of novelty in the colonial case throughout the years
of controversy. Again and again, Reid's work demonstrates
the extraordinary learning in legal and constitutional matters displayed by colonial polemicists and leaders, and their
remarkable adroitness as political tacticians, whose pursuit
of the strategy of constitutional avoidance enabled them to
head off an open rupture for almost a decade. Repeatedly, he
demonstrates the anachronism of the view that an authoritative center had unilateral authority to define the imperial constitution. The list of Reid's contributions on this level could
be stretched out to enormous length.

Third, in his latest body of work Reid develops two important theses about the origins of the Revolution to which his
earlier work paid relatively little attention. Put simply, the
first thesis is that the dispute, not over Parliament's authority
to *tax* the colonies, but over its authority to *legislate* for the
colonies, was what "took the constitutional quarrel to the
point of armed conflict" and thereby "cast the constitutional
die for rebellion."[25] In this point, he strongly reinforces one of
my central points in *Peripheries and Center*. His second thesis

---

[25] Reid, *Authority to Legislate*, 4–5.

is that the colonial appeal to the Crown for support against Parliament, by raising the specter of a resurgent prerogative, alarmed British Whigs and significantly shaped metropolitan responses to colonial demands. Although neither of these points is new, Reid perhaps offers the most systematic exposition of them.

Even though this large body of work confirmed, reinforced, and amplified the interpretation I put forward in *Peripheries and Center*, it did not revise it in any fundamental way. Hence, when, earlier in this decade, Christopher Tomlins and Michael Grossberg, as editors of *The Cambridge History of Law in America*, approached me about writing a chapter on the subject of "Law and the Origins of the American Revolution," I produced what was mainly a distillation of the central chapters of that book. When, as editors of the new series the Cambridge History of Law in America, Tomlins and Grossberg again approached me earlier this year about writing a short volume that would amplify my contribution to *The Cambridge History of Law in America*, I reminded them that in the central chapters of *Peripheries and Center* I had already covered that subject at roughly the same length as the proposed volume. Knowing that I seldom change my mind about problems once I have dealt with them, I have always been reluctant to revisit them, and even though *Peripheries and Center* had been out of print for the better part of a decade, except for an on-demand edition available through the American Council of Learned Societies, my immediate inclination was to decline the invitation. Besides, Reid's abridged edition of his 1995 *Constitutional History of the American Revolution*, a volume of approximately the same length and scope, though with a topical organization, was still in print.

As I pondered the matter more thoroughly, however, I realized that neither *Peripheries and Center* nor Reid's massive body of work had managed to persuade scholars of the American Revolution to assign more weight to constitutional and legal issues in explaining that event. Both Reid and I had offered constitutional interpretations at a time when constitutional history was no longer at the forefront of scholarly interest in the American Revolution. Wrapped within a text that spanned the entire era from 1607 to 1788 and within an argument that concentrated on demonstrating the colonial roots of U.S. federalism, the interpretive force of those chapters of *Peripheries and Center* that offered a constitutional explanation for the Revolution had been lost on a generation more concerned with exploring the character than the causes of the Revolution, whereas Reid's work, notwithstanding its extent and compelling persuasiveness, had been almost entirely neglected by mainstream historians.

Three recent examples can be cited to illustrate this neglect. First, at a John Carter Brown Library seminar in 2007 on a paper on why there had been no significant work done on the origins of the Revolution since the mid-1970s, when I objected that the paper's author had left out any reference to Reid's voluminous writings and by implication to my own *Peripheries and Center*, the author and two other senior historians of the Revolution present at that seminar responded that they did not take Reid's work as seriously as I did. Indeed, I heard no evidence that they or anybody else at that seminar had even read, much less mastered, it. Second, at the 2008 annual meeting of the American Historical Association in Washington, a panel of historians, participating in a session the underlying premise of which was that virtually nothing of importance had been done on this subject since 1976 and that the main lines of interpretation now remained essentially where the scholarly discussion had brought them by that date, considered the question of whether the origins of the American Revolution was a subject that, after so many decades of neglect, was worth revisiting. That constitutional questions, including Reid's extensive contribution, got not even a mention at this session powerfully underlines the extent to which mainstream historians have failed even to acknowledge, much less to absorb, this impressive literature. Third, in a forum now being considered by the *Journal of American History* on the origins of the Revolution, not one of the six contributions emphasizes the legal and constitutional dimensions of the underlying contest.

The almost total neglect of this point of view by mainstream historians would be an interesting subject for scholarly speculation in itself. Is it because the body of Reid's work is so formidable that scholars are reluctant to try to come to terms with it? Because the boundaries between history and law are so impermeable? Because early American historians have yet to come to a full appreciation of the fundamental importance of law in the formation of colonial British American identities throughout the early modern era, a subject about which Reid himself has relatively little to say?[26] Because the whole thrust of Reid's work, which suggests that the Revolution was a British revolution that has to be understood as an episode in British imperial history and not as the first step in the creation of the American nation, runs powerfully against the grain of revolutionary scholarship since the late 1960s? Or because of some other reason altogether?

Legal historians have been somewhat more attentive to constitutional issues. Although such issues did not figure in Christopher L. Tomlins and Bruce H. Mann's impressive 2001 collection of new work in early American legal history, *The Many Legalities of Early America*,[27] none of the seventeen chapters taking up the origins of the American Revolution or building on Reid's arguments, two recent and impressive legal history monographs focus directly on the constitution-making process in the early modern British overseas world, one by Mary Sarah Bilder on Rhode Island[28] and the other by Daniel J. Hulsebosch on New York.[29] Primarily interested in

[26] On this subject, see Jack P. Greene, "'By Their Laws Shall Ye Know Them': Law and Identity in Colonial British America," *Journal of Interdisciplinary History*, 33 (Autumn 2002), 247–60.

[27] Christopher L. Tomlins and Bruce H. Mann, eds., *The Many Legalities of Early America* (Chapel Hill: University of North Carolina Press, 2001).

[28] Mary Sarah Bilder, *The Transatlantic Constitution: Colonial Legal Culture and the Empire* (Cambridge, Mass.: Harvard University Press, 2004).

[29] Daniel J. Hulsebosch, *Constituting Empire: New York and the Transformation of Constitutionalism in the Atlantic World, 1664–1830* (Chapel Hill: University of North Carolina Press, 2005).

the colonial era and, particularly in the Hulsebosch study, the way colonial constitutional developments informed those of the national era, neither of these works focuses on the origins of the American Revolution per se.

To an important extent, both Bilder and Hulsebosch concentrated on two aspects of imperial governance: the legal, as in the extension to and modification of British common law culture in the colonies, and the judicial, as in the operation of the British Privy Council as a final court of appeals within the empire. Inasmuch as neither aspect became a central issue in the debate of the 1760s and 1770s, colonists regarding them as protective of the rights they were trying to defend, Bilder and Hulsebosch pay relatively little attention either to the disputes over the distribution of authority between the Crown and colonial legislatures that had been the principal focus of constitutional debate during the colonial era or to the debate over the competing legislative jurisdictions of Parliament and the assemblies, the principal issue behind the crisis that led to the secession of thirteen out of the thirty-two American colonies from the British Empire in 1776. Nevertheless, each of these studies makes an important contribution to understanding the legal dimensions of the origins of the Revolution in the colony it studies by showing how after 1750 legal disputes became entangled with the larger debate over the reach and nature of metropolitan authority, and each provides much new detail about the ways antagonists used the law to argue whatever case they were trying to make.

Moreover, these two works, having thoroughly absorbed and endeavored to move beyond the central insights in Reid's work and in *Peripheries and Center*, powerfully reinforce my arguments about the distinction among the British, colonial, and imperial constitutions and the indeterminancy and contested nature of the colonial and imperial constitutions. Excellent examples of what needs to be done for all the colonies to achieve a comprehensive history of colonial constitutional development from the ground up, these path-breaking studies highlight the returns that can be gained from close study of colonial legal and constitutional history and, we can hope, herald a new era of interest in and investigation of that subject.

This hope encouraged me to conclude that a succinct volume on the constitutional and legal dimensions of the controversies that led to the American Revolution might both accomplish the avowed aims of the series in providing a volume that would be suitable for students in legal and general history at the undergraduate level and encourage both students and interested scholars to move beyond the interpretive orthodoxies we have inherited from the last great flowering of historical literature on the origins of the Revolution. I began to think about a volume that would revolve around the relevant chapters from *Peripheries and Center*, augmented by some new research I have been doing on the polemical literature of the 1760s and 1770s and lightly revised to reflect the insights of Reid and others who have published on this subject over the past quarter century. When I suggested this possibility to the editors, they agreed to take it up with the editors at Cambridge University Press, who, once I determined that the University of Georgia Press would allow me to republish in extenso material from the earlier book, offered to move ahead with it. I put together the basic text of the manuscript while I was teaching in the John F. Kennedy Institute at the Free University of Berlin during the summer term of 2009 and completed it during the early weeks of my tenure as a Fellow at the National Humanities Center in Research Triangle Park, North Carolina.

I offer this relatively brief narrative account of the constitutional origins of the American Revolution in the conviction that the debate it analyzes is central to any satisfactory explanation of that event. For a more legally informed study of the same subject, I refer the reader to the abridged edition of John Phillip Reid's *Constitutional History of the Revolution*, a short and accessible guide to that author's many penetrating insights and arguments.

I am grateful to several people who helped in the preparation of this volume. RST Stoermer provided computer and database advice and did the index. Amy Turner Bushnell scrutinized the prose text and footnotes, caught many errors, and sometimes persuaded me to shorten some long sentences. Marianne Wasson helped with the dust jacket illustrations. Series editors Christopher Tomlins and Michael Grossberg offered much useful advice. Newgen Imaging Systems did an excellent job of copy editing. Eric Crahan and Jason Przybylski at Cambridge University Press guided the manuscript smoothly through production.

Research Triangle Park
November 15, 2009

PROLOGUE: INHERITANCE

The revolution that occurred in North America during the last quarter of the eighteenth century was the unintended consequence of a dispute about law. During the dozen years between 1764 and 1776, Britons on both sides of the Atlantic engaged in an elaborate debate over the source and character of law within the larger British Empire. Whether the king-in-Parliament, the ultimate source of statute law in Great Britain, could legislate for British colonies overseas was the ostensible question in dispute, but many other related and even deeper legal issues involving the nature of the constitution of the empire and the location of sovereignty within the empire emerged from and were thoroughly canvassed during the debate. On neither side of the Atlantic was opinion monolithic, but two sides, one representing the dominant opinion in metropolitan Britain and the other the principal view in the colonies, rapidly took shape. The failure to reconcile these positions led in 1775 to open warfare and in 1776 to the decision of thirteen of Britain's more than thirty American colonies to declare their independence and form an American union. The nature and shifting character of this dispute can only be understood by placing it in the larger temporal process of imperial legal and constitutional thought and practice over the previous century and a half.

As recent literature on European state formation reveals, the problem of how to organize and theorize an extended polity was intrinsic to late medieval and early modern state building. As the national states emerging in western Europe sought through conquest, dynastic unions, or annexations to expand their authority over areas already well peopled and possessed of their own peculiar socioeconomic, legal, and political traditions, they could sometimes absorb those areas into the central polity, as England did with Wales in the fifteenth century, but often lacked the resources for such consolidation and had to settle for some form of indirect governance and limited sovereignty, the form of which had to be negotiated with local power holders in those areas. In the resulting constitutional arrangements, authority did not flow outward from a powerful central core but was constructed through a process of reciprocal bargaining between the core and newly acquired territories that usually left considerable authority in the hands of provincial leaders.[1]

Increasingly, imperial historians have come to realize that the process of governance and constitution making in early modern overseas empires represented an extension of this model. In those empires, fiscal resources were never sufficient to support the bureaucratic, military, and naval machinery necessary to impose central authority on the dominant, self-empowered possessing classes in the new peripheries without their consent or acquiescence. To obtain the cooperation of those classes, metropolitan officials had little choice but to negotiate systems of authority with them in a bargaining process that produced varieties of indirect rule that at once set clear boundaries on central power, recognized the rights of localities and provinces to varying degrees of self-government, and ensured that under normal circumstances metropolitan decisions affecting the peripheries should consult or respect local and provincial interests. For historians of

---

[1] The foundational works are Charles Tilly, *Coercion, Capital, and European States, AD 990–1990* (Cambridge, Mass.: Basil Blackwell, 1990) and Mark Greengrass, ed., *Conquest and Coalescence: The Shaping of the State in Early Modern Europe* (London: Arnold, 1991).

empire, this new perspective has led to a new appreciation of
the extraordinary agency of the dominant settler populations
in overseas territories in creating and managing the polities
by which they were governed and of the critical role of
those polities in forming the constitutional arrangements that
characterized those empires.

Settler agency was directly related to the limited resources
of colonizing nations. At the beginning of the era of early
modern colonization, none of the emerging nation-states
of Europe had either the coercive resources necessary to
establish its hegemony over portions of the New World or
the financial wherewithal to mobilize such resources. As a
result, during the early stages of colonization, any nation-
state contemplating overseas ventures farmed out that task,
either to private groups organized into chartered trading
companies or to influential individuals. In return for authorization from the Crown and in the expectation of realizing
extensive economic and social advantages, these *adventurers*
agreed to assume the heavy financial burdens of founding,
defending, and succoring beachheads of European occupa-
tion in America. In effect, European rulers gave these private
agents licenses with wide discretion to operate in domains
to which their claims were highly tenuous and over whose
indigenous inhabitants they exercised no effective control. If
the gamble was successful, European rulers secured at least
minimal jurisdiction over American territories and peoples at
minimal cost to royal treasuries.

Some of these early private agents of European imperial-
ism, especially the trading companies operating under the
aegis of the Portuguese and the Dutch, enjoyed considerable
success in establishing commercial footholds to exploit some
of the economic potential of the New World. However, unless
they encountered wealthy native empires, rich mineral depos-
its, or vast pools of native labor – things that in America happened on a large scale only in Mexico and Peru – few private
adventurers had the resources to sustain the high costs of settling, administering, and developing a colony. Most of them
were quickly forced to seek cooperation and contributions

from settlers, traders, and other individual participants in the colonizing process.

These efforts to enlist such cooperation acknowledged the fact that the actual process of establishing effective centers of European power in America was often less the result of the activities of colonial organizers or licensees than of the many groups and individuals who took actual possession of land, built estates and businesses, turned what had previously been wholly aboriginal landscapes into ones that were at least partly European, constructed and presided over a viable system of economic organization, created towns or other political units, and subjugated, reduced to profitable labor, killed off, or expelled the original inhabitants. Making up for their scarcity of economic resources, thousands of Europeans, by dint of their industry and initiative, created social spaces for themselves and their families in America and thereby created for themselves status, capital, and power.

Throughout the new European Americas during the early modern era, independent individual participants in the colonizing process were thus engaged in a deep and widespread process of individual and corporate self-empowerment. In contemporary Europe, only a small fraction of the male population ever managed to rise out of a state of socioeconomic dependency to achieve the civic competence, the full right to have a voice in political decisions that was the preserve of independent property holders. By contrast, as a consequence of the easy availability of land or other resources, a large proportion of adult male white colonists acquired land or other resources, built estates, and achieved individual independence.

This development produced strong demands on the part of the large, empowered settler populations for the extension to the colonies of the same rights to security of property and civic participation that appertained to the empowered, high-status, and independent property holders in the polities from which they came. In their view, colonial governance, no less than metropolitan governance, should guarantee that men of their standing would not be governed without being consulted or in ways that were patently against their interests. Along with the vast distance of the colonies from Europe, these circumstances powerfully drove those who were nominally in charge of the colonies toward the establishment and toleration of political structures that involved active consultation with, if not the formal consent of, local settlers. Consultation meant that local populations would more willingly both acknowledge the legitimacy of the authority of private agencies of colonization and contribute to local costs. The earliest stages of colonization thus resulted in the emergence in new colonial peripheries of many new and relatively autonomous centers of European power that were effectively under local control.

These centers invariably were reflections of the European worlds from which the settlers came. Intending to create offshoots of the Old World in the New, the large numbers of emigrants to the colonies took their laws and institutions with them and made them the primary foundations for the new societies they sought to establish. For these societies, these laws and institutions functioned as "a concomitant of emigration." They were not, as one scholar has noted, "imposed upon settlers but claimed by them."[2] They served as a vivid and symbolically powerful badge of the emigrants' deepest aspirations to retain in their new places of abode their identities as members of the European societies to which they were attached, identities that, in their eyes, both established their superiority over and sharply distinguished them from the seemingly rude and uncivilized people they were seeking to dispossess.

The English settlements established in North America, the West Indies, and the Atlantic islands of Bermuda and the Bahamas provide a case study of the way this process worked. Among the main components of the emerging identity of

---

[2] Jorg Frisch, "Law as a Means and as an End: Remarks on the Function of European and Non-European Law in the Process of European Expansion," in W. J. Mommsen and J. A. De Moor, eds., *European Expansion and Law: The Encounter of European and Indigenous Law in 19th- and 20th-Century Asia and Africa* (Oxford: Oxford University Press, 1992), 21.

English people in early modern England, the Protestantism and, increasingly during the eighteenth century, the slowly expanding commercial and strategic might of the English nation were both important. Far more significant, however, were the systems of law and liberty that, contemporary English and many foreign observers seemed to agree, distinguished English people from all other peoples on the face of the globe.[3] The proud boast of the English was that, through a variety of conquests and upheavals, they had been able, in marked contrast to most other political societies in Europe, to retain their identity as a free people who had secured their liberty through their dedication to what later analysts would call the rule of law.

A long-developing tradition of jurisprudential political discourse supported this dedication. Emphasizing the role of law as a restraint on the power of the Crown, this tradition was rooted in such older writings as Sir John Fortescue, *De Laudibus Legum Angliae*, written during the fifteenth century but not published until 1616, and elaborated in a series of important works by several of the most prominent judges and legal thinkers of the early seventeenth century, including Sir Edward Coke, Sir John Davies, and Nathaniel Bacon. Writing in an age when, except for the Netherlands, every other major European state was slipping into absolutism and England's own first two Stuart kings seemed to be trying to extend the prerogatives of the Crown and perhaps even to do away with Parliaments in England, these early seventeenth-century legal writers were anxious to erect legal and constitutional restraints that would ensure security of life, liberty, and property against such extensions of royal power.[4]

---

[3] See Richard Helgerson, *Forms of Nationhood: The Elizabethan Writing of England* (Chicago: University of Chicago Press, 1992); Linda Colley, *The Britons: Forging the Nations, 1707–1787* (New Haven: Yale University Press, 1992); and Benedict Anderson, *Imagined Communities: Reflections on the Origin and Spread of Nationalism* (London: Verso, 1983).

[4] The best analysis of this tradition is still to be found in J. G. A. Pocock, *The Ancient Constitution and the Feudal Law: English Historical Thought in the Seventeenth Century* (Cambridge: Cambridge University Press, 1957).

This emerging jurisprudential tradition rested on a distinction, already fully elaborated by Fortescue, between two
fundamentally different kinds of monarchy, *regal* and *political*.
Whereas in a regal monarchy such as that in France, *"What
pleased the prince,"* as Fortescue wrote, had *"the force of law,"*
in a political monarchy such as that in England, "the regal
power" was "restrained by political law." Bound by their coro-
nation oaths to the observance of English laws, English kings
could neither "change laws at their pleasure" nor "make new
ones" "without the assent of the subjects." The happy result of
this system, according to Fortescue, was that English people, in
contrast to their neighbors, were governed by laws to which they
had consented, and, as Coke and other writers pointed out, this
was as true for the common law, to which the people assented
through long usage and custom, as it was for the statute law
passed by the Parliaments to which they sent representatives.[5]

With a wide variety of other contemporary political
writers, the exponents of the English jurisprudential tradition
agreed that the happy capacity of English people to preserve
their liberty rested largely on two institutions for determining and making law: Juries and Parliaments. By guaranteeing
that no legal case would be determined "but by the Verdict
of his Peers, (or Equals) his Neighbours, and of his own
Condition," wrote the Whig political publicist Henry Care,
the first, juries, gave every person "a Share in the executive
Part of the Law." By giving each independent person through
"his chosen Representatives" a share "in the Legislative (or
Lawmaking) Power," the second, Parliament, insured that no
law should be passed without the consent of the nation's property holders. These "two grand Pillars of *English* Liberty,"
declared Care in paraphrasing Coke, provided English people
with "a greater inheritance" than they had ever received from
their immediate "Progenitors." For Englishmen, liberty was,
thus, not just a condition enforced by law but the very essence
of their emerging national identity.[6]

[5] Sir John Fortescue, *De Laudibus Legum Angliae* (Cambridge, 1942), 25,
27, 31, 33, 79, 81.
[6] Henry Care, *English Liberties*, 5th ed. (Boston, 1721), 3–4, 27.

For English people migrating overseas to establish new communities of settlement, the capacity to enjoy – to possess – the English system of law and liberty was thus crucial to their ability to maintain their identity as English people and to continue to think of themselves and be thought of as English. For that reason, as well as because they regarded English legal and constitutional arrangements as the very best way to preserve the properties they hoped to acquire in their new homes, it is scarcely surprising that, in establishing local enclaves of power during the first few years of colonization, English settlers all over America made every effort to construct them on English legal foundations. As the legal historian George Dargo has observed, "the attempt to establish English law and the 'rights and liberties of Englishmen' was constant from the first settlement to the [American] Revolution" and beyond.[7]

Nevertheless, as Yunlong Man has shown in his careful study of the first half century of development of provincial political institutions in England's five most successful colonies, English authorities did not anticipate the development of such demands when trying to work out a mode of governance for the colonies. "During the first half of the seventeenth century, the formative years of the colonial polities," Man finds, "English authorities never devised, or even conceived of," an arrangement by which colonial governance would be modeled on "the national government of England." Instead, they remained committed to a conciliar form of colonial governance of the kind they devised for Virginia during its early years. This form consisted of an appointed governor and councilors and included no formal devices for consulting the broader population, and they continued for several decades to think of this conciliar form as the norm for English colonial governance.[8]

---

[7] George Dargo, *Roots of the Republic: A New Perspective on Early American Constitutionalism* (New York: Praeger, 1974), 58.

[8] Yunlong Man, "English Colonization and the Formation of Anglo-American Polities, 1606–1664" (unpublished Ph.D. dissertation, Johns Hopkins University, 1994), 17–61, 455.

But several developments during the early stages of the colonizing process encouraged the development of a representative component in the emerging colonial constitutions. To entice settlers, colonial organizers found early that they not only had to offer them property in land but also guarantee them the property in rights by which English people had traditionally secured their real and material possessions. Thus in 1619, the Virginia Company of London found it necessary to establish a polity that included a representative assembly through which the settlers could, in the time-honored fashion of the English, make – and formally consent to – the laws under which they would live. Directed by company leaders "to imitate and follow the policy of the form of government, laws, customs, and manner of trial; and other administration of justice, used in the realm of England," the new assembly, the first such body in England's still small American world, immediately claimed the right to consent to all taxes levied on the inhabitants of Virginia.[9]

The legal instruments of English colonization – letters patent, charters, proclamations – encouraged this attempt in three ways. First, they often specified that the settlers and their progeny should be treated as "natural born subjects of England" and thereby strongly suggested that there would be no legal distinctions between English people who lived in the home island and those who resided in the colonies. Second, they required that colonies operate under no laws that were repugnant to "Laws, Statutes, Customs, and Rights of our Kingdom of England" and thereby powerfully implied that the laws of England were to provide the model, and the standard, for all colonial laws. Third, beginning with the charter to Maryland in 1632, they also stipulated that colonies should use and enjoy "all Privileges, Franchises and Liberties of this our Kingdom of England, freely, quietly, and peacefully to have and possess ... in the same manner as our Liege-Men

---

[9] Ordinance, July 24, 1621, Virginia Laws, March 1624, in Jack P. Greene, ed., *Great Britain and the American Colonies, 1606–1783* (New York: Harper and Row, 1970), 28, 30.

born, or to be born within our said Kingdom of England, without Impediment, Molestation, Vexation, Impeachment, or Grievance," and thereby guaranteed that no laws would be passed without the consent of the freemen of the colony.[10]

In no case more than twenty years after the founding of a colony, and often much earlier, these conditions and developments encouraged the establishment of representative institutions. Between roughly 1620 and 1660, every American colony with a substantial body of settlers adopted some form of elected assembly to pass laws for the polities they were creating: Virginia and Bermuda in the 1620s, Massachusetts Bay, Maryland, Connecticut, Plymouth, New Haven, and Barbados in the 1630s, St. Kitts, Antigua, and Rhode Island in the 1640s, and Montserrat and Nevis in the 1650s. By 1660, all thirteen settled colonies in the Americas had functioning representative assemblies. From New England to Barbados, colonial English America proved to be an extraordinarily fertile ground for Parliamentary governance.[11]

Even in situations in which company officials or proprietors took the initiative in establishing these early lawmaking bodies, as was the case with Virginia, Bermuda, and Maryland, the representative bodies never acted as the "passive servants and petitioners of the prerogative" as had been the case with the medieval House of Commons. On the contrary, modern historians have been impressed by their "effectiveness and spirit of assertiveness." "Usually from their very first meetings," Michael Kammen has noted, they acted as the aggressive spokesmen for the proliferating settlements within the colonies. Claiming their constituents' rights to the traditional English principles of consensual governance, they early insisted that no laws or taxes might go into effect without their assent, demanded the initiative in legislation,

---

[10] David S. Lovejoy, *The Glorious Revolution in America* (New York: Harper & Row, 1972), 39; Maryland Charter, June 30, 1632, in Greene, *Great Britain and the American Colonies*, 24.

[11] See Michael Kammen, *Deputyes & Libertyes: The Origins of Representative Government in Colonial America* (New York: Knopf, 1969), 11–12.

turned themselves into high courts of appeal and original jurisdiction in the manner of the medieval House of Commons, and rarely shrank from controversy with "local executives, proprietors, or the Crown."[12]

To be sure, it took about twenty years for these bodies "to materialize, stabilize, and take permanent form in each colony." During the early years, they usually did not sit as a separate body but met together with the governor's council or even with the governor himself to hear cases and pass laws.[13] But they set course early toward achieving their independence from the executive, and by the 1640s the four largest colonies, each of them on its own initiative, had all moved toward a bicameral legislature, with the lower house sitting separately from the governor and council: Virginia in 1643, Massachusetts Bay in 1644, Maryland in 1650, and Barbados in 1652. Local exigencies, not emulation, drove this development. In every case, the specific shape of a provincial polity was the product of what Yunlong Man calls an "indigenous development." Some popular provincial governors, such as Sir William Berkeley in Virginia and Philip Bell in Barbados, fostered these developments, but in doing so they were invariably merely consolidating the political frameworks earlier worked out by emerging local leaders and acknowledging that the capacity to govern, in Man's formulation, "compelled [Crown, company, or proprietary] recognition of the indigenous structures of colonial government that had emerged out of colonial conditions." For its part, the Crown remained suspicious of representative government, not officially acknowledging the permanence of the assembly in Virginia until 1639, nearly fifteen years after it had assumed direct governmental responsibility for that colony.[14]

By the end of the second quarter of the seventeenth century, the tradition of consensual governance was thus "firmly

---

[12] Ibid., 7, 9, 62, 67.

[13] Ibid., 11.

[14] Man, "English Colonization and the Formation of Anglo-American Polities," 232–414, traces these developments in detail. The quotations are from pp. 416, 455.

rooted" in colonial English America.[15] Moreover, once their governments had acquired a bicameral form, provincial magnates had no difficulty in noting "the remarkable resemblance" between colonial polities and the traditional form of metropolitan English governance, and they began, as did the Barbadian government in 1651, to defend the polities they had created on the grounds that they represented "the nearest model of conformity to that under which our predecessors of the English nation have lived and flourished for above a thousand years." English officials were also impressed by the structural similarities between the colonial polities and the metropolitan government. At the same time, the enunciation and proliferation in England of the classical theory of mixed government during and after the English Civil War and its rapid installation as the official interpretation of the English constitution provided additional justification for the application of that theory to the "indigenous colonial tri-partite government of governor, council, and assembly." Additionally, the Stuart monarchy provided "official sanction" for this "conceptual transformation" in 1661 when it "introduced just such a government in Jamaica," recently captured from the Spanish and only the second English colony to come under royal control, instructing its new governor "to proceed 'according to such good, just and reasonable customs and institutions as are exercised and settled in our colonies and plantations.'"[16]

Yet, this action with regard to Jamaica did not completely settle the issue of the structure of English colonial governance. Most of the new proprietary colonies created during the Restoration – in the Carolinas, the Jerseys, and Pennsylvania – and the new royal colony of New Hampshire, separated from Massachusetts in 1679, quickly moved to institute the sort of tripartite polities that had developed in the older colonies. But the Duke of York – the future James II and the proprietor

[15] Kammen, *Deputyes & Liberties*, 61.
[16] Man, "English Colonization and the Formation of Anglo-American Polities," 15–16, 391–92.

of the colony of New York, captured from the Dutch in the mid-1660s – resisted the creation of an assembly for nearly twenty years until 1683, and immediately reversed this concession when he became king. Moreover, James II's attempt to consolidate the New England colonies into a single polity, the Dominion of New England, without representative institutions, deeply threatened the long-established tradition of representative government in those colonies.

Such actions were part of an effort by English officials during the Restoration to impose metropolitan authority on the local centers of power that had emerged in America. Throughout the decades from 1660 to 1690, the metropolitan government undertook a variety of measures intended to reduce the colonies to what it called "an absolute obedience to the King's authority."[17] These included subordinating the economies of the colonies to that of the metropolis through the navigation acts, passed between 1651 and 1696; bringing as many as possible of the still mostly private colonies under the direct control of the Crown; and curtailing the powers of colonial political institutions. As a theoretical support for these efforts, metropolitan officials in the late 1670s enunciated the new doctrine that the extension of representative government to the colonies was an act of royal grace.

Everywhere in the colonies, these metropolitan intrusions into colonial affairs encountered stiff resistance. In response, provincial assemblies expressed the determination of the property holders they represented to secure both their estates and their claims to an English identity by obtaining metropolitan recognition that, as English people or the descendants of English people, they were entitled to enjoy all the rights and legal protections of English people in the home island. This determination stimulated an extensive constitutional discussion intended to identify explicit legal defenses that would put colonial claims to English rights and legal protections on

---

[17] Report of the Commissioners sent to New England, [April 30,] 1661, in W. Noel Sainsbury et al., eds., *Calendar of State Papers, Colonial*, 44 vols. (London: His Majesty's Stationary Office, 1860–), *1661–8*, 25.

a solid foundation and thereby protect the colonies from such wholesale intrusions of metropolitan power.[18]

In these discussions, colonial spokesmen articulated an elaborate argument designed to strengthen their early claims to what they thought of as their inherited rights as English people. According to this argument, the original settlers and their descendants were all equally free-born English subjects who had left their native country to establish English hegemony over portions of the New World. Denying that they could lose any of their inherited rights simply by migrating to America, they pointed out that they had created their own civil governments with the specific purpose of securing those rights to themselves. At the same time, they argued that, so far from being a grant from the Crown, their assemblies derived from their basic English right to representative government and many decades of customary practice. No charter or other instrument could grant to English people a right they already enjoyed as part of their inheritance, they contended. Such instruments, like Magna Charta, merely constituted an acknowledgment on the part of the Crown that such rights inhered in the people themselves.

But it was far easier for inhabitants of distant and dependent colonies to lay claim to the rights of Englishmen than it was for them actually to secure them, and the quest to secure those rights against the power of the metropolis was everywhere an enduring feature of colonial political life. In general, leaders of individual colonies pursued this quest along two parallel lines. First, they sought explicit guarantees of the rights of colonists to the laws of England. Second, they sought to enhance the authority of the elected assemblies. In the colonies, no less than in the metropolis, colonial leaders were determined that law and parliaments should be the bulwark of the people's liberties and properties.

---

[18] This subject is discussed more fully in Jack P. Greene, *Peripheries and Center: Constitutional Development in Extended Polities of the British Empire and the United States 1607–1788* (Athens, Ga.: University of Georgia Press, 1986), 12–18.

The colonists' quest for explicit guarantees of their right to English laws was a recurrent subject of debate for more than a half century beginning around 1670.[19] This debate revolved around two questions. The first was whether the colonies were conquered countries, to be governed at the will of the King, or settled territories whose inhabitants, enjoying the privileges of Englishmen as their birthright, were to be governed by the laws of England. If the latter, then a second question arose of which English laws should apply, the common law, statute law, or both? Despite a series of contradictory rulings on the first question by metropolitan authorities, which left metropolitan authorities in confusion well into the 1770s, few colonial leaders had any doubt that the colonies were polities of settlement whose inhabitants were entitled to all the traditional rights of Englishmen, including whatever laws of England they found useful. Between 1670 and 1700 the legislatures of several colonies sought explicit confirmation of this position in public declarations and statutes, and these efforts continued during the early decades of the eighteenth century, particularly in Jamaica, where, perhaps because the colony had been acquired by conquest, settlers were especially anxious to have some positive codification of their rights, and in Maryland, where antiproprietary leaders viewed English laws as a safeguard against possible arbitrary rule by the proprietor. Only the Jamaican Assembly succeeded in this quest, granting the Crown a permanent revenue of £8,000 per year in return for confirmation of a clause acknowledging the right of Jamaican settlers to English laws.

But the failure of other colonies to gain such statutes did not deprive their free inhabitants of the use of English law. Indeed, throughout the colonial era, and probably at no time more than in the half century after 1725, lawyers and judges seem to have applied all kinds of English law, common as well as statute, as it suited local and temporal needs and conditions.[20] In so doing, local legal and judicial

---

[19] Ibid., 23–28, provides a distinct discussion of this subject.
[20] William E. Nelson, *The Common Law of Colonial America: Volume I: The Chesapeake and New England 1607–1660* (Oxford: Oxford

officials, operating through colonial courts, fashioned a legal system for each colony that, as Sir William Gooch, lieutenant governor of Virginia from 1727 to 1749, observed, was both "exactly suited to the Circumstances of the Respective Governments, and as near as possible [as] it can be to the Laws and Customs of England."[21] The colonies thus gained in practice what they had, except in a few cases, been unable to obtain by statute: traditional English guarantees of life, liberty, and property. This development helps to account for the virtual disappearance of colonial legislative attempts to secure such laws after the mid-1730s. That after more than a century they had still not managed to obtain positive legal confirmation of their entitlement to the benefits of English law, however, continued to sustain a lingering unease was powerfully evidenced during the 1760s and 1770s by the frequency and vehemence of colonial denials that the colonies fell into the category of conquered countries or were without the benefits of the common law and English statutes that secured the rights and liberties of English subjects.

Much more enduring was a second issue: The extent and foundations of colonial legislative authority.[22] To be sure,

University Press, 2008), provides an authoritative analysis of the earliest stages of this process, the later manifestations of which, the author intends to treat in subsequent volumes, limited to colonies that subsequently became part of the United States.

[21] Gooch's remarks, written in the late 1720s, are reprinted in Jack P. Greene, *Great Britain and the American Colonies*, 196–212, The quotations are from p. 203. How colonial courts adapted English common law to contribute to the creation of provincial constitutions in Rhode Island and New York and to the formation of a wider imperial constitution for the empire are the subjects of two relatively recent monographs: Mary Sarah Bilder, *The Transatlantic Constitution: Colonial Legal Culture and Empire* (Cambridge, Mass.: Harvard University Press, 2004), and Daniel J. Hulsebosch, *Constituting Empire: New York and the Transformation of Constitutionalism in the Atlantic World, 1664–1830* (Chapel Hill: University of North Carolina Press, 2005). These excellent volumes suggest that comparable studies of all the colonial polities, not just those that became part of the United States, will be essential for the achievement of a comprehensive discussion of the constitutional development of the early modern British Empire.

[22] Greene, *Peripheries and Center*, 28–42, provides an extended treatment of this subject.

the Glorious Revolution and the overthrow of the Dominion of New England effectively ended any efforts to do away with representative government in the colonies. By the first decade of the eighteenth century, representative assemblies had become a fixed feature of English colonial governance. Some of the earliest colonies lost their separate status over the course of the seventeenth century, Plymouth amalgamating with Massachusetts and New Haven with Connecticut, and East Jersey and West Jersey joining to form the single colony of New Jersey, but every one of the eighteen settled colonies still in existence in 1700 had its own elected legislature.

Thereafter, each new British colony acquired an assembly as soon as it had sufficient settlers to support one: the Bahamas in 1729, Georgia in 1755, and Nova Scotia in 1758. In 1749, the Boston essayist and historian Dr. William Douglass could credibly refer to those few English "Settlements with a Governor only[,] ... such [as] ... *Newfoundland, Nova Scotia, Hudson's Bay*, and *Georgia*," as "not [yet fully] colonized." Because they had no assembly, these plantations, according to Douglass, lacked the "Essence of a *British* Constitution."[23] With the notable exception of Quebec, whose majority French population initially showed little interest in adapting to English political institutions, all of the new colonies acquired as a result of the Seven Years' War – East Florida, West Florida, Grenada, St. Vincent, Tobago, and Dominica – established assemblies in the 1760s and 1770s. The new colony of St. John convened an assembly soon after it was established in 1773. By the time of the American Revolution, twenty-five provincial parliaments, not counting the Irish Parliament, were functioning in the British overseas world.

Notwithstanding this massive expansion of representative institutions throughout the American empire and the fact that, already by 1700, the assemblies in the older colonies had "achieved a position, if not superior to, at least parallel

---

[23] William Douglass, *Summary, Historical and Political, of the First Planting, Progressive Improvement, and Present State of the British Settlements in North America*, 2 vols. (London: R. and J. Dodsley, 1749–51), 1: 207.

to and independent from" the governors and councils[24] and in most cases had gained a degree of independence, customary assurances of frequent elections, and traditions of regular meeting that exceeded those of the House of Commons before the Glorious Revolution, the legal and constitutional status of the assemblies remained a hotly and frequently contested issue down to and after the American Revolution. Metropolitan authorities and their supporters in the colonies repeatedly affirmed the doctrine, first enunciated by the Lords of Trade in 1679, that the assemblies' lawmaking power and indeed their very existence depended on the grace and favor of the Crown as extended to them by royal charter or some other official document such as the king's commission or instructions to governors and that the Crown might therefore change the constitutions of the colonies whenever and however it saw fit. In answer, assemblies and their supporters elaborated on the arguments advanced by earlier generations to counter such prerogative claims, citing charters, their English libertarian inheritance, and both English and local custom to justify not only the existence of their assemblies but also their claims to full legislative authority and to rights peculiar to their specific polities.

Whether the Crown could – or could not – alter colonial rights and privileges established through usage and founded on either custom or the colonists' inherited rights as English people was certainly the most divisive issue separating metropolis and colonies during the seven decades following the Glorious Revolution. That issue was at the heart of the recurring controversies over the applicability of English law in the colonies and the status of the colonial assemblies. Revolving around the explicit question of the balance of power between colonial legislatures and the Crown and the implicit issue of the relationship of these bodies to the metropolitan Parliament, this dispute would have an important bearing on the events that led to the American Revolution.

---

[24] Man, "English Colonization and the Formation of Anglo-American Polities," 391.

I

EMPIRE NEGOTIATED, 1689–1763

Throughout the first century and a half of the British Empire, the precise constitutional relationship between the colonies and the metropolitan state remained unsettled and subject to continuous negotiation between colonial polities and metropolitan authority. "The chiefest Thing wanting to make the Inhabitants of these Plantations happy," an anonymous Virginian told his English readers in 1701, "is a good Constitution of Government." By a good constitution, he explained, he meant one that would not only settle the nagging questions of "what is Law, and what is not in the Plantations" and "how far the Legislative Authority is in the Assemblies of the several Colonies" but also settle them in such a way as to leave the colonies with "a Just and Equal Government." Such a constitution, he insisted, was necessary to guarantee the colonists the equal and impartial administration of justice and the full enjoyment of "their Liberties and Estates" that were the proud distinguishing marks of Englishmen whether they remained at home or lived in distant colonies. But the Crown's continuing claims for "a more absolute Power in the Plantations than in England" meant that the colonists would never be able to extract such formal and explicit guarantees from metropolitan authorities. That "a Regular Settlement" of this question had "never yet been made," that, as another writer phrased it, the precise "bounds between the chief power and the people" in the colonies, between metropolitan authority and colonial rights, had never been explicitly settled, left the British–American world with two competing definitions of the constitutional situation within the expanding British Empire and remained a source of deep anxiety for both colonial leaders and metropolitan authorities.[1]

CROWN AND COLONIES

Although the colonists never succeeded in persuading Crown officials in London to establish a "regular Constitution of Government" for the British Empire that explicitly and formally put the colonists on an equal footing with Englishmen with respect to their liberties and property, in actual practice, a variety of factors mitigated the Crown's claims for greater authority in the colonies than it exercised in Britain. These included distance, inherited traditions of governance, metropolitan reluctance to commit substantial resources to colonial governance, and the extraordinary economic success of the empire.

In the early 1720s, in a passage in *Cato's Letters* that many later writers on the colonies would find worthy of quotation, John Trenchard and Thomas Gordon remarked that distant colonies could be kept dependent on their parent states either "by Force" or by "using them well."[2] Unlike later empires, however, the early modern British Empire was not held together by force. Before 1760, metropolitan authorities sometimes considered using force to control the colonies and

[1] Charles D'Avenant, *Political and Commercial Works*, 4 vols. (London, 1771), 2:35, 55; [Benjamin Harrison II], *An Essay upon the Government of the English Plantations on the Continent of America* (1701); *An Anonymous Virginian's Proposals for Liberty under the British Crown, with Two Memoranda by William Byrd*, ed. Louis B. Wright (San Marino, Calif.: Huntington Library, 1945), 15–24; *The Groans of Jamaica, Expressed in a Letter from a Gentleman Residing there, to his Friend in London* (London, 1714), iv; William Wood, *A Survey of Trade*, 2d ed. (London, 1719), 177.

[2] John Trenchard and Thomas Gordon, *Cato's Letters*, 4 vols. (London, 1724), 3:286.

even wished that they had larger forces in the colonies for that purpose. With the significant exception of the small army that was sent to Virginia to suppress Bacon's Rebellion in the late 1670s, however, the few military units stationed by the metropolitan government in the colonies were intended not to police the colonies but to defend them against attacks either from the colonies of rival powers or from their own slaves. The defensive character of the British army in America is obvious. Most of the troops were stationed in the more exposed Caribbean colonies, and those few troops on the continent were strategically placed to guard the mainland colonies against attack from French Canada or Louisiana or Spanish Florida.

Without a much larger force than it could afford to keep in the colonies, the British government had no other choice than to use them well. That "public opinion sets bounds to every government,"[3] that no government could function, as Burke put it, "without regard to the general opinion of those who were to be governed,"[4] was a truism among political theorists during the early modern era, and although those people who were most closely involved in colonial administration in London often demanded tighter controls over the colonies, during the seven decades following the Glorious Revolution the metropolitan government never made a sustained effort to govern the colonies in ways that were at serious variance with colonial opinion. Despite much bluster from the Board of Trade and governors and other royal and proprietary officials in the colonies, the metropolitan government consistently governed the colonies in such a way as to reveal that it had no intention of trying "to streighten or oppress them."[5]

Indeed, especially over the decades following the close of the first series of intercolonial wars between 1689 and 1713,

---

[3] James Madison, "Public Opinion," Dec. 19, 1791, in Gaillard Hunt, ed., *The Writings of James Madison*, 9 vols. (New York: G. P. Putnam's, 1900–1910), 6:70.

[4] Edmund Burke, "Letter to the Sheriffs of Bristol," in *The Works of Edmund Burke*, 16 vols. (London: C. & J. Rivington, 1826), 3: 179.

[5] A Merchant, *A Discourse of the Duties on Merchandize, more Particularly of that on Sugars* (London, 1695), 6–7.

the growth of the British colonies in population, wealth, and strategic importance was so rapid in comparison with that of the American colonies of rival European nations that by the middle of the eighteenth century it had become a widely accepted "Maxim" among British colonial experts "that *Liberty and Encouragement*" were "the *Basis of [successful] colonies.*" The remarkable development of the British colonies exceeded that of other European colonies, observers often asserted, precisely because they had been so "very singularly indulged in many respects above [the colonies of] all other nations; particularly in the power of making laws" for themselves. Along with "Plenty of good land," Adam Smith wrote in his section on the "Causes of Prosperity of New Colonies" in *The Wealth of Nations*, "liberty to manage their own affairs [in] their own way" was one of "the two great causes of the prosperity" of the British colonies in America. If, as another writer declared, "those free systems of provincial government" that encouraged such a demonstrable "regard to the rights of men" were what primarily "distinguished the English colonies above all others," it followed that "nothing but our arbitrary treatment of them and our misgovernment" could "make them otherwise than beneficial to the nation in general."[6]

The lax administration thus thought to have been in some major part responsible for the rapid growth of the colonies was especially evident during the long ministry of Sir Robert Walpole from 1721 until 1742, and it derived largely from the application to colonial affairs of many of the underlying principles and techniques that he had employed with such

---

[6] Archibald Kennedy, *Observations on the Importance of the Northern Colonies under Proper Regulations* (New York, 1750), 12, 30–1; The Watchman, #4, *Pennsylvania Journal & Weekly Advertiser*, Apr. 27, 1758; George Chalmers, *An Introduction to the History of the Revolt of the American Colonies*, 2 vols. (Boston: J. Monroe, 1845), 1:16; Malachy Postlethwayt, *The Universal Dictionary of Trade and Commerce*, 2 vols. (London, 1757), 1: 535; Josiah Tucker, *A Brief Essay on the Advantages and Disadvantages...* (London, 1750), 95–6; Adam Smith, *An Inquiry into the Nature and Causes of the Wealth of Nations* (Chicago: Encyclopedia Britannica, 1952), 246.

brilliant success in managing domestic affairs. To avoid any issues involving fundamentals and all debates over basic principles, to restrict the active role of government as much as possible and act only when it was expedient or necessary to do so, to attempt to bind potentially disruptive groups to the administration by catering to their interests, to seek to adjust all disputes by compromise and manipulation, and, if a choice must be made between competing interests, always to align the government with the stronger – each of these characteristically Walpolean modes of procedure inevitably spilled over into and affected the handling of the colonies. Based on a clear recognition that the continued prosperity of the colonies – which had been such an important "Cause of enriching this Nation"[7] – depended to a considerable degree on their having, as one writer put it, "a Government ... as Easy & Mild as possible to invite people to Settle under it" and to keep them happy once they were there, the new metropolitan posture toward the colonies was succinctly characterized by Charles Delafaye, one of Walpole's subordinates. "One would not Strain any Point," Delafaye warned Governor Francis Nicholson of South Carolina early in Walpole's administration, "where it can be of no Service to our King and Country, and will Create Enemys to one[']s Self." To promote the economic well-being of the empire in general and, not incidentally, to avoid political difficulties for the administration at home thus became the central objectives of British colonial policy in the decades after 1720. Although the Board of Trade continued to press for measures that would bring the colonies under closer metropolitan supervision, it regularly failed to get full ministerial support for its recommendations during these years.[8]

Walpole's tendency to let the colonies proceed on their own without much interference from the central administration

---

[7] Joshua Gee, *The Trade and Navigation of Great-Britain* (London, 1729), 98.

[8] Charles Delafaye to Francis Nicholson, Jan. 16, 1722, in Jack P. Greene, ed., *Settlements to Society, 1584–1763* (New York: McGraw-Hill, 1966), 231–2.

in London except in matters that were of serious and pressing concern to powerful interest groups in Britain actually
gave colonial governors more room for political maneuver
than they had had at any time since the Restoration. For
those governors operating from an actual or potential position of political strength, this relaxation of pressure meant
that they could pursue the "real Advantage" of the parent
state without having to be constantly on guard against
reprimands from home for failing to enforce the "long
established Maxims" of the Board of Trade. Those with significant patronage at their command were able to distribute the growing number of royal offices in the colonies to
influential members of local elites and thereby parry opposition to British policy and secure support from a critical
segment of colonial society. This was precisely the course
of action through which Walpole had solidified his political
control in Britain. Ever since the 1670s, however, metropolitan officials had been slowly taking into their own hands
the patronage to most key offices in the colonies with the
result that most governors controlled the appointment to few
offices and thus had few of the utilitarian resources through
which they might have enhanced metropolitan authority in
the colonies. By thus depriving them of their "only means
of rewarding Merit and creating and [exerting] Influence,"
governors complained, metropolitan officials had assigned
them the task of preserving British authority "without giving
[them] the power of performance."[9]

Under these conditions, many governors chose simply not
to "consider any Thing further than how to sit easy" and
to be careful "to do nothing, which upon a fair hearing ...
can be blamed." Because the surest way to "sit easy" was
to reach a political accommodation with local interests, they

9 William Gooch, "Some Remarks on a Paper transmitted into America ...,"
   in Jack P. Greene, ed., *Great Britain and the American Colonies,*
   1606–1763 (New York: Harper and Row, 1970), 196–7, 208, 212;
   Chalmers, *Introduction to the History of the Revolt*, 2:354. See also,
   Bernard Bailyn, *The Origins of American Politics* (New York: Knopf,
   1968), 72–80.

frequently aligned themselves with dominant political factions in the colonies. Such governors sought to avoid disputes with the representative assemblies by taking special care not to challenge their customary privileges and, if necessary, even quietly giving way before their demands. As a consequence, royal and proprietary governors in many colonies were fully integrated into the local political community and came to identify and to be identified as much with the interests of the colonies as with those of the metropolis. This cooption, or domestication, of metropolitan governors significantly eased tensions between London and the colonies: The personal prestige and sometimes even the political influence of governors actually increased, and the assemblies contented themselves with the rather large amount of de facto power they could wield whenever it became necessary to do so.[10]

In this situation, the character of the long struggle over the distribution of authority within the British Empire changed substantially. Although the colonial assemblies did not usually shrink from any challenges from metropolitan representatives to the rights of people and institutions within their respective jurisdictions, they virtually ceased to demand the explicit recognition of those rights they had so often sought between 1660 and 1720. Thereafter, the unstated strategy of the assemblies seems to have been to secure local rights against metropolitan power in much the same way that those rights had been achieved within the metropolis itself: Through practice and usage that with the implicit acquiescence of the metropolis would gradually acquire the sanction of custom. The effort of the Jamaica Assembly in the 1720s to obtain the Crown's specific acknowledgment that Jamaicans were entitled to all the rights of Englishmen in return for voting a perpetual revenue to the Crown was notable because it was

[10] "Of the State of the British Plantations in America," in Joseph E. Johnson, ed., "A Quaker Imperialist's View of the British Colonies in America: 1732," *Pennsylvania Magazine of History and Biography* 60 (1936): 114; Gabriel Johnston to Lord Wilmington, Feb. 10, 1737, Historical Manuscripts Commission, *The Manuscripts of the Marquess of Townshend* (London: H. M. Stationary Office, 1887), 262–64.

the last such attempt by any assembly before the disturbances that immediately preceded the American Revolution.

Ever since the establishment of the colonies, their inhabitants mostly through their assemblies had been slowly building their own local inheritances and "Establishing the Constitution[s] of their Countrey[s]" on what they hoped was a firm foundation that would secure their inherited rights as Englishmen. Initially, it was entirely plausible for metropolitan officials to think of the colonies as "so many petty Corporations at a distance," with degrees of local authority equivalent only to those of "municipal corporations" in England. "As the colonies [had] prospered and increased to a numerous and mighty people, spreading over a great tract of the globe," however, they had gradually, in their "Corporate Capacity[s]," become full and distinct "Communities, deriving their Authority from the Crown."[11] Under these conditions, as Edmund Burke later remarked, "it was natural that they should attribute to [their] assemblies, so respectable in their formal constitution, some part of the dignity of the great nations which they represented."[12]

Metropolitan officials might speak derisively of these assemblies' pretensions "to have an equal power with the parliament of England." They might insist that these assemblies would never be "suffer[ed] ... to erect themselves into the power, and authority, of the British House of Commons." But the fact was that during the century and a half after the first establishment of the colonies, the assemblies had changed the constitutions of those colonies much in the same manner as Parliament was at the very same time changing the constitution of Britain. Thus, the assemblies were no longer limited to making by-laws but "made acts of all sorts and in all cases whatsoever. They levied money, not for parochial

[11] *The Charter of Maryland Together with the Debates and Proceedings of the ... Assembly* (Annapolis, 1725), iii; Gooch, "Some Remarks on a Paper," in Greene, ed., *Great Britain and the American Colonies*, 200; Ferdinand John Paris to Jeremiah Allen, July 26, 1738, "Talcott Papers," *Collections of the Connecticut Historical Society* 5 (1896): 83.

[12] Burke, "Letter to the Sheriffs of Bristol," in *Works*, 3: 189.

purposes, but upon regular grants to the Crown, following all the rules and principles of a parliament to which they approached every day more and more nearly." In comparison with the British House of Commons, these "Plantation Assemblies" might indeed be "circumscribed by very narrow Bounds." They did not, after all, preside over "a great and independent empire." But if these "little Senate[s]" did not have "all" the authority of Parliament, they nonetheless were, as James Otis said in the case of the Massachusetts House of Representatives, "the great council of this province, as the British parliament is of the kingdom" of Great Britain. "However contemptuously some … affect[ed] to speak of" them, they were thus, Otis implied, the most important and certainly the most cherished components of the colonists' "Ancient Constitution[s]."[13]

Notwithstanding the very great extent to which London officials had acquiesced in the many changes that had helped to shape these "long established Constitutions in [the] Colonies," they never came to regard those constitutions as fixed and inviolable On the contrary, as a later observer acidly remarked, while they suffered "the real and substantial Authority of the British Government … to be sapped, and at length overturned" within the colonies, metropolitan authorities constantly "kept up in words" their "high Claims of Prerogative." Indeed, those claims became more strident over time.[14]

[13] Opinions of Rawlins, n.d., and Pratt, [1757–8], in George Chalmers, ed., *Opinions of Eminent Lawyers* (Burlington, Vt.: C. Goodrich, 1858), 267, 376; Gooch, "Some Remarks on a Paper," and Sir John Randolph's Speech, [Aug. 6, 1737], in Greene, ed., *Great Britain and the American Colonies*, 200, 244–5; Burke, "Letter to the Sheriffs of Bristol," in *Works*, 3:189; [Nicholas Bourke], *Privileges of the Island of Jamaica Vindicated with an Impartial Narrative of the Late Dispute between the Governor and House of Representatives* (London, 1766), 31; *Remarks upon a Message Sent by the Lower House to the Upper House of Assembly, Apr. 4, 1762* ([Philadelphia], 1764), 14; J. N., *The Liberty and Property of British Subjects Asserted* (London, 1726), 22; James Otis, *A Vindication of the Conduct of the House of Representatives of the Province of Massachusetts-Bay* (Boston, 1762), 52; *Charter of Maryland Together with the Debates*, iii.

[14] Gooch, "Some Remarks on a Paper," in Greene, ed., *Great Britain and the American Colonies*, 198; Jack P. Greene, ed., "William

Almost from the beginnings of English colonization, people in London had worried that as the distant colonies became stronger and more powerful they would seek to shake off their dependence on the metropolis. Increasingly during the first half of the eighteenth century, such fears as well as a growing awareness of the economic and strategic importance of the colonies to Britain had led to demands for the Crown "to revise the Constitutions of the Settlements abroad, and to regulate them" by restricting the scope of their local legislative powers and compelling them "to follow the commands sent them by your Majesty." Invariably, these demands to bring the colonies under a more "absolute and immediate dependancy" became more vociferous during wartime, when colonial resistance to or incomplete compliance with defense requisitions and directions from London underlined for people in the metropolis the tenuousness of metropolitan controls in the colonies and made them acutely aware of the extent to which the enforcement of metropolitan measures in the colonies depended on the approval of colonial governments.[15]

During the late 1740s, London authorities responded to this situation by undertaking a new and reasonably systematic campaign to bring the colonies under closer supervision by reducing their autonomy and, if necessary, remodeling their constitutions. To achieve these ends, Crown officials initially relied almost entirely on traditional instruments of metropolitan control, including legislative review and royal instructions. Their efforts evoked considerable colonial resentment over the expanded use of the royal veto of

Knox's Explanation for the American Revolution," *William and Mary Quarterly*, 3d ser., 30 (1973): 302.
[15] Anonymous letter, ca. early 1730s, in Greene, ed., *Great Britain and the American Colonies*, 268–9; Board of Trade to King, Sept. 8, 1721, and Joshua Gee to Board of Trade, [Oct. 27, 1721], in W. Noel Sainsbury et al., eds., *Calendar of State Papers, Colonial*, 44 vols. (London: H. M. Stationary Office, 1860–), 1720–1, 444–9, 475. See also John Bumstead, "'Things in the Womb of Time': Ideas of American Independence, 1633 to 1763," *William and Mary Quarterly*, 3d ser., 31 (1974): 533–64.

colonial laws. Even more seriously, perhaps, they revived and intensified a long-standing controversy over the legal force of Crown and proprietary instructions in the colonies. As a consequence, during the 1750s and early 1760s, attention on both sides of the Atlantic focused ever more directly on the continuing tensions within the British Empire between central control and colonial rights.[16]

At various times following the Glorious Revolution, metropolitan officials had sought through formal instructions to colonial governors to achieve a variety of objectives, many of which were intended to curtail the powers of the assemblies while maintaining the authority of the prerogative in the colonies. Thus, they instructed governors not to consent to the passage of temporary laws that would expire before they could be reviewed in London, to insist on the inclusion of suspending clauses in any legislation that seemed to interfere with the royal prerogative or the navigation acts, not to permit the assemblies to determine their internal constitutions or to enjoy traditional parliamentary privileges, to make sure that the royal-appointed upper houses exercised equal rights with the assemblies in framing money bills, to secure from the assemblies permanent revenues so that governors and other members of the colonial civil establishments would not be dependent on the assemblies for their support, to deny the assemblies the power to nominate or to appoint persons to executive offices, and to pass no bills for the emission of paper currencies.[17]

The assumption behind both these instructions and the insistence that they were binding on the colonies was, as one

---

[16] A fuller analysis of this new metropolitan campaign will be found in Jack P. Greene, "'A Posture of Hostility': A Reconsideration of Some Aspects of the Origins of the American Revolution," *American Antiquarian Society Proceedings* 87 (1977): 5–46.

[17] See, on this point, Leonard W. Labaree, *Royal Government in America: A Study of the British Colonial System before 1783* (New Haven: Yale University Press, 1930), 420–48, and Jack P. Greene, *The Quest for Power: The Lower Houses of Assembly in the Southern Royal Colonies, 1689–1763* (Chapel Hill: University of North Carolina Press, 1963), 13–14, 52, 129, 380–7, 439–40.

official phrased it early in the eighteenth century, that legislative authority in the colonies operated "within the limits of the Governor's commission and Her Majesty's instructions."[18] As William Knox would subsequently explain, because, according to metropolitan theory, the constitutions of the royal colonies derived from the Crown's commissions to his governors and because each of those commissions specifically directed the governor to "guide himself by the Instructions he ... therewith receive[d] and also by such other Instructions as he receive[d] [t]hereafter," Crown officials invariably took the position that the king's instructions were "part of the Commission itself, and of equal authority."[19] In Maryland and Pennsylvania, provincial officials used the same argument to urge the constitutional character of proprietary instructions.

Just as few colonial leaders were disposed to admit that the royal commission was the sole basis of their local constitutions, so also did they deny that the instructions had any constitutional status. Commissions at least had been passed under the great seal in Britain and were routinely entered into the public records of the colonies. But instructions passed only under the lesser authority of the privy seal and, on the explicit directions of metropolitan authorities, were usually "kept secret by the Governor[s]." Thus, colonial advocates pointed out, for the colonists to accord constitutional standing to instructions would be an open admission that, as one writer phrased it, the colonies were "without any Constitution at all, and could have no permanent form of Government, but might have one secretly modelled by the King's Ministers and privately introduced, without their ever being able to know what it was." In proprietary colonies, the same objections were made to instructions from the proprietors.[20]

Because almost no colonial leaders were willing to admit that the colonies had no constitution or any permanent form

---

[18]   Opinion of William Rawlin, n.d., in Chalmers, ed., *Opinions of Eminent Lawyers*, 376.
[19]   Greene, ed., "Knox's Explanation for the American Revolution," 301.
[20]   Ibid., 301–2.

of government, it is not surprising that governors of both royal and proprietary colonies never had much success in securing compliance with any instructions that the assemblies opposed. Time after time, officials in the colonies complained that those bodies showed "no regard ... to H[is] M[ajesty's] Instructions." In defense of this behavior, assemblies argued that they had no obligation to comply with what one writer referred to as "unconstitutional Instructions," by which they meant instructions that were either contrary to existing colonial statutes or were incompatible with either the colonists' inherent rights as Englishmen or the customary powers and privileges of their assemblies. As the New Jersey Assembly pointed out in 1707, the "last clause of the *Petition of Right*" had stipulated that the Crown's servants were obliged to act "according to Law, and not otherwise."[21]

Similar arguments served as the basis for the colonies' adamant opposition to the Crown's expanded use of instructions after 1748. As a South Carolinian explained in 1756, the Crown's instructions might be obligatory upon governors and councils "because, if either should disregard them, they might be immediately displaced." But, colonial advocates argued, no instruction could bind the inhabitants of any colony "unless the people whom it concerns, adopt[ed] it, and their representatives, in their legislative capacity, confirm[ed] it by a law."

For, they contended, if instructions not thus ratified by the people's representatives "should be laws and rules to the people, ... then there would be no need of assemblies, and all our laws and taxes might be made by an instruction." For the king to "make his instructions the rule and measure of the

[21] Samuel Shute to Board of Trade, [Sept. 8, 1721], Oct. 29, 1722, *Calendar of State Papers, Colonial, 1720–21*, 407, *1722–23*, 157–8; [Joseph Galloway], *A True and Impartial State of the Province of Pennsylvania* (Philadelphia, 1759), 31–2; *Pennsylvania Gazette*, Sept. 18, 1729; *Boston Weekly News-Letter* (Boston), Jan. 27, 1732; William Douglass, *Summary, Historical and Political, of the First Planting, Progressive Improvements, and Present State of the British Settlements in North America*, 2 vols. (Boston, 1749–51), 2:33–4; *The Reply of the House of Representatives of the Province of New Jersey* [New York, 1707], 8.

people's obedience" would be "to govern by Instructions and not by Laws" and thereby to make "his will their only law." If, as the colonists believed, each assembly had "the same freedom and independence of legislature, as the parliament of Great Britain has," then it followed that it could not "be governed, directed, restrained or restricted, by any posterior instructions or commands" that diminished that legislative "freedom and independence."[22]

But these arguments carried little weight in the metropolis. "You Americans have wrong Ideas of the Nature of your Constitution," Lord Granville, president of the Privy Council throughout the 1750s, told Benjamin Franklin in 1757, "you contend that the King's Instructions to his Governors are not Laws, and think yourselves at Liberty to disregard them at your own Discretion. But, those Instructions," Granville insisted, could not be thus treated "as not binding, and no Law … they are first drawn up by grave and wise Men learned in the Laws and Constitutions of the Nation; they are then brought to the [Privy] Council Board, where they are solemnly weigh'd and maturely consider'd, and after receiving such Amendments as are found proper and necessary, they are agreed upon and establish'd. The Council is over all the Colonies," Granville continued: "The King and Council is THE LEGISLATOR of the Colonies; and when his Majesty's Instructions come there, they are the LAW OF THE LAND; they are, said his L[ordshi]p, repeating it, the Law of the Land, and as such ought to be OBEYED." Given the depth and extent of colonial opposition to this view, however, metropolitan officials had no way to ensure that the Crown's instructions would be thus "OBEYED" in the colonies.[23]

This stalemate over whether royal and proprietary instructions were binding on the colonies was emblematic of the

[22] C. G., *South Carolina Gazette*, Dec. 3, 1764; T. W., ibid., May 13, 1756; The Inhabitant, ibid., Dec. 10, 1764; Lewis Morris to Board of Trade, Jan. 28, 1745, in "The Papers of Lewis Morris," *Collections of the New Jersey Historical Society* 4 (1852): 221; Thomas Pownall, *The Administration of the Colonies* (London, 1764), 40–1.

[23] Benjamin Franklin to the Proprietors, Aug. 20, 1757, in Leonard W. Labaree et al., eds., *The Papers of Benjamin Franklin*, 30 vols.

ongoing struggle within the British Empire over how power should be allocated between the metropolis and the colonies. For the first time in many decades, metropolitan officials, beginning in 1748, had made a concerted effort to bring the colonies more thoroughly under London authority. Although the colonial assemblies had been able to thwart most of their specific initiatives, the assemblies' success in this regard in no way diminished metropolitan determination to augment the Crown's authority in the colonies. Rather, as Benjamin Franklin reported from London in 1759, a decade of failure and frustration had left "the Ministers and great Men here" more persuaded than ever that the colonies had "too many and too great Privileges" and that it was "not only the Interest of the Crown but of the Nation to reduce them" by "Clipping the Wings of Assemblies in their Claims of all the Privileges of a House of Commons" and reducing the colonies to an "absolute Subjection to Orders sent from hence in the Shape of Instructions."[24]

This continuing "zeal" among metropolitan authorities "for making the Crown absolute in America" more and more caused "informed" and "sensible Men" on the opposite side of the Atlantic to "look ... with Jealousy and Distrust upon the Royal Authority." By reminding colonial leaders that the Crown had not abandoned its claims for a more unlimited power in the colonies than it enjoyed at home and reviving inherited memories of "the arbitrary reigns of a Charles and a James ... when prerogative was unlimited, and liberty undefined," it enhanced the colonists' awareness that "nothing but a free and independent Assembly" could give them adequate "protection against arbitrary power" and intensified their determination to hold "fast those Privileges," including especially their inherent rights to strong representative assemblies, "that tend[ed] to balance ... or keep ... down" the power of the Crown.[25]

   (New Haven: Yale University Press, 1959–), 7: 249–50; to Isaac Norris, Mar. 19, 1759, ibid., 8:293.
[24] Franklin to Norris, Mar. 19, 1759, ibid., 8: 293–5.
[25] Greene, ed., "Knox's Explanation for the American Revolution," 302; [Bourke], *Privileges of the Island of Jamaica Vindicated*, 2, 27–8, 42,

Thus stirred by new fears that "the natural, and legal, and constitutional rights of the people" in the colonies might "be annihilated," colonial leaders responded to this campaign with intense resentment that the Crown's servants in the colonies should yet "be so infatuated, as to seek every occasion for alarming the fears, and exciting the jealousy, of his majesty's subjects; by endeavouring, to extend the prerogative, and advance the power, of the Crown, to the diminution, if not the total extinction, of the natural and indisputable rights of the people" in the colonies. Whether their constitutions would ever be settled or would be constantly exposed "to a *perpetual mutability*," and whether metropolitan authorities would ever "*explicitly* ... acknowledge, and put out of farther danger of unconstitutional attempts" the "essential rights of the people" in the colonies were persistent and worrisome questions for the colonists during the late 1750s and early 1760s.[26]

In 1724, the Crown's law officers had complained that "so many things, of no little consequence" to the constitutions of the colonies, were still "left in [such] great uncertainty, at this day." Forty years later, such an observation was still appropriate. Whereas the colonists lamented that the constitutions of the colonies were yet "so imperfect, in numberless instances, that the rights of the people lie, even now, at the mere mercy of their Governours" and profoundly wished that "our Liberties & Privileges as free born British Subjects were once properly defin'd," metropolitan authorities were more than ever persuaded that they should, could at any time, and had every "right to [re]moddle the Constitution[s]" of the distant and increasingly valuable colonies in such a way as finally to set "some bounds" to their inflated privileges and extensive autonomy. This wide divergence of opinion powerfully illustrates the fact that as late as the early 1760s the

66; Pennsylvanus, *Pennsylvania Journal* (Philadelphia), Supplement, Mar. 25, 1756.
[26] The Inhabitant, *South Carolina Gazette*, Dec. 10, 1764; [Galloway], *True and Impartial State*, 11; C. G., *South Carolina Gazette*, Dec. 17, 1764.

vexing constitutional problem of the distribution of power within the British Empire had not yet been resolved.[27]

PARLIAMENT AND THE COLONIES

In relations between the colonies and the home government before the mid-1760s, Parliament's authority over the colonies was an infinitely less important issue than that of the Crown. When, in 1649, during the Interregnum, the House of Commons asserted its authority not just over the realm of England but over "all the Dominions and Territories thereunto belonging,"[28] significant proportions of the populations of Barbados and Virginia, both predominantly royalist strongholds, resisted. In defense of their actions, the Barbadians explicitly raised the issue that would bring the British Empire into open conflict 120 years later: no legislation without representation. Any effort to bind them "to the Government and Lordship of a Parliament in which we have no Representatives, or persons chosen by us, for there to propound and consent to what might be needful to us, as also to oppose and dispute all what should tend to our disadvantage and harm," they protested, "would be a slavery far exceeding all that [any other part of] the English nation hath yet suffered."[29] Similarly, over the next fifty years, several colonies resisted the navigation acts at least partly on the

[27] Opinion of Yorke and Wearg, May 18, 1724, in Chalmers, ed., *Opinions of Eminent Lawyers*, 216; William Smith, Jr., *The History of the Province of New York*, ed. Michael Kammen. 2 vols. (Cambridge, Mass.: Harvard University Press, 1972), 1: 259; Virginia Committee of Correspondence to Edward Montague, July 28, 1764, "Proceedings of the Virginia Committee of Correspondence," *Virginia Magazine of History and Biography* 12 (1905): 5–14; Robert Hunter Morris to William Pitt, [1758–9], Miscellaneous Manuscripts, Clements Library; Benning Wentworth to Board of Trade, Dec. 23, 1755, Colonial Office Papers, 5/926, Public Record Office, London.

[28] "An Act Declaring and Constituting the People of England to be a Commonwealth and Free-State," [May 19, 1649], in C. H. Firth and R. S. Rait, eds., *Acts and Ordinances of the Interregnum, 1642–1660*, 2 vols. (London: H. M. Stationary Office, 1911), 2: 122.

[29] N. Darnell Davis, *The Cavaliers and Roundheads of Barbados, 1650–1652* (Georgetown, British Guinea: Argosy Press, 1883), 198.

grounds that the removal of their inhabitants out of England had simultaneously left them without any of "those privileges in the Parliament of England which their fathers had" and left Parliament with no legislative authority over them.[30]

But there were no such bold assertions from any of the colonies during the seventy-five years following the Glorious Revolution, and the virtual absence of any systematic attention either in Britain or in the colonies to the nature of Parliament's specific relationship to the colonies stands in pointed contrast to the seemingly perpetual debates over the extent to which royal authority was or was not limited in the colonies by charters, customs, and the colonists' rights as Britons. What was the meaning of this silence?

During the late Middle Ages, both the House of Lords and the House of Commons, as Robert L. Schuyler has explained, functioned less as modern legislative bodies with independent initiating powers than as advisers of or counselors to the king. This essentially conciliar role was not very different from that of the king's own appointed Privy Council under the Tudors. As the Crown's advisers, both Parliament and the Privy Council made regulations for the Crown's dominions outside the realm of England. In practice, however, most such regulations were the work not of the king-in-Parliament but of the king-in-council, which also heard appeals from all of the king's external dominions. Nevertheless, the king-in-Parliament did occasionally legislate for the dominions, and this custom of occasional legislation gradually, as in the case of Ireland, "evolved into a legally recognized right" – recognized, that is, within England.[31]

---

[30] Samuel Nadhorth to Secretary Morrice, Oct. 26, 1666, in *Calendar of State Papers, Colonial, 1661–68*, 418. See also A. Berriedale Keith, *Constitutional History of the First British Empire* (Oxford: Clarendon Press, 1930), 104–6.

[31] Robert Livingston Schuyler, *Parliament and the British Empire* (New York: Columbia University Press, 1929), 1–39; A. Donaldson, "The Application in Ireland of English and British Legislation Made before 1801" (Ph.D. dissertation, Queen's University, Belfast, 1952), 357, as quoted by Barbara A. Black, "The Constitution of Empire: The Case for the Colonists," *University of Pennsylvania Law Review* 124 (1976): 1183.

With the establishment of the American colonies, Parliament simply assumed that it could legislate for the colonies. Although the Stuarts, who still had veto power, were careful not to let Parliament assert too wide a jurisdiction in the colonial sphere and although the colonies, like the king's external dominions in the medieval empire, generally came to be considered possessions of the Crown and not parts of the realm, throughout the seventeenth century Parliament did on occasion bind both Ireland and the American colonies through acts that specifically applied to them, most notably in the series of navigation acts adopted between 1651 and 1696. Nevertheless, throughout the seventeenth century the king-in-council, not the king-in-Parliament, assumed most of the burden for overseeing the administration of both Ireland and the colonies.[32]

Notwithstanding the Crown's paramount role in colonial administration, however, the founding and development of the American colonies took place in a period of "great constitutional change," a period that, in A. F. M. Madden's words, saw "a shift of balance between king and parliament" from a situation of "royal dictatorship" under Henry VIII to "one of parliamentary omnicompetence" by the time of George III. "Ruled by convention," Britain's constitution, as H. T. Dickinson has emphasized, "was the product of time and the result of specific responses to practical problems." "Not fixed and immutable," it "developed almost imperceptibly through the ages" through custom, usage, and precedent. During the seventeenth century, Parliament had sought, with modest success, to diminish the relative authority of the Crown by appeals to fundamental law and "customary restraints on arbitrary power," the Whig case against unlimited prerogative being

---

[32] See Leo Francis Stock, ed., *Proceedings and Debates of the British Parliaments respecting North America*, 5 vols. (Washington, D.C.: Carnegie Institution, 1924–41), 1: 31; A. F. M. Madden, "1066, 1776 and All That: The Relevance of English Medieval Experience of 'Empire' to Later Imperial Constitutional Issues," in J. E. Flint and G. Williams, eds., *Perspectives of Empire* (London: Longman, 1973), 10–11, 13, 15.

based on an "ideology of customary law, regulated monarchy and immemorial Parliamentary right." From the early 1640s on, as Corinne C. Weston has shown, radical advocates of the expansion of parliamentary power had invoked the coordination principle in lawmaking in an effort to redefine the "relationships between the king and the two houses of Parliament by elevating the two houses at the expense of the king." A "theory of shared legal sovereignty by which the two houses became the predominant partners in lawmaking," this doctrine held that sovereignty rested not in the king alone but in the king-in-Parliament.[33]

But the diminution of the king's power within England during the seventeenth century was relatively minor compared to that which took place in the wake of the Glorious Revolution. As a result of that revolution, the principle of coordination was enshrined as the new orthodoxy. As Jennifer Carter has observed, England now "had a monarch depending on a parliamentary title, and a constitution based on [parliamentary] law." The "two salient features of the post-Revolution constitution were, first, that however much it was disguised a parliamentary monarchy had replaced a divine right monarchy; and, secondly, that since 1689 the monarch had learned somehow to live with Parliament." As Carter has emphasized, however, these developments were by no means a "foregone conclusion" at the time of the Glorious Revolution. Only gradually over the next half century did Parliament grow from what Burke called "a mere representative of the people, and a guardian of popular privileges for its own immediate

[33] Madden, "1066, 1776, and All That," 24; Black, "Constitution of Empire," 1193; H. T. Dickinson, "The Eighteenth-Century Debate on the 'Glorious Revolution,'" *History* 61 (1976): 42–3; John Phillip Reid, *In Defiance of the Law: The Standing-Army Controversy, the Two Constitutions, and the Coming of the American Revolution* (Chapel Hill: University of North Carolina Press, 1981), 3; Quentin Skinner, "History and Ideology in the English Revolution," *Historical Journal* 8 (1965): 151; Corinne C. Weston, "Co-ordination – A Radicalising Principle in Stuart Politics," in Margaret Jacob and James Jacob, eds., *The Origins of Anglo-American Radicalism* (London: Allen & Unwin, 1984), 85–104.

constituents . . . into a mighty sovereign," from a body that was
not simply "a control on the Crown on its own behalf" to one
that, as Burke put it, "communicated a sort of strength to the
royal authority." As several historians recently have pointed
out, the "concept of a sovereign parliament" had not been
"reasonably foreseeable in 1689," was largely "a development
of the mid-eighteenth century," and was only just "hardening
into an orthodoxy" during the 1760s. Nevertheless, the long-
term effect of this great constitutional change, as Dickinson
has noted, was to transform the ancient "doctrine of non-
resistance from a buttress of divine right monarchy into the
strongest defence of an existing constitution, whatever form
it might take." Increasingly during the eighteenth century, the
constitution came to be seen – in Britain – as virtually identical with Parliament itself: The constitution became precisely
what Parliament said it was, and many contemporaries within
the British political nation recognized that this "Modern
Constitution" was both a recent development and "infinitely
better than the Ancient Constitution."[34]

Precisely what this domestic constitutional change in
the metropolis meant for the colonies was never explicitly
worked out. Much evidence suggests that the colonists recognized and accepted the growing omnipotence of Parliament
within Britain.[35] How they regarded Parliament's authority over the rest of the empire is much more problematic.
No American produced a treatise comparable to William
Molyneux's *The Case of Ireland's Being Bound by Acts of
Parliament in England Stated*, a 1698 publication which, as
the title implies, argued that Ireland was a separate kingdom

[34] Jennifer Carter, "The Revolution and the Constitution," in Geoffrey
Holmes, ed., *Britain after the Glorious Revolution, 1689–1715* (New
York: St. Martin's, 1969), 39–40, 47, 55; Edmund Burke, "Letter to the
Sheriffs of Bristol," in *Works*, 3: 188; H. T. Dickinson, "The Eighteenth-
Century Debate on the Sovereignty of Parliament," *Transactions of the
Royal Historical Society*, 5th ser., 26 (1976): 189; Black, "Constitution
of Empire," 1210–11; Dickinson, "Eighteenth-Century Debate on the
Glorious Revolution," 33, 39.

[35] See, for instance, the essay signed "Z" in *Pennsylvania Gazette*, Apr. 8,
1736.

with its own parliament and that the English Parliament had no jurisdiction over it.[36]

Some contemporary reports, however, suggested that at least some prominent colonials questioned Parliament's legislative capacity in the colonies. In May 1744, for example, William Fairfield, speaker-elect of the Massachusetts House of Representatives, reportedly "openly in his Discourse bid Defiance to the Act of Parliament then lately pass'd for the Suppression of the *Land Bank* Scheme" in Massachusetts Bay.[37] Similarly, Governor Stephen Hopkins of Rhode Island allegedly declared in July 1757 "that the King & Parliament had no more Right to make Laws for us than the Mohawks" and that whatever might be said "concerning the Arbitrary Despotic Government of the Kingdom of France, yet nothing could be more tyrannical, than our being Obliged by Acts of Parliament To which we were not parties to the making; and in which we were not Represented."[38] The Earl of Loudoun, the king's first commander-in-chief of forces in America, charged that such notions were widespread in the colonies, complaining to his London superiors in December 1756 that it was "very common for the people in the Lower and more inhabited Country [in America] to say" that "they would be glad to see any Man durst Offer to put an English Act of Parliament in Force in this country."[39]

But such attitudes seem to have been unusual. From very early in the eighteenth century, most colonial political leaders appear to have admitted the legitimacy of acts of Parliament

[36] William Molyneux, *The Case of Ireland's Being Bound by Acts of Parliament in England Stated* (Dublin, 1698); Caroline Robbins, *The Eighteenth-Century Commonwealthman: Studies in the Transmission, Development and Circumstance of English Liberal Thought from the Restoration of Charles II until the War with the Thirteen Colonies* (Cambridge, Mass: Harvard University Press., 1961), 137–43, contains an excellent short discussion of Molyneux and his treatise.

[37] *An Account of the Rise, Progress, and Consequence of the Land Bank* (Boston, 1744), 39–40.

[38] Deposition of Samuel Peabody, Sept. 15, 1758, Rhode Island Manuscripts, 12: 21, Rhode Island Historical Society, Providence.

[39] Loudoun to Earl of Halifax, Dec. 26, 1756, Loudoun Papers 2416C, Huntington Library, San Marino, Calif.

in which the colonies were "particularly named," even when they "abhor[red] the very thought of them."[40] On a few occasions and when it was for their own advantage, some people even argued that certain acts of Parliament that did not specifically mention the colonies, such as the Act of Toleration, were actually in force there.[41] Similarly, people on the losing side of an argument in the colonies several times threatened to appeal to Parliament for redress of grievances on the grounds that its members, having "been in the Practice of these Things for Ages past," were obviously "better Judges ... than we who are but of Yesterday."[42] Thus, in the 1730s and 1740s, people who opposed the Massachusetts Assembly's measures for emitting paper money urged "the supreme Legislature[,] the *Parliament of Great Britain*," to take some "*summary Method[s]*" to "abridge the Plantations of this Privilege which they have assumed, of making their *publick Bills of Credit, a Tender.*"[43] Although people sometimes looked to Parliament for redress against colonial assemblies, the assemblies themselves occasionally appealed to Parliament against what they regarded as the arbitrary behavior of the Crown. For example, in 1701 the Jamaica Assembly tried to address the English House of Commons against what it took to be the arbitrary behavior of Governor Sir William Beeston, and in the early 1730s, some Massachusetts leaders advocated an appeal to Parliament to protect the colony from measures "projected by the Crown," which they regarded as "inconsistent with the Liberties of their Country."[44]

[40] George Larkin to Board of Trade, Oct. 14, 1701, *Calendar of State Papers, Colonial*, 1701, 576.

[41] [Francis Mackemie], *A Narrative of a New and Unusual American Imprisonment* ([New York], 1707).

[42] *The Melancholy State of this Province Considered in a Letter from a Gentleman in Boston to his Friend in the Country* (Boston, 1736), 4.

[43] William Douglass, *A Discourse Concerning the Currencies of the British Plantations in America* (Boston, 1740), 20–1, 41.

[44] Sir William Beeston to Board of Trade, July 30, 1701, *Calendar of State Papers, Colonial*, 1701, 379–80; [Jonathan Belcher], *Extracts from the Political State of Great Britain, December, 1730* [Boston, 1731], 14; Declaration of the House of Commons, May 10, 1733, in Stock, ed., *Proceedings and Debates*, 4: 214–15.

If the range of colonial attitudes reveals enormous uncertainty in the colonies over the relationship of Parliament to the British dominions on the American periphery, few in Britain following the Glorious Revolution had any doubt that Parliament had the right to legislate for the colonies whenever it chose to do so. Throughout the eighteenth century, Parliament continued to pass legislation affecting the external commerce and sometimes even the internal economies of the colonies. Metropolitan authorities proposed parliamentary intervention in several other areas. When the Board of Trade concluded early in the eighteenth century that the private colonies would have to be brought under the direct supervision of the Crown if they were ever to be properly subordinated to the metropolis, it automatically assumed that the recall of the charters would be handled by parliamentary statute.

Charles II or James II would have denied Parliament's competence in this area. After 1688, however, metropolitan administrators counted on the assistance of Parliament to handle difficult colonial situations. Between 1701 and 1715 they brought four separate bills into Parliament calling for the Crown's resumption of the private colonies. Because of the opposition of the proprietors, a genuine reluctance by many members of Parliament to tamper with private property, the vagaries of party politics, and, after the beginning of Queen Anne's war in 1702, an uncertain international situation that made any measure likely to produce discontent in the colonies seem highly imprudent, none of these bills got a full hearing and all failed to pass. Nevertheless, no one in Britain questioned the authority of Parliament to act in this area.[45]

Also during the early decades of the eighteenth century, the refusal of some colonial legislatures to comply with royal requests twice brought demands from metropolitan authorities

---

[45] Board of Trade to King, Feb. 26, 1698, Sept. 2, 1714, *Calendar of State Papers, Colonial, 1697-98*, 121-2, *1714-15*, 19-20; Board of Trade to Queen, Mar. 26, 1701, Jan. 10, 1706, ibid., *1701*, 141-3, *1706-8*, 3-6; House of Commons Committee to Board of Trade, Aug. 17, 1715, ibid., *1714-15*, 269; Opinion of Edmund Northey, July 22, 1714, in Chalmers, ed., *Opinions of Eminent Lawyers*, 338-41. See also the documents in Stock, ed., *Proceedings and Debates*, 3: 16-17, 114, 118, 361-5.

for parliamentary intervention into the internal administration of specific colonies. First, when the New York Assembly failed to vote as large a salary to Governor Robert Hunter as stipulated by his instructions or to provide salaries for other executive officials, the Privy Council, on the recommendation of the Board of Trade, took the unprecedented step in March 1711 of threatening to bring before Parliament a bill "for Enacting a Standing Revenue ... within the Province of New York for the Support of the Governor there, and the necessary Expenses of the Government" if the assembly would not itself provide the "Necessary Support." Although the Board repeated this threat several times and the Privy Council twice ordered bills to be brought before the House of Commons, the assembly stood firm for over two years. Finally, Hunter, despairing of ever getting any effective backing from London, agreed to a compromise in the summer of 1713 that led to the resolution of the conflict and the metropolitan authorities' abandonment of any plans to turn to Parliament.[46]

Similarly, during the late 1720s and early 1730s, when the Massachusetts House of Representatives repeatedly refused to comply with the Crown's directions to vote a permanent salary for the royal governor, the Board of Trade, in desperation, threatened in early 1729 to turn to Parliament. When the Massachusetts House would not yield, however, the Board again was unable to carry through on its threats and in 1736 finally abandoned the cause and permitted the governor to accept annual grants from the House.[47]

46 Board of Trade to Privy Council, Mar. 1, 1711, in W. L. Grant and J. Munro, eds., *Acts of the Privy Council, Colonial Series*, 6 vols. (London: H. M. Stationary Office, 1908–12), 2: 641–2; Board of Trade to Dartmouth, Apr. 1, 1713, *Calendar of State Papers, Colonial, 1712–14*, 168. See also Board of Trade to Gov. Robert Lowther of Barbados, July 20, 1713, and Gov. Lord Archibald Hamilton of Jamaica, Mar. 22, 1714, ibid., 207–9, 322.

47 Board of Trade to Newcastle, Mar. 27, 1729, and Newcastle to William Burnett, June 26, 1729 (two letters), *Calendar of State Papers, Colonial, 1728–29*, 339–40, 412–14; Jonathan Belcher to Newcastle, June 11, 1734, and Board of Trade to King, Aug. 29, 1734, ibid., *1734–35*, 130–1, 194–5; *Acts of the Privy Council, Colonial*, 3: 259–64; *Boston Gazette*, Sept. 1, 1729; *Boston Weekly News-Letter*, Sept. 18, 1729; *Pennsylvania Gazette*, Sept. 18, 1729.

Following the Board of Trade's failure to bring its recommendations for a permanent revenue for either New York or Massachusetts before Parliament, that body during the 1730s and 1740s refused on three separate occasions to use its legislative authority to strengthen royal authority in the colonies. In 1734, a House of Lords committee proposed a bill to prevent any colonial laws from taking effect until they had been approved by the Crown, but the Lords never formulated this proposal into a bill. Similarly, two bills to regulate colonial paper currencies considered by the House of Commons in 1744 and 1749 contained clauses that would have given royal instructions the force of law in the colonies. When these clauses provoked a "general opposition" from the colonial agents in London, however, the Commons dropped both bills, and the currency law it finally did enact in 1751 included no such provision.[48]

Parliament's reluctance to act on these and earlier matters affecting the charters and internal administration of the colonies contrasted pointedly with its willingness to legislate on a wide range of other problems. During the first six decades of the eighteenth century, it passed legislation to encourage the production of naval stores (1706) and indigo (1748) in the colonies, to regulate the value of foreign coin (1708), to restrict colonial manufacture of hats (1732) and iron (1750), to make it easier for metropolitan creditors to secure payment of colonial debts (1732), to discourage trade with foreign sugar islands (1733), to prohibit private banks of issue in the colonies (1741), and to forbid the emission of legal tender paper money in the four New England colonies (1751). Although it also enacted a few measures of concern to the colonies as a whole, including statutes to establish a colonial post office (1710) and to provide for the naturalization of foreigners who migrated to the colonies (1740), Parliament, as Martin Bladen, a member of Parliament and of the Board

---

[48] See Stock, ed., *Proceedings and Debates*, 4: 236–7, 5: 183–7, 298, 360–6; William Cobbett and T. C. Hansard, eds., *The Parliamentary History of England from the Earliest Period to 1803*, 36 vols. (London: T. C. Hansard, 1806–20), 14: 563–4.

of Trade, observed in 1739, in practice had thus very largely limited its activities with regard to the colonies to "laying Duties on their Produce, and with Enacting Laws, to secure the Advantage of their Commerce to Us."[49]

By not legislating on the noneconomic and internal affairs of the colonies, Parliament was acting toward them very much as it acted toward Ireland. In response to repeated claims by Irish leaders for exemption from its authority, Parliament passed a Declaratory Act in 1720 asserting its jurisdiction over Ireland in "all cases whatsoever." As J. C. Beckett has emphasized, however, Parliament continued thereafter, as it had done since the Tudor period, to exercise its right to legislate for Ireland "with great caution." After 1720, as before, British legislation for Ireland "was, in fact, very largely economic or administrative," and the Crown, as had long been its custom, usually sought the concurrence of the Irish Parliament to any British statutes that applied specifically to Ireland. According to Beckett, "there was never any question of taxing Ireland by British legislation; and even in less vital matters ministers were very unwilling to stir up trouble by using the authority of a British statute to over-ride the will of the Irish Parliament."[50]

Nor did the British Parliament customarily legislate on Irish internal affairs. With a "nervous regard for Irish opinion" and a grave "apprehensive[ness] of the consequences that might follow rash punitive measures," the British government in Ireland occasionally threatened to take unpopular measures but repeatedly backed down in the face of Irish resistance. The result was that the constitutional relationship between Ireland and Great Britain underwent "a practical change, due to the pressure of political circumstances." Even the application of Poyning's Law, which required the

[49] Jack P. Greene, ed., "Martin Bladen's Blueprint for a Colonial Union," *William and Mary Quarterly*, 3d ser., 17 (1960): 522.
[50] J. C. Beckett, "The Irish Parliament in the Eighteenth Century," *Belfast National History and Philosophical Society Proceedings*, 2d ser., 4 (1955): 22–3, and "Anglo-Irish Constitutional Relations in the Later Eighteenth Century," *Irish Historical Studies*, 14 (1964–5): 20–3.

prior approval in London of all bills brought before the Irish Parliament, "became little more than formal," and the British Parliament rarely legislated in areas likely to produce a "popular clamour" in Ireland. And in Ireland, as in America, British trade laws were routinely evaded by smuggling whenever they were regarded as unfair and detrimental to Irish interests.[51]

The suggestion, sometimes made by scholars, that in resisting parliamentary authority during the 1760s and 1770s the American colonies were "reject[ing] the results of" the Glorious Revolution presents major difficulties.[52] The ascendancy of Parliament within Britain and the eventual triumph of the doctrine of parliamentary omnipotence during the mid-eighteenth century may have been the most important results of that revolution, but they were by no means the only ones. Within Britain, as Jennifer Carter has pointed out, another consequence of the revolution was "a distinct, though not complete, withdrawal of central authority from local affairs." Earlier in the seventeenth century, Charles I had undertaken an extensive effort to exert the authority of the central government over county and local affairs in both the civil and the religious realms, and, although this effort was interrupted during the Civil War, the later Stuarts resumed it after the Restoration. "Perhaps nothing done in the 1680s by Charles II and James II," Carter has noted, "caused so much reaction against them as their interference with local privilege and the accustomed pattern of existing hierarchies – in counties, in corporations, or in university colleges." At least in the short run, the revolution effectively put an end to this effort and thereby created the conditions necessary for "the

[51] Beckett, "Anglo-Irish Constitutional Relations," 21–2; J. L. McCracken, "The Conflict between the Irish Administration and Parliament, 1753–6," *Irish Historical Studies*, 3 (1942–3): 169, 179; F. G. James, "Irish Smuggling in the Eighteenth Century," ibid., 12 (1961): 299–317.
[52] For instance, Alison Gilbert Olson, "Parliament, Empire, and Parliamentary Law, 1776," in J. G. A. Pocock, ed., *Three British Revolutions: 1641, 1688, 1776* (Princeton: Princeton University Press, 1980), 289.

typical eighteenth-century situation of gentry and aristocratic independence in the localities."[53]

Within Britain, the localities, along with the people who dominated them, enjoyed much less interference from the central government than they had at any time under the Stuart monarchy. During the eighty years following the Glorious Revolution, Britain seems to have experienced a significant redistribution of power to the localities as English, Welsh, and (after 1707) Scottish counties became what Edward Shils has referred to as "pockets of approximate independence." The same development was evident in Britain's more distant peripheries in Ireland and America, and this localization of power ensured that, in contrast to contemporary continental monarchies, Britain's expanding nation-state and overseas empire would not be founded on "methods of centralisation and absolutism."[54]

In both Ireland and the American colonies, the growth of parliamentary institutions during the eighteenth century epitomized this development. Before the Glorious Revolution, the Irish Parliament had convened only rarely. Though it met somewhat more frequently under Charles I, only three Irish parliaments met under Elizabeth and only one under both James I and Charles II. Between 1666 and 1692, it did not meet at all. Hence, as Beckett has noted, "the Irish parliament as we know it in the eighteenth century begins in 1692," when the ascendancy of the Protestant population as a result of the revolution enabled it "to take a more independent

---

[53] Carter, "Revolution and the Constitution," 53, 56; T. H. Breen, *Puritans and Adventurers: Change and Persistence in Early America* (New York: Oxford University Press, 1980), 4–24.

[54] Edward Shils, *Center and Periphery: Essays in Microsociology* (Chicago: University of Chicago Press, 1975), 10. See also Norma Landau, *Justices of the Peace, 1679–1760* (Berkeley and Los Angeles: University of California Press, 1984), on the continuing independence of county elites in regard to the internal affairs of the counties, and E. P. Thompson, "The Grid of Inheritance: A Comment," in Jack Goody, Joan Thirsk, and E. P. Thompson, eds., *Family and Inheritance: Rural Society in Western Europe, 1200–1800* (Cambridge: Cambridge University Press, 1976), 328–60, on the "tenacity and force of local custom" in determining patterns of social and legal relations in English local society.

line than formerly," while the insufficiency of the Crown's hereditary revenues to meet the usual costs of government provided it with an opportunity "to assert its rights, even against England," in exchange for granting funds to make up the difference. As a result of these developments, the Irish Parliament beginning in 1692 both met regularly and developed a vigorous "spirit of independence." Comparable developments occurred in the American colonies.[55]

For the development of the British Empire as a whole, then, perhaps the most important results of the Glorious Revolution were the localization of power and the growth of parliamentary institutions, not just within Britain but also in Ireland and the American colonies. At the same time that the British Parliament was growing "into a mighty sovereign," Ireland and the American colonies, "advancing by equal steps, and governed by the same necessity," had, as Burke would subsequently remark in relation to the American colonies, "formed within themselves, either by royal instruction or royal charter, assemblies so exceedingly resembling a parliament, in all their forms, functions, and powers, that it was impossible they should not imbibe some opinion of a similar authority."[56] To be sure, there were very important distinctions among these British legislatures. Those in Britain and Ireland had a House of Lords and the representative portions of the legislature were both much larger and considerably less representative than the colonial lower houses. At the same time, both the Irish Parliament, through the operation of Poyning's Law, and the colonial assemblies, through the process of metropolitan review of colonial legislation, had far more serious restrictions on their legislative power than had the British Parliament.[57]

Notwithstanding these differences, the growth in the power of all these bodies during the eighteenth century depended on the same circumstance: The Crown's inability

[55] Beckett, "Irish Parliament in the Eighteenth Century," 18–20.
[56] Burke, "Letter to the Sheriffs of Bristol," in *Works*, 3: 188–9.
[57] Beckett, "Irish Parliament in the Eighteenth Century," 17–28.

to cover either the normal costs of government or extraordinary wartime expenses without formal grants from local legislative bodies.[58] Moreover, they all performed the same legislative functions within their respective political societies. For the political nations in both Ireland and the colonies to assume that their "mimic parliament[s]" rested on the same "Foundations" and had the same rights and powers within their several political jurisdictions as did the British Parliament within Britain was therefore entirely reasonable.[59] "The parliament of Great-Britain, and the general assembly (or parliament) of ... any American Province," the South Carolina merchant Christopher Gadsden declared in the early 1760s, "though they differ widely with regard to the extent of their different spheres of action, and the latter's may be called a sphere within the former's, yet they differ not an iota" in their functions.[60] There was therefore no reason, added an anonymous contemporary from Maryland, why "the same Rights cannot be common to both, where they may be exercised without clashing or interfering with one another."[61]

Just as the growth of parliamentary power after 1689 had changed the constitution of Britain in fundamental ways, so also had similar developments in Ireland and the colonies altered the constitutions there. Throughout the British Empire, both in the metropolis and in the overseas polities, constitutions were customary. That is, in the best English constitutional tradition, they were all the products of evolving usage. In Burke's words, they had been slowly "formed by imperceptible habits, and old custom, the great support of all governments in the world."[62] "No Government ever was built at once or by the rules of architecture, but like an old house

[58] Clayton Roberts, "The Constitutional Significance of the Financial Settlement of 1690," *Historical Journal* 20 (1970): 59–76.

[59] Herman Merivale, *Lectures on Colonization and Colonies* (London: Longman, 1861), 74.

[60] Christopher Gadsden to the Gentlemen Electors of the Parish of St. Paul, Stono, *South Carolina Gazette*, Feb. 5, 1763.

[61] *Remarks upon a Message Sent by the Lower House to the Upper House of Assembly, Apr. 4, 1762* ([Philadelphia], 1764), 14.

[62] Burke, "Letter to the Sheriffs of Bristol," in *Works*, 3: 190.

at 20 times up & down & irregular," observed Sir George
Saville, an English member of Parliament in the 1760s, in
commenting on the nature of constitutional change within
the British Empire, "I believe," he continued, that "principles
have less to do than we suppose. The Critics['] rules were
made after the poems. The Rules of architecture after ye
houses, Grammar after language and governments go *per
hookum & crookum* & then we demonstrate it *per bookum.*
There is not that argument or practice so bad that you may
have precedents for it."[63]

If by the early 1760s the British, Irish, and American colonial constitutions were thus all well "established by long custom and ... sanctioned by accepted usage,"[64] the unformulated
and unasked question was whether in the process of changing the constitutions of their respective political jurisdictions,
these legislatures were also changing the constitution of the
whole to which they all belonged. Without as yet having formulated a fully articulated and coherent sense of empire,[65] the
British political nation had not, before the 1760s, developed
any explicit concept of an imperial constitution. Indeed, the
tendency within Britain was to conflate the British constitution with the imperial constitution. Yet the absence of the
concept did not mean that an imperial constitution was not
slowly being formed through the same evolutionary process that was shaping and reshaping the constitutions of the
several entities that composed the British Empire. As Burke
would subsequently remark, during the eighteenth century
an imperial constitution had gradually evolved out of "mere
neglect; possibly from the natural operation of things, which,
left to themselves, generally fall into their proper order."[66] In

---

[63] Sir George Saville to [Mr. Acklom], [Aug. 1768], Saville Papers, William
L. Clements Library, Ann Arbor, Mich.

[64] John Phillip Reid, "In Accordance with Usage: The Authority of Custom,
the Stamp Act Debate, and the Coming of the American Revolution,"
Fordham Law Review 45 (1976): 341.

[65] Richard Koebner, *Empire* (Cambridge: Cambridge University Press,
1961), 61–193.

[66] Burke, "Letter to the Sheriffs of Bristol," in *Works*, 3: 190.

this constitution, as Andrew C. McLaughlin, the doyen of American constitutional historians, pointed out three-quarters of a century ago, the metropolitan government exercised general powers that "from the necessity of the case ... could not well be exercised by [Ireland or] the colonies: the post-office, naturalization, war and peace, foreign affairs, intercolonial and foreign commerce, establishment of new colonies, etc.," and the Irish and American colonial governments exerted de facto and virtually exclusive jurisdiction over all matters of purely local concern, including matters of taxation.[67]

This arrangement meant that people outside the metropolis, Irishmen and American colonists, were subject to what Burke called a "double legislature": The legislature at Westminster and their own. As the two legislatures operated within well-defined and distinct spheres, they did not, in Burke's words, "very grossly or systematically clash."[68] Parliament usually limited its actions with regard to the colonies to the general or external sphere and was obviously not "clearly *informed [about]* ... the Constitutions and Governments [with]in the Colonies,"[69] while the Crown, through its governors and its powers of legislative and judicial review, exerted the predominant role in metropolitan interactions with the colonies. The colonists, therefore, as Barbara Black has argued persuasively, could reasonably develop a sense that the colonies were primarily "the king's dominions" and that Parliament's involvement with them was "essentially conciliar" – that is, advisory to, reinforcive of, and operating through the Crown – much as it had in the medieval empire. Inasmuch as Parliament's colonial authority thus derived from the Crown, it followed that as the colonial assemblies had succeeded in reducing the Crown's authority in the colonies, they had also diminished the authority of Parliament and that the developing constitution of the empire was, as the seventeenth-century English constitution had been in theory, a

---

[67] Andrew C. McLaughlin, *The Foundations of American Constitutionalism* (New York: New York University Press, 1932), 138.
[68] Burke, "Letter to the Sheriffs of Bristol," in *Works*, 3: 190.
[69] *American Magazine* 1 (Jan. 1741): viii.

constitution of "principled limitation," in which by long custom
Parliament's authority did not usually extend to the internal
affairs of the colonies and virtually all segments of the empire
enjoyed "the benefits of government by consent" in matters
pertaining to their own particular interior concerns.[70]

This is not to suggest that colonists thought of the colonies as "Independent State[s]" nor yet of their assemblies
as bodies "politick coeordinate with (claimeing equal powers) and consequently independent of the Great Councell of
the Realme."[71] But colonial leaders certainly understood that
their precise relationship to Parliament remained unsettled.
Benjamin Franklin spoke for many colonists during the Stamp
Act crisis when he questioned the extent of Parliament's jurisdiction over the colonies. "Planted in times when the powers of parliament were not supposed so extensive as they are
become since the Revolution" and "in lands and countries
where the parliament had not then the least jurisdiction," all
of the colonies except Georgia and Nova Scotia, Franklin
pointed out, had been settled without "*any money* granted
by parliament" by people who, with "permission from the
Crown, purchased or conquered the territory, at the expence
of their own private treasure and blood." "These territories,"
Franklin contended, "thus became new dominions of the
Crown, settled under royal charters, that formed their several

---

[70] Black, "Constitution of Empire," 1202–3. The colonists were not the
only people in the empire who believed that jurisdiction over the colonies
was largely the concern of the Crown. In a House of Commons debate in
December 1754, Henry Fox argued against passage of "a particular and
distinct Mutiny Bill" for the colonies on those grounds. Because the colonies were "more immediately under the eye of the Crown than any other
part of the British dominions," Fox declared, such a bill would be "too
great an encroachment upon the prerogatives of the Crown, or at least ...
would be intermeddling in an affair with which we have no call to have
any concern" (R. C. Simmons and P. D. G. Thomas, eds., *Proceedings
and Debates of the British Parliament Respecting North America, 1754–
1783*, 5 vols. to date (Millwood, N.Y.: Kraus, 1982–), 1: 36).
[71] *A Letter to a Gentleman chosen to be a Member of the Honourable
House of Representatives* ([Boston,] 1732), 15; Gov. Robert Hunter
to Sec. St. John, Sept. 12, 1711, *Calendar of State Papers, Colonial,
1711–12*, 103–4.

governments and constitutions, on which the parliament was *never consulted*; or had the *least participation*." Like the Irish settlers, the American colonists "from the beginning," Franklin noted, had had "their separate parliaments, called modestly assemblies: by these chiefly our Kings have governed them. How far, and in what particulars, they are subordinate and subject to the British parliament; or whether they may not, if the King pleases, be governed as *domains of the Crown*, without that parliament, are points newly agitated, [and] never yet ... thoroughly considered and settled."[72]

In the absence of such a thorough consideration, the colonists' experience taught them that, "since the Settlement made at the Revolution," the constitutions of the colonies, no less than that of Britain itself, had entered "*a new Aera*" in which "the main strong lines" of "the people's rights (including Americans)" had "been more particularly pointed out and established." Far from rejecting the results of the Glorious Revolution, colonists simply assumed that they were entitled to all its benefits. As a result of the revolution, they felt, their "Liberties & Constitution[s]" had been "secur'd & establish'd upon [just as] ... firm and lasting [a] foundation" as had been those of Britons in the home islands. Based "on the same rational, constitutional foundation" laid down during the revolutionary settlement, Parliament and the assemblies, colonial leaders could reasonably surmise, differed from each other "ONLY as a greater circle from a less[er]."[73]

According to the practice of the extended polity of the British Empire as it had developed during the three-quarters of a century following the Glorious Revolution, there were thus three separate sorts of constitutions. First, there was a British constitution for the central state and its immediate dependencies, including Cornwall, Wales, and, after 1707, Scotland. Second, there were separate provincial

---

[72] Benjamin Franklin, "On the Tenure of the Manor of East Greenwich," 1766, in Verner W. Crane, ed., *Benjamin Franklin's Letters to the Press* (Chapel Hill: University of North Carolina Press, 1950), 48.

[73] A Freeholder, *Maryland Gazette*, Mar. 16, 1748; C. G., *South Carolina Gazette*, Dec. 17, 1764; *New York Gazette*, Oct. 21, 1734.

constitutions for Ireland and for each of the colonies in America. Third, there was an as yet undefined, even unacknowledged, imperial constitution – the constitution of the British Empire – according to the practice of which authority was distributed in an as yet uncodified and not very clearly understood way between the metropolis and the overseas polities with Parliament exercising power over general concerns and the local legislatures handling local affairs within their respective jurisdictions.

Practice to the contrary notwithstanding, no one in power in Britain accepted *in theory* any limitations on the authority of Parliament to act in the colonial sphere. Parliament might hesitate to undertake any measure that would raise "a general opposition from our colonies and plantations," as it did during the 1740s, when the Crown proposed legislation to make royal instructions law in the colonies and as it repeatedly did in Irish affairs. Through such restraint, Parliament acknowledged the truth of the adage that government was founded on the consent of the governed. But metropolitan authorities, in both the colonies and Britain, never doubted that Parliament had authority to take any action it thought necessary with regard to the colonies, even to the point of "alter[ing] ... or intirely abolish[ing]" any "Concessions or Constitutions" formerly "granted by any of the Kings of England, or the first proprietors" if they thought those "Concessions or Constitutions inconvenient or Injurious" to the metropolis. Even those who believed that the Crown could not of its own authority change the constitutions of the colonies in any fundamental way also thought that there was absolutely no "mischief" that could not "be remedied ... by act of parliament of Great Britain." As occasion required, Parliament could levy taxes to defray the cost of the internal administration of specific colonies, revoke charters, new "moddle the Constitution[s] of those governments," or otherwise abridge the colonies of the "many valuable Privileges which they enjoy[ed]" in exactly the same way as it had ostensibly already done in the case of Ireland with the Declaratory Act of 1720. "In all *British* Cases and over all Persons according to the British Constitution," they were convinced, the "Legislature of *Great Britain*" was "absolutely supreme and the *Dernier Resort*" not just for Britain but for the entire British Empire.[74]

By the time the outbreak of the Seven Years' War in the mid-1750s forced them to suspend the campaign begun in the late 1740s to tighten metropolitan controls over the colonies, Crown officers in Britain had decided that they would never be able to accomplish their objectives with the prerogative powers at their command. Their largely ineffective efforts to enhance Crown authority in the colonies during the six years from 1748 to 1754 had taught them that "no other Authority than that of the British Parliament" would either "be regarded by the Colonys, or be able to awe them into acquiescence." Increasingly, during these prewar years, frustration had driven them to threaten the intervention of Parliament to force colonial compliance with metropolitan commands. Except in the case of the Currency Act of 1751, however, metropolitan ministries had proven reluctant to involve Parliament in their reform efforts. During the war the failure of several colonies to support the military effort and the expansion of colonial legislative power at the expense of the Crown brought forth a veritable chorus of demands for Parliament to intervene in colonial governance, including proposals for Parliament to form "a Parliamentary Union"

---

[74] Cobbett and Hansard, eds., *Parliamentary History of England*, 14: 563; Lewis Morris to Board of Trade and to Newcastle, Jan. 28, 1745, "The Papers of Lewis Morris," *Collections of the New Jersey Historical Society* 4 (1852): 220–1, 226–8; Opinion of Edmund Northey, July 22, 1714, in Chalmers, ed., *Opinions of Eminent Lawyers*, 339; Sir Nathaniel Lawes to Board of Trade, Nov. 13, 1720, Apr. 20, June 12, Oct. 30, 1721, *Calendar of State Papers, Colonial, 1720–21*, 194, 290, 334, 480; Robert Hunter Morris to William Pitt, [1758–59], Miscellaneous Mss., William L. Clements Library; William Douglass, *Summary, Historical and Political, of the First Planting, Progressive Improvements, and Present State of the British Settlements in North-America*, 2 vols. (Boston, 1749–51), 1: 212, 2: 34; *Weekly News-Letter* (Boston), Sept. 11, 1728; Richard Jackson's Opinion on Changing the Pennsylvania Constitution, [1758], in Carl Van Doren, ed., *Letters and Papers of Benjamin Franklin and Richard Jackson, 1753–1785* (Philadelphia: American Philosophical Society, 1947), 83–4; *Some Observations on the [Excise] Bill . . .* (Boston, 1754), 7–8; *New York Gazette Revived in the Post-Boy*, Jan. 18, 1748.

among the colonies for their defense, to tax the colonies to pay the costs of the war, to curtail colonial trading with the enemy, and to act to "restore ye Authority of ye Crown & settle ye Rights of ye People according to the true Spirit of ye British Constitution."[75]

That Parliament might indeed act to shore up metropolitan authority in the colonies was suggested in 1757. The House of Commons intervened in the purely domestic affairs of a colony for the first time since 1733 in May of that year, when, with the full approval of the Crown, it censured the Jamaica Assembly for making extravagant constitutional claims while resisting instructions from London. The pains metropolitan authorities took to inform all of the colonies of the Commons' action in this important precedent strongly suggested the possibility that they might take similar actions with regard to other colonies.[76]

Whether a more extensive exertion of parliamentary authority over the colonies would be readily accepted by the colonists seems not to have been doubted in Britain, and many colonials,

[75] Thomas Pownall to Halifax, Oct. 29, 1757, Force Papers, vol. 9, Box 7, Library of Congress, Washington, D.C.; Thomas C. Barrow, "A Project for Imperial Reform: 'Hints Respecting the Settlement for our American Provinces,' 1763," *William and Mary Quarterly*, 3d ser., 24 (1967): 118; Charles Townshend to Newcastle, Nov. 7, 1754, Newcastle Papers, Add. Mss. 32737, ff. 57–8, British Library, London; William Shirley to *Sir Thomas Robinson, Feb. 4, 1755*, in C. H. Lincoln, ed., *Correspondence of William Shirley*, 2 vols. (New York: Macmillan, 1912), 2: 123–4; Robert Dinwiddie to Robinson, Feb. 12, 1755, in Robert A. Brock, ed., *The Official Records of Robert Dinwiddie*, 2 vols. (Richmond: Virginia Historical Society, 1883–4), 1: 493; [Henry McCulloh], *Proposals for Uniting the English Colonies on the Continent of America* (London, 1757), 15–16; *State of the British and French Colonies in North America* (London, 1755), 57, 67–8; Malachy Postlethwayt, *Britain's Commercial Interest Explained and Improved*, 2 vols. (London, 1757), 2: 424–5, and *The Universal Dictionary of Trade and Commerce*, 2 vols. (London, 1757), I: 373; T – -s W – -t, *South Carolina Gazette*, Supplement, May 13, 1756.
[76] *Journals of the House of Commons* (London), 27: 910–11 (May 23, 1757); John Pownall to governors, June 3, 1757, Colonial Office Papers, 324/6, Public Record Office, London; "Some Instances of Matters relating to the Colonies in which the House of Commons have interfered," 1757, Hardwicke Papers, Add. Mss. 35909, ff. 275–80, British Library, London.

especially those who held Crown offices or otherwise supported the executive in its contest with the local legislatures,
agreed that there would be "no contending" with Parliament.
That august body, they believed, had the power and the right
to do whatever it thought necessary with regard to the colonies. It could pass measures "for their better Regulation," even
to the point of abridging the colonists' "Privileges & put[ting
them] ... under a more Despotick Govern[men]t." "A *British*
Parliament," Governor Lewis Morris told the New Jersey
Assembly in April 1745, could "abolish any Constitution in
the Plantations that they deem inconvenient or disadvanta-
geous to the ... Nation" as a whole.[77]

How the colonists might respond if Parliament did indeed
try to legislate for the colonies in unaccustomed ways might
have been predicted from their reactions to earlier proposals
for such measures. When Parliament was considering legislation to resume the charters of the private colonies during the
first decades of the eighteenth century, Jeremiah Dummer,
agent for the New England charter colonies, produced the
most systematic colonial commentary on Parliament's authority over the colonies before the 1760s. In *A Defence of the
New England Charters*, first published in London in 1721,
Dummer admitted that Parliament's "Legislative Power"
was "absolute and unaccountable, and [that] King, Lords
and Commons" might "do what they please[d]." But, he
added, in elaborating a point that would be frequently made
by partisans of the colonies between 1764 and 1776, "the
Question here is not about Power, but *Right: And shall not*

---

[77] A New-England Man, *A Letter to the Inhabitants of the Province of
the Massachusetts-Bay* (Boston, 1751), 4; [Archibald Kennedy], *Serious
Considerations on the Present State of the Affairs of the Northern
Colonies* (New York, 1754), 23–4; *American Magazine* 1 (Jan.
1741): viii; Cadwallader Colden's "Observations on the Balance of Power
in Government," 1744/45, in *The Letters and Papers of Cadwallader
Colden, New-York Historical Society Collections*, 68 (1937), 257;
New-York Post-Boy, Apr. 9, 1745; Douglass, *Summary, Historical
and Political*, 1: 243–4; *South Carolina Gazette*, June 5, 1756; William
Smith, *A Brief State of the Province of Pennsylvania*, 3d ed. (London,
1756), 41–2.

the Supream Judicature of all the Nation do right?" Denying
that it was "right" for colonies, which had "no Representatives
in Parliament," to be "censur'd and depriv'd" of their rights
by that body," Dummer suggested "that what the Parliament
can't do justly, they can't do at all." "The higher the Power
is," he concluded, "the greater [the] Caution is to be us'd in
the Execution of it."[78]

The colonists' view of an unjust action was revealed during the 1740s, when Parliament was considering legislation to
make royal instructions law in the colonies. Such legislation,
the colonists contended, was *"contrary to the Constitution[s]
of Great Britain & of the Plantations"* and *"inconsistent
with the Liberties & Privileges inherent in an Englishman
whilst he is in a Brittish Dominion."* By subjecting them to "a
Despotick Power vested in the Crown," such a measure, they
protested, would deprive them of their "inestimable privilege of" being "governed by the laws of their own making"
and "annihilate all the Legislative Power" formerly exercised
by the colonies. Such a measure, asserted William Bollan,
agent for Massachusetts in London, "was plainly ... an
unconstitutional attempt" that would "wholly subvert" the
"Constitution[s] of the Colonies."[79]

The colonists were implying in these protests that, as
the New Jersey Assembly resolved in 1745, Parliament
had no right through legislation to encroach "upon *the
fundamental Constitution[s]*" of the colonies or to alter "*the
Concessions made to the first Settlers ... by his Majesty's*

---

[78] Jeremiah Dummer, *Defence of the New-England Charters* (London,
   1721), 76, 78.
[79] Cadwallader Colden to Archibald Kennedy, Apr. 4, 1745, *Colden
   Papers, New-York Historical Society Collections,* 67 (1934): 310–12;
   William Bollan to Massachusetts Speaker, July 12, 1751, Bollan Papers,
   Manuscript A B62, New England Historical and Genealogical Society,
   Boston; Petition of Eliakin Palmer, Mar. 5, 1749, in Stock, ed., *Proceedings
   and Debates,* 5: 304–6; William Greene to Richard Partridge, [June 18,
   1749], in Gertrude S. Kimball, ed., *Correspondence of the Colonial
   Governors of Rhode Island, 1723–1775,* 2 vols. (Boston: Houghton
   Mifflin, 1902–3), 2: 94.

Royal Ancestors."[80] Although no colonists at this time seem
to have explicitly denied that Parliament, as well as the
assemblies, could legislate for the internal affairs of the colonies, the obvious logic of their argument was that legislation
without representation was a violation of the entire British
constitutional tradition as it had evolved in both Britain and
the colonies and that Parliament therefore had no authority over the internal concerns of the colonies. Certainly, this
was the obvious inference behind the assertion, made by the
historian Daniel Neal in his 1720 *History of New-England*,
that because the inhabitants of Massachusetts had been
guaranteed "all English liberties" by the 1691 charter, they
could "be touched by no Law, by no Tax, but of their own
making."[81]

Adherents to this emerging colonial interpretation of the
eighteenth-century British and imperial constitutions had
obviously not accepted the postrevolutionary metropolitan
concept of a constitution based on parliamentary supremacy.
Rather, they were espousing the older seventeenth-century
theory of a constitution of customary restraints on arbitrary
power, a theory that seemed to them to be more compatible
with – and more explanatory of – their own constitutional
experience both within the colonies and, with regard to
metropolitan-colonial relationships, within the empire at
large. Questioning whether Parliament had "a Right to enact
any Thing contrary to a fundamental Part of the British
Constitution," they argued that Magna Charta and the
Petition of Right were expressive of *"reserv'd Rights"* that
were antecedent to and therefore binding on Parliament.
"To imagine that a Parliament is Omnipotent, or may do
any Thing," a Freeholder argued in the *Maryland Gazette* in
February 1748, was "a vulgar Mistake … for … they can't
alter the Constitution. There are certain Powers, Rights, and
Privileges invested in every Branch of the Legislature, by the

---

[80] *New-York Post-Boy*, Apr. 9, 1745.
[81] Daniel Neal, *The History of New-England*, 2 vols. (London, 1720),
    2: 479.

Constitution," he explained, "no Part of which can be given up by any of them without breaking thro' that Constitution, which is the Basis of the whole." "Even the Authority of Parliament," concluded another writer in accordance with the best seventeenth-century thought on the subject, "is circumscribed by Law, and has its Bounds."[82]

The practical question, of course, was what agency could prevent Parliament from trampling on these fundamental rights whenever it decided to do so: in the words of another Maryland writer, "Who, or what, can disable the Legislature?" Though some colonial thinkers suggested in early hints of the later concept of judicial review that the courts might do so, colonial thinkers could come up with no better answer than the people themselves. Strictly speaking, observed still a third Maryland author who quoted extensively from John Locke, it was untrue that the legislative power was "accountable to no Power of Earth." Although he admitted that there was "no Power on Earth (that is, no Body politic, entrusted by the Society) superior to the legislative Power," he insisted that that power was always limited by the willingness of the governed to obey it. Legislative power was therefore always "accountable to the *Community*," members of which could judge whether the legislature "acted agreeably to … *Reason* [and to] … the *Fundamental Rule[s] of society*" and withhold support from any measures that "Breach[ed] the *Constitution*." But the emerging imperial constitution contained no formal and theoretically neutral mechanism to which people in the colonies could appeal against an erring Parliament.[83]

---

[82] A Freeholder, *Maryland Gazette* (Annapolis), Feb. 10, 1748; *Boston Gazette or Country Journal*, May 10, 1756; The Watchman, #1, *Pennsylvania Journal and Weekly Advertiser* (Philadelphia), Feb. 23, 1758. For an example of the contrary view, see *Pennsylvania Gazette*, Apr. 8, 1736.

[83] Philanthropos, *Maryland Gazette*, Apr. 27, May 18, 1748; Americano-Britannus, ibid., June 4, 1748; A Native of Maryland, ibid., May 11, 1748; *Pennsylvania Journal and Weekly Advertiser*, July 4, 1754, Feb. 23, 1758; [Daniel Fowle], *An Appendix to the Late Eclipse of Liberty* (Boston, 1756), 20–1, 24.

In this situation, colonists could do little else but hope that "so great" a body as the British Parliament would take no action that by "preparing Slavery to us would give a presedent" that could subsequently be used "against themselves." Although some people fretted lest after the war Parliament should try "to make general Colony Laws" that would "deeply ... enter into our *Constitution[s]* and affect our most *valuable Priviledges*," most seem to have remained far more fearful of attacks on their rights and constitutions from the "long hand of the Prerogative" than from Parliament. Indeed, rather than thinking of Parliament as a source of danger or as a competitor to their own legislative jurisdictions, they seem to have regarded it, in the phrase of Christopher Gadsden, as "their best and most interested friends" in Britain, the ultimate protector of colonial as well as British rights and privileges, and a body to which they could appeal for help if the Crown persisted in its efforts to violate their established constitutions.[84]

Acting in their executive capacity, the Crown's ministers might very well, as they had so often done in the past, through either ignorance or malice, take up oppressive measures against the colonies. But colonial writers cited the House of Commons' condemnation of the Earl of Clarendon under Charles II for having tried to introduce "an arbitrary government *in[to] his Majesty's ... plantations*" as evidence that "*that August Assembly*, the Protectors of English Liberties," would never lend its weight "to enforce illegal or arbitrary orders" or, indeed, to "*do any thing that shall be to our disadvantage.*" Parliament's refusal in 1744 and 1749 to give the royal instructions the force in law in the colonies seemed

[84] Henry Beekman to Henry Livingston, Jan. 7, 1745, as quoted by Philip L. White, *The Beekmans of New York in Politics and Commerce, 1674–1877* (New York: New-York Historical Society, 1956), 190; Isaac Norris to Benjamin Franklin, May 18, 1765, *Franklin Papers*, 12: 130–1; *A Letter to a Gentleman*, 15; William Smith, Jr., to Thomas Clap, [1757–1759], as quoted in Smith, *History of the Province of New York*, ed. Kammen, 1: xxxiv; Watchman, #2, *Pennsylvania Journal and Weekly Advertiser*, Mar. 26, 1758; C. G., *South Carolina Gazette*, Dec. 17, 1764.

to confirm this opinion. When "the clause [for that purpose] was thrown out by the Commons," Franklin later recalled, "we adored them as our friends and [as] friends of liberty." The widespread feeling seems to have been that Parliament simply had too much wisdom and too much regard for the preservation of British liberty – in the colonies as well as in Britain – ever to interfere with the jurisdictions of its sister parliaments, the colonial legislatures. The ministry did not again try to enlist Parliament in its schemes to make instructions law in the colonies, Franklin believed, because it feared that if it permitted Parliament to "meddle at all with the Government of the Colonies," it "would establish more Liberty in the Colonies," at the expense of the powers and prerogatives of the Crown.[85]

Of course, this roseate view ignored some powerful evidence pointing in the opposite direction. Especially foreboding were the implications behind the precise wording of the House of Commons' condemnation of the Jamaica Assembly in 1757. Whereas a committee report had denounced the assembly's claims as "illegal unconstitutional and dirogatory of the Rights of the Crown and People of Great Britain," William Knox later recounted, the House of Commons itself "ordered the Word *Unconstitutional* to be struck out, and [in its place] inserted [the phrase] *repugnant to His Majesty's Commission to His Governor of the said Island.*" The grounds for this change, "as it was said in the Debate and reported in America, where I then was, and well remember the alarm it excited," Knox wrote, was that "the Island had no Constitution but the King's Commission." By this change in wording, the House of Commons in effect subscribed to the Crown's long-standing contention that, as Knox put it, "the Colonys have no Constitution, but that the mode of Government in each of them depends upon the good pleasure of the King, as expressed in his Commission, and Instructions to his Governor."[86]

The colonists' failure to give major weight to such evidence provides impressive testimony to their basic trust in Parliament, which, it is clear in retrospect, was founded on Parliament's not having acted toward the colonies before the 1760s in ways that could be perceived as unusual, arbitrary, or threatening. Indeed, because it had almost entirely refrained from interfering in internal colonial matters, Parliament had done precisely the opposite. So long as Parliament continued to take only a limited role in colonial affairs and otherwise to behave in ways to which colonists had become accustomed, they had little cause to be jealous of, much less to challenge, its authority. But the colonists' failure to challenge Parliament's authority did not mean that they would accept it "in all cases whatsoever," as the Irish Declaratory Act asserted. Nor did their high regard for Parliament indicate that they endorsed the doctrine of parliamentary omnipotence that was then gaining ascendance in Britain as a result of what C. H. McIlwain has called the "unforeseen constitutional consequences" of the Glorious Revolution. Because Parliament had never tried to intrude into their internal affairs in any sustained or serious way, they had never been required to consider the legitimacy of its authority to do so. Neither by explicit declaration nor by long-standing practice had they ever accepted – or rejected – the doctrine of parliamentary omnipotence insofar as it extended to the colonies. However thoroughly it had come to be accepted in Britain as an essential attribute of the British constitution, that doctrine could not, without colonial acceptance, become an established principle of the emerging imperial constitution, that cluster of conventions that defined and structured relationships between colonies and metropolis in the mid-eighteenth-century British Empire.[87]

[86] Greene, ed., "William Knox's Explanation for the American Revolution," 301; Barrow, ed., "Project for Imperial Reform," 117.
[87] Charles H. McIlwain, *The American Revolution: A Constitutional Interpretation* (New York: Macmillan, 1923), 14.

Even though Parliament's precise relationship to the colonies had, in Franklin's words, "never yet [been] ... thoroughly considered and settled," well before the 1760s it could be viewed from two well articulated and opposing perspectives. One, the perspective of London, derived from the metropolitan understanding of the nature of the British constitution as it had evolved since the Glorious Revolution. The other, from the overseas polities, was shaped by the colonists' experience with their own local constitutions and the developing imperial constitution. The weight of much recent historical argument has been that the perspective of the metropolis was the "correct" one. But this interpretation falls into the trap of equating correctness with centrality and strength. As subsequent events would prove, the position of the metropolis on this question could never be regarded as "correct," in the sense of enjoying unchallenged supremacy until it had been ratified in the colonies, either by explicit consent or by implicit acquiescence.[88]

That the colonists would not readily ratify the doctrine of parliamentary omnipotence could easily be surmised from the thrust of their own constitutional thought between 1660 and 1760. Their view of the constitution was developmental in the sense that they saw their own constitutions and, by implication, the constitution of the empire as moving in the same direction as had the British constitution in the wake of the Glorious Revolution, that is, toward increasing limitations on prerogative power and greater security for individual and corporate rights under the protection of a strong legislature. According to this view, further gains in this direction might yet be made but those achieved could not – constitutionally, at least – be lost. From this perspective, any effort to impose the principle of unlimited parliamentary authority on the colonies was bound to appear to the colonists as retrogressive and unacceptable. In this unsettled and uncodified situation, practice was the best, indeed, the only, guide to

---

[88] Franklin, "On the Tenure of the Manor," in Crane, ed., *Franklin's Letters to the Press*, 48.

what was "constitutional" in relations between metropolis and colonies within the empire, and, as McLaughlin pointed out in the 1930s, the British Empire "as a practical working system" was characterized "by diversification and not by centralization." According to metropolitan theory, the central government in London "had complete and unalloyed power." In "actual practice," however, "the empire of the mid-eighteenth century was a diversified empire" with power "actually distributed [among] and exercised by various governments." Ireland and the American dominions "had long existed" as "bodies, corporate, constituent members of the Empire," each with its own constitution and a government "with many powers and with actual authority." Each inhabitant of both Ireland and the American colonies thus lived under two governments, one imperial in scope and exercising full general powers over foreign affairs, war and peace, and external trade and the other a colonial government that "was peculiarly his own." Although the several colonial governments were by no means "in possession of complete authority," they had long exercised actual and virtually exclusive jurisdiction over almost all matters of purely local concern.[89]

To a remarkable extent, the colonial legislatures, like Parliament in Britain, exercised full legislative powers over their respective jurisdictions. They claimed those powers on the basis of their constituents' inherited rights as Britons not to be subjected to any laws passed without their consent, on their having actually exercised those powers, according to their customary constitutions, for many decades and in some cases for over a century, and on metropolitan confirmation of their rights to those powers through either explicit charters or long-standing custom. Because the metropolitan government never explicitly admitted in theory what had developed in practice, however, the authority of the colonial assemblies vis-à-vis that of the British Crown and the Parliament remained

[89] McLaughlin, *Foundations of American Constitutionalism*, 132–3, 138; McLaughlin, A *Constitutional History of the United States* (New York: Appleton-Century, 1935), 14.

in an uncertain state as late as the 1760s. Meanwhile, notwithstanding this lack of theoretical resolution or agreement as to the actual and customary distribution of power within the empire, the empire continued to function in practice with a clear demarcation of authority, with virtually all internal matters being handled by the colonial governments and most external affairs and matters of general concern by the metropolitan government.

2

EMPIRE CONFRONTED, 1764–1766

At the conclusion of the Seven Years' War in 1763, the only certainty about constitutional arrangements within the large, extended polity that constituted the early modern British Empire was their uncertainty. The balance of authority between metropolis and colonies remained undefined. Recurrent disputes over the extent of the Crown's colonial authority had left that issue unresolved, and the nature of Parliament's relation to the colonies had never been explicitly examined. As Massachusetts Governor Francis Bernard remarked in August 1764, the relationship of the "Subordinate Governments ... to the Sovereign power" had "never been formally settled" and was certainly not "generally understood."[1]

Parliament's efforts to impose taxes on the colonies in the mid-1760s precipitated the first intensive and systematic exploration of this problem on either side of the Atlantic. Ostensibly, the issue raised by these efforts, especially by the Stamp Act of 1765, was no more than whether, in the succinct words of Bernard, "America shall or shall not be Subject to

[1] Francis Bernard to Richard Jackson, Aug. 18, 1764, in Edmund S. Morgan, ed., *Prologue to Revolution: Sources and Documents on the Stamp Act Crisis, 1764–1766* (Chapel Hill: University of North Carolina Press, 1959), 29.

the Legislature of Great Britain.["] But the controversy rapidly moved on to a more general level. In the process, it provoked a broad-ranging consideration of fundamental issues involving the nature of the constitutional relationship between Britain and the colonies and the distribution of power within the empire. Far from producing either a theoretical or a practical resolution of these issues, however, the Stamp Act crisis of 1764–6 revealed a deep rift in understanding between the colonies and metropolis that would never be bridged within the structure of the empire.

Historians have tended to agree that the administration of George Grenville had no reservations about the legitimacy of its actions when it initiated these efforts to impose taxes in March 1764. But Grenville's speech introducing his American measures suggests otherwise. No M. P. arose to challenge the legitimacy of his proposals. Indeed, one observer reported that they "gained the applause of the whole House." Yet, by acknowledging that "the path" might be "thorny," Grenville betrayed both an awareness of the novelty of his proposals and a pronounced uneasiness about the reception that they might receive in the colonies.[3] As Bernard would later remark, Grenville and his aides could scarcely have failed to realize "that such an Innovation as a Parliamentary Taxation would cause a great Alarm & meet with much Opposition in most parts of America."[4]

Some metropolitan supporters later admitted that the Stamp Act was the "first Instance of parliament's imposing an internal tax upon the colonies for the single purpose of a revenue." For at least three decades, however, metropolitan officials had casually assumed that Parliament's colonial

---

[2] Bernard to Lord Barrington, Nov. 23, 1765, in Edward Channing and Archibald Cary Coolidge, eds., *The Barrington-Bernard Correspondence* (Cambridge, Mass.: Harvard University Press, 1912), 96.

[3] Commons Proceedings, Mar. 8, 1764, in R. C. Simmons and P. D. G. Thomas, eds., *Proceedings and Debates of the British Parliament Respecting North America, 1754–1783*, 5 vols. to date (New York: Kraus, 1980–87), I: 492.

[4] Bernard to Barrington, Nov. 23, 1765, Channing and Coolidge, eds., *Barrington-Bernard Correspondence*, 94.

authority was unlimited. For over a century, Parliament had routinely laid duties upon colonial exports and imports for the purposes of regulating trade. But it was also true that parliamentary legislation for the colonies had been confined almost entirely to commercial and other economic regulations of general scope. The only precedent for a tax for any other purpose was the Post Office Act of 1710, and that measure, as William Beckford, the wealthy Jamaican sugar planter and M. P., noted on the floor of the House of Commons, had "certainly [been] for the convenience of the colonies themselves."[5] If there were no clear precedents for Parliament's taxing the colonies for revenue before the Stamp Act, neither had anyone ever explicitly articulated a theoretical justification for the exertion of parliamentary authority in that area.

Because of the traditional link between taxation and representation in British constitutional thought and practice, this problem was potentially troublesome – for metropolitans as much as for colonials. Indeed, metropolitan disquiet over this problem was clearly revealed during the Stamp Act crisis by proposals from several writers for colonial representation in Parliament. More important, the Grenville administration itself implicitly acknowledged the importance of this problem by the pains it took to deal with it. During the winter of 1764–5, in the months preceding the final passage of the Stamp Act, Grenville's lieutenant, Thomas Whately, ingeniously developed the doctrine of virtual representation, according to which the colonists, like those individuals and groups who resided in Britain but had no voice in elections, were nonetheless *virtually* represented in Parliament.[6]

5 [William Knox], *The Claim of the Colonies to an Exemption from Internal Taxes Imposed by Authority of Parliament Examined* (London, 1765), 30; Commons Proceedings, Feb. 6, 1765, in Simmons and Thomas, eds., *Proceedings and Debates*, 2: 11.
6 [Thomas Whateley], *The Regulations Lately Made Concerning the Colonies and the Taxes Imposed upon Them, Considered* (London, 1765), 100–14. Examples of metropolitan calls for colonial representation in Parliament may be found in *Reflexions on Representation in Parliament* (London, 1766), 41–2, and [Thomas Crowley], *Letters and Dissertations on Various Subjects* (London, 1776), 8–9, 16.

When Grenville first brought the proposal for colonial stamp duties before Parliament, however, neither he nor Whately had apparently yet applied this doctrine to the colonies, and he tried to finesse the problem created by the lack of colonial representation in Parliament with a simple – and categorical – assertion of Parliament's right. Indeed, by insisting on that occasion that Britain had "an inherent right to lay inland duties there," Grenville himself first raised the question of parliamentary right. In addition, by going out of his way to assert that the "very sovereignty of this kingdom depends [up]on it," he also managed to establish the framework within which most metropolitans would subsequently consider the issue by ensuring that they would thenceforth interpret colonial resistance to the exertion of that right as a challenge not simply to the authority of Parliament per se but to the sovereignty of the metropolis in general.[7]

As soon as it was raised, the specter of parliamentary taxation stimulated "great inquiry and some apparent puzzle" in the colonies. That it was both "new and unprecedented" most colonial leaders seemed to agree. In the "long period of more than one hundred and fifty years" since the founding of the colonies, the Pennsylvania lawyer John Dickinson subsequently remarked, "no statute was ever [previously] passed [by the British Parliament] for the sole purpose of raising a revenue on the colonies." However, notwithstanding the fact that the entire subject "had never been canvassed before" and was "yet new to the whole British Nation," few colonists seem to have doubted that, at least from their perspective from overseas polities, it was obviously unconstitutional.[8]

---

[7] Commons Proceedings, Mar. 8, 1764, in Simmons and Thomas, eds., *Proceedings and Debates*, 1:492.

[8] The Earl of Clarendon [John Adams] to William Pym, Jan. 1766, in Charles F. Adams, ed., *The Works of John Adams*, 10 vols. (Boston, 1856), 3: 477; [Thomas Fitch et al.], *Reasons Why the British Colonies, in America, Should Not Be Charged with Internal Taxes* (New Haven, 1764), in Bernard Bailyn, ed., *Pamphlets of the American Revolution, 1750–1776* (Cambridge, Mass.: Harvard University Press, 1965), 404; John Dickinson, *Letters from a Farmer in Pennsylvania to the Inhabitants of the British Colonies* (Philadelphia, 1768), in Forrest McDonald, ed., *Empire and Nation* (Englewood Cliffs, N.J.: Prentice Hall, 1962), 26;

Beginning with their earliest protests against the proposed Stamp Act, they insisted that no community of Englishmen and their descendants could be taxed without their consent, an exemption they claimed "as their Right" and not "as a *Privilege*."[9] "To be subject to no ... taxation ... but [that] which is authorized by the representative body of each society in concert with the representative of the Crown presiding over it," declared the Barbados Assembly, was "a privilege which we imagined the subjects of Great Britain had been particularly entitled to in every settlement, however distant, of the British Empire as a birthright and blessing indeed capable of making every settlement, even the most distant of that Empire[,] grateful to a British spirit."[10] Throughout the entire British world, the colonists asserted, in colonies as well as in the metropolis, representation was the only basis for the authority to tax. Because Parliament represented only the inhabitants of Britain, it necessarily followed that its taxing power did "not extend ... to such parts of the British dominions as are not represented in that grand legislature of the nation."[11]

Colonial analysts dismissed the idea of virtual representation out of hand. Founded on no more secure foundation than "a Defect in the Constitution of England," namely, the "Want of a full Representation in Parliament of all the People of England," the "Phantasie of virtual Representation," they declared, was obviously a "far-fetched" notion "of late date" that had been fabricated for the sole purpose of arguing the colonists "out of their civil Rights." If they were virtually represented in 1765, the colonists contended, they must always have been so, and if they had always been represented, why,

New York Gazette & Post-Boy, May 22, 1766; [Kenneth Morrison], *An Essay towards the Vindication of the Committee of Correspondence in Barbados* (Barbados, 1766), 9.

9 New York Petition to the House of Commons, Oct. 18, 1764, in Morgan, ed., *Prologue to Revolution*, 9–10.

10 Barbados Assembly to Gov. Charles Pinfold, Nov. 26, 1765, as quoted in David H. Makinson, *Barbados: A Study of North-American-West-Indian Relations* (London: Mouton, 1964), 72.

11 [Fitch], *Reasons Why*, in Bailyn, ed., *Pamphlets*, 385, 387.

for a century and more, as one anonymous writer asked, had "the Mother Country ... continually applied to the assemblies of the various provinces, whenever she wanted their assistance?" Indeed, he queried, why in the first place had she granted "a provincial legislature to her Colonies, and from the time of their first existence, invest[ed them] ... with the sole power of internal taxation?"[12]

Besides, they complained, the very concept was incompatible with that ancient and basic British constitutional principle that no tax could be "justly laid on any People ... when the People taxed have not contributed to the Law, and agreed by their Representatives to receive it." Quoting Joseph Addison to show that in the British tradition true liberty always required a community of interest between legislators and constituents, an anonymous Barbadian pointed out that this notion of a "common interest" was so fundamental to the British constitution that it even extended "beyond the legislative Line, into the civil Administration of Justice. Juries to determine on a Point of Life and Property," he observed, "must come in a Manner qualified for the Office, by having lived in the Neighbourhood of the Party" under prosecution. Thus, in "Cases of [both] Taxations and Verdicts," he noted, a "Man's Neighbours alone" were, according to British constitutional practice, the only people who had "an exclusive Right to determine all his Questions." Hence, it seemed evident to this writer that virtual representation was "a Notion no less absurd than virtual Neighbourhood would be, if set up in a Court of Law." "*To have any Authority*," he concluded in quoting David Hume, "*a Law ... must be derived from a Legislature* WHICH HAS A RIGHT"; for a legislature to have a right, it had to have a common interest and a direct connection with the people for whom it presumed to legislate.[13]

---

[12] Maurice Moore, *The Justice and Policy of Taxing the American Colonies in Great Britain, Considered* (Wilmington, 1765), in William S. Price, Jr., ed., *Not a Conquered People: Two Carolinians View Parliamentary Taxation* (Raleigh: North Carolina Department of Archives and History, 1975), 44–6; *Candid Observations on Two Pamphlets Lately Published* (Barbados, 1766), 22; *The Crisis, or, A Full Defence of the Colonies* (London, 1766), 5–7.

[13] *Candid Observations*, 19–22, 30.

For people in the far reaches of an extended polity like that of the early modern British Empire, this emphasis upon the local foundations of both legislative and judicial authority made sense, and, whatever Parliament might declare, few colonists had any doubt that their rights as Englishmen demanded both that they be exempt from taxes levied in a distant metropolis without their consent and that their own local assemblies have an exclusive power to tax them. Indeed, as most colonial leaders seem to have recognized, the "exclusive Right" of the assemblies to tax the colonies constituted "what the Lawyers call the very Git of the Colony Argument."[14]

In analyzing the colonial response to the Stamp Act crisis, most scholars have tended to treat the colonists' claims as demands for their individual rights as Englishmen, as indeed they were. But this emphasis has tended to obscure the very important extent to which, especially during the Stamp Act crisis, the colonists seem to have believed that, as Robert W. Tucker and David C. Hendrickson have reminded us, "there could be no effective guarantee of individual rights without the effective guarantee of collective rights (or powers)," which they thought of as virtually synonymous with "the rights of the provincial assemblies." As was stressed in Chapter 1, the status and authority of the assemblies had "always been the central issue in the metropolitan-colonial [constitutional] relationship." Whereas earlier the conflict had been between the assemblies and the Crown, it was now between the assemblies and Parliament. In view of the close relationship in colonial thinking between individual rights and corporate rights, it is by no means an exaggeration to argue, as do Tucker and Hendrickson, "that the central issue raised by the measures of the Grenville ministry concerned the role and power of the provincial assembly."[15]

Throughout the Stamp Act crisis, colonial spokesmen put enormous stress upon the traditional conception of their

[14] Ibid., 12.
[15] Robert W. Tucker and David C. Hendrickson, *The Fall of the First British Empire: Origins of the War of American Independence* (Baltimore: Johns Hopkins University Press, 1982), 162, 187–8.

assemblies as the primary guardians of both the individual liberties of their constituents and the corporate rights of the colonies. Noting that it was precisely because their great distance from the metropolis had prevented them from being either fully incorporated into the British nation or represented in the metropolitan Parliament that "their own assemblies" had been "established in its stead," they insisted that each of their own local legislatures enjoyed full legislative authority and exclusive power to tax within its respective jurisdiction.[16] "As the legislative, deliberative body" in each colony, the assembly, in the words of former Massachusetts Governor Thomas Pownall, represented the collective "will of that province or colony."[17]

This identification of individual rights with the corporate rights of the assemblies ran through the entire colonial argument. Thus, the Connecticut Assembly argued against Parliamentary taxation on the grounds that it would both deprive its constituents of "that fundamental privilege of Englishmen whereby, in special, they are denominated a free people" and, no less important, leave them with "no more than a show of legislation." "May it not be truly said in this case," it asked, "that the Assemblies in the colonies will have left no other power or authority, and the people no other freedom, estates, or privileges than what may truly be called a tenancy at will; that they [will] have exchanged, or rather lost, those privileges and rights which, according to the national constitution, were their birthright and inheritance, for such a disagreeable tenancy?"[18]

But the colonists based their claims for exemption from parliamentary taxation not merely on "their right to the general principles of the British constitution," nor on "the [many] royal declaration[s] and grant[s] in their favor" in their charters from the Crown. They also grounded those claims on "Prescription, or long Usage, which," they insisted,

---

[16] *Letter to G. G.* (London, 1767), 27.
[17] Pownall's speech, May 15, 1767, in Simmons and Thomas, eds., *Proceedings and Debates*, 2: 482.
[18] [Fitch], *Reasons Why*, in Bailyn, ed., *Pamphlets*, 393–4.

was "generally understood to give Right." "Ever since the
first establishment of ... civil government" in the colonies "to
the present time," their protagonists argued, "for more than
100 years," they had "uniformly exercised and enjoyed the
privileges of imposing and raising their own taxes, in their
provincial assemblies"; and those privileges, they asserted,
had been "constantly ... acknowledged, and allowed to be
just in the claim and use thereof by the Crown, the ministry,
and the Parliament." Originally confirmed "by solemn acts
of government," their rights, one writer declared in language
redolent of the colonists' ancient disputes with Crown authorities, had thus subsequently been "sanctified by successive
usage, grounded upon a generous reliance on English Faith
and Compact, and that usage – ratified by repeated authoritative acquiescence." Such "constant and uninterrupted usage
and custom," it seemed to them, was, in the best traditions
of English constitutional development, "sufficient of itself
to make a constitution." In these appeals to their rights as
Englishmen, their charters, and long-standing custom, colonial spokesmen were merely turning against Parliament the
defenses that they and their ancestors had developed over the
previous century to protect colonial rights against abuses of
prerogative.[19]

Whatever the sources of the legislative authority of the
assemblies, the most significant questions posed by the new
intrusion of Parliament into the domestic affairs of the colonies – the most vital issues raised by the Stamp Act crisis

[19] Ibid., 392; [Morrison], *Essay towards the Vindication*, 10–11;
Barbados Committee of Correspondence to London agent, [1765], in
John Dickinson, *An Address to the Committee of Correspondence in
Barbados* (Philadelphia, 1766), in Paul Leicester Ford, ed., *The Writings
of John Dickinson* (Philadelphia, 1895), 255–56; *Letter to G. G.*, 35–6;
Aequus, letter from the *Massachusetts Gazette*, Mar. 6, 1766, in Charles
S. Hyneman and Donald S. Lutz, eds. *American Political Writing dur-
ing the Founding Era, 1760–1805*, 2 vols. (Indianapolis: Liberty Fund,
1983), 1: 63, 65; Richard Bland, *The Colonel Dismounted: or the Rector
Vindicated* (Williamsburg, 1764), in Bailyn, ed., *Pamphlets*, 323; John
Gay Alleyne, *A Letter to the North American, On Occasion of his
Address to the Committee of Correspondence in Barbados* (Barbados,
1766), 4.

vis-à-vis the constitutional organization of the early modern British Empire – were how extensive that authority was and how it related to the authority of the British Parliament. Few colonists could accept the metropolitan position that there were no limits to Parliament's colonial authority. They did not deny that Parliament's power was extraordinary. They knew that, at least within Britain, its privileges were then "as undetermined as were formerly the Prerogatives of the Crown." Just as the prerogative had eventually been "fixed and settled," however, "So in like Manner," they believed, "ought all other Claims of Privilege to be," including those of Parliament. "Power of every Sort has its Boundary," declared an anonymous Barbadian, and it "would tend to the Happiness of all English Subjects" if Parliament's "Privileges were as well known and ascertained as the Prerogatives of the Crown." "To presume to adjust the boundaries of the power of Parliament" might be beyond its competence, the Massachusetts House of Representatives admitted in October 1765, but it had no doubt that "boundaries there undoubtedly are."[20]

In trying to fix for themselves the boundaries of parliamentary authority, colonial spokesmen carefully distinguished between power and authority. For a legislature to have "Authority," they argued, it "must have a Right over the Persons whomsoever it may affect," and such a right, they believed, could only be "derived by Compact, and must have a legal and open Commencement" that "carried with it not only Marks of Notoriety, but of the Consent of all Parties." Nor, they contended, could that compact be changed without the mutual consent of all parties. Consent was thus not merely "a bare Circumstance to the Rise and vesting of Authority."

[20] Tucker and Hendrickson, *Fall of the First British Empire*, 73; Richard Bland, *An Inquiry into the Rights of the British Colonies* (Williamsburg, 1766), in William J. Van Schreeven and Robert L. Scribner, eds., *Revolutionary Virginia: The Road to Independence*, 4 vols. to date (Charlottesville: University of Virginia Press, 1973–), 1: 42; Massachusetts House to Bernard, Oct. 23, 1765, in Harry Alonzo Cushing, ed., *The Writings of Samuel Adams*, 4 vols. (New York: G. P. Putnam, 1904–8), 1: 16.

It was "the very Essence of ... Jurisdiction." Without it, a legislature had no authority, and its actions could be "supported
on no other Base than Power." However great had been the
increase in Parliament's authority as a result of the constitutional changes that had occurred in England since the founding of the colonies, those changes were perforce confined to
the "People of England only" and had "nothing to do with"
the colonies unless the colonists had themselves consented to
them. Great as was the "Power of Parliament," its colonial
authority was therefore necessarily confined to those areas in
which the colonies had given their consent.[21]

But what were these areas and how could they be described?
A few colonists concluded that there were no areas in which
Parliament had "lawful authority over" the colonies. The del-
egation of legislative power to the colonies, they believed, had
to be "considered not only as uncurrent with, but as exclusive
of all parliamentary participation in the *proper subjects* of
their legislation, that is to say, in cases not repugnant to the
laws of Great-Britain." According to this line of argument,
Parliament had "no power but what is delegated to them by
their constituents," and because those constituents had "no
power over our liberty and property," it followed that the
authority of Parliament was "(over these things at least) ...
purely local, and confined to the places they are chosen to
represent," and, as at least one writer asserted, that any exertion of that authority over the colonies was "most inconsistent with civil liberty."[22]

But most colonists took a far more cautious approach to
this subject. They neither claimed "an independent legislature" nor denied that the colonies were "all subordinate to
and dependent upon the mother country." Rather, most seem

[21] *Candid Observations*, 26–31.
[22] [William Goddard?], *The Constitutional Courant: Containing Matters
      Interesting to Liberty, and No Wise Repugnant to Loyalty* ([Burlington,
      N.J.], 1765), in Merrill Jensen, ed., *Tracts of the American Revolution,
      1763–1776* (Indianapolis: Bobbs Merrill, 1967), 87, 90; Aequus, in
      Hynemann and Lutz, eds., *American Political Writing*, 1: 64; Philalethes,
      in *New York Gazette*, May 8, 1766.

to have agreed with the Maryland lawyer Daniel Dulany that because the colonies were "dependent upon Great Britain," the "supreme authority vested in the King, Lords, and Commons" could "justly be exercised to secure, or preserve their dependence whenever necessary for that purpose." Such authority, wrote Dulany, "results from and is implied in the idea of the relation subsisting between England and her colonies." As Dulany quickly added, however, there could "very well exist a *dependence* ... without absolute *vassalage* and *slavery*," and he was persuaded that the extent of that dependence could be located in "what the superior may *rightfully* control or compel, and in what the inferior ought to be at liberty to act without control or compulsion."[23]

The colonies might thus, as the Virginia lawyer Richard Bland acknowledged, be "subordinate to the Authority of Parliament," but they were subordinate only "in Degree" and "not absolutely so." "When powers compatible with the relation between the superior and inferior have by express compact been granted to and accepted by the latter, and have been, after that compact, repeatedly recognized by the former – when they may be exercised effectually upon every occasion without injury to that relation," Dulany explained, "the authority of the superior can't properly interpose, for by the powers vested in the inferior is the superior limited." As free-born Britons, the colonists assumed, they could not be subjected to any but what Bland referred to as "a constitutional Subordination" to the parent state.[24]

But what was the nature of that "constitutional Subordination"? Where should the line be drawn between the authority of Parliament at the center and that of the legislatures in the colonies? The traditional view has been that during the Stamp Act crisis the colonists drew that line between taxation

[23] James Otis, *The Rights of the British Colonies Asserted and Proved* (Boston, 1764), in Bailyn, ed., *Pamphlets*, 457; [Fitch], *Reasons Why*, in ibid., 395; Daniel Dulany, *Considerations on the Propriety of Imposing Taxes in the British Colonies* (Annapolis, 1765), in ibid., 619.

[24] Dulany, *Considerations*, in Bailyn, ed., *Pamphlets*, 619; Bland, *Inquiry*, in Van Schreeven and Scribner, eds., *Revolutionary Virginia*, 1: 41, 43.

and legislation, that they denied Parliament's authority to tax the colonies for revenue but not its authority to legislate for the colonies. That neither the Stamp Act Congress nor many of the assemblies explicitly commented on Parliament's authority outside the realm of taxation seems to support this argument. Probably because "the issue of the day was taxation" and "Parliament at this time was not attempting to interfere in" other aspects of the internal affairs of the colonies, these bodies, as Edmund S. Morgan has observed, saw no need to consider Parliament's legislative authority in other areas, and "what the colonies insisted on most vigorously was that Parliament's supreme legislative authority did not include the right to tax." But the failure of most of these bodies to challenge Parliament's legislative authority outside the area of taxation by no means constituted an admission of that authority, especially in view of the explicit denial of that authority by several official bodies.[25]

Indeed, considerable evidence suggests that the colonists' strong initial impulse was to exclude Parliament from all jurisdiction over the domestic affairs of the colonies. They claimed a right not merely to no taxation without representation but to no legislation without representation. Thus, did the Connecticut Assembly in the summer of 1764 in its protest against the proposed stamp duties invoke that "fundamental principle of the British constitution that 'NO LAW CAN BE MADE OR ABROGATED WITHOUT THE CONSENT OF THE PEOPLE BY THEIR REPRESENTATIVES.'" And thus did the Virginia Assembly in its petition to the king the following December claim for its constituents the "ancient and inestimable Right of being governed by such Laws respecting their internal Polity and Taxation as are derived from their own Consent" – a claim reiterated by the Virginia House of Burgesses when it adopted Patrick Henry's defiant resolutions in May 1765 and repeated in one form or another

---

[25] Edmund S. Morgan, "Colonial Ideas of Parliamentary Power," *William and Mary Quarterly*, 3d ser., 5 (1948): 311–41. The quotation is from p. 326.

in public resolutions by the legislatures of Rhode Island, Maryland, and Connecticut in September and October. Although the Massachusetts Assembly did not go so far in its resolutions against the Stamp Act, it unequivocally asserted, in a late October message to Governor Bernard, its right to make laws for the province's "internal government and taxation." And that authority, it added, had "been never ... questioned; but has been constantly recognized by the King and Parliament."[26]

Precisely what the several assemblies were claiming in 1764–6 when they denied Parliament's authority to pass laws respecting the internal polity of the colonies can be surmised from contemporary comment by several prominent political writers. These included the Virginians Richard Bland and Landon Carter; Rhode Island's elected governor, Stephen Hopkins; and the Massachusetts political leader Samuel Adams. An analysis of the works of these and other writers suggests that, as Bernard Bailyn has emphasized, the supposed colonial distinction between taxation and legislation was less important to the colonial attempt to demarcate the

---

[26] [Fitch], *Reasons Why*, in Bailyn, *Pamphlets*, 391, 406; Virginia Petition, Dec. 18, 1764, Virginia Resolutions, May 30, 1765, Rhode Island Resolves, Sept. 1765, Maryland Resolves, Sept. 28, 1765, Connecticut Resolves, Oct. 25, 1765, in Morgan, ed., *Prologue to Revolution*, 14, 48, 50–1, 53, 55; Massachusetts House to Bernard, Oct. 23, 1765, in Cushing, ed., *Writings of Samuel Adams*, 1: 17–18. Of the nine older North American colonies whose assemblies passed resolutions against the Stamp Act (those of Georgia, North Carolina, Delaware, and New Hampshire did not), four claimed exclusive jurisdiction over both taxation and internal legislation. If, on the basis of its letter to Bernard, the Massachusetts Assembly is added to this list, that makes five – or a majority – of the nine assemblies that subscribed to this more sweeping assertion. Indeed, except for that of Pennsylvania, all of the assemblies that passed resolutions before the Massachusetts Resolves of October 29, 1765, followed the Virginia formula, and all of those who acted after that date limited their explicit claims to an exemption from taxation. This temporal differentiation would seem to support the argument suggested previously that the colonists' initial impulse was to adhere to a more expanded conception of their rights and that they only gradually focused their protests exclusively upon taxation. All of the assembly resolutions are conveniently collected in Morgan, ed., *Prologue to Revolution*, 47–62.

jurisdictional boundaries between Parliament and the colonial assemblies than the distinction between "'internal' and 'external' spheres of government."[27]

Bland provided the most extensive and systematic exploration of this distinction. In *The Colonel Dismounted*, published in late October 1764, just a few weeks before the Virginia Assembly prepared to petition against the proposed stamp duties, he argued that because Virginians were entitled to all of the "liberties and privileges of English subjects, they must necessarily have a legal constitution," which he defined as "a legislature composed in part of the representatives of the people who may enact laws for the INTERNAL government of the colony and suitable to its various circumstances and occasions." "Without such a representative," Bland made "bold enough to say, no law can be made." Thus, by definition, Parliament, in which the colonists were not represented, had no authority to pass laws for the "INTERNAL government" of the colonies without blatantly violating "the most valuable part" of the colonists' "Birthright" as Englishmen, the right "of being governed by laws made with our own consent." The constitution, said Bland, demanded that Parliament be excluded from "all power" over any colony "but such as respects its EXTERNAL government," and, he observed in a pointed reference to the proposed stamp duties, any law "respecting our INTERNAL polity which may hereafter be imposed on us by act of Parliament is arbitrary, as depriving us of our rights, and may be opposed."[28]

Fifteen months later, early in 1766, after Parliament had passed the Stamp Act and it had met with widespread colonial resistance, Bland enlarged upon this position in a second pamphlet, *An Inquiry into the Rights of the British Colonies*. Once again claiming for the colonists the authority "of directing their *internal* Government by Laws made with their Consent," he argued that each colony was "a distinct State,

[27] Bernard Bailyn, *The Ideological Origins of the American Revolution* (Cambridge, Mass.: Harvard University Press, 1967), 213, n. 55.

[28] Bland, *Colonel Dismounted*, in Bailyn, ed., *Pamphlets*, 320.

independent, as to their *internal* Government, of the original Kingdom, but united with her, as to their *external* Polity,
in the closest and most intimate LEAGUE AND AMITY,
under the same Allegiance, and enjoying the Benefits of a
reciprocal Intercourse." Though Bland did not make clear in
either pamphlet exactly what matters were subsumed under
the terms *internal* and *external*, his clear implication was
that Parliament's authority – to legislate as well as to tax –
stopped short of the Atlantic coast of the colonies and did not
extend over any affairs relating exclusively to the internal life
of the colonies. Such matters, according to Bland's formulation, were the exclusive preserve of the colonial assemblies.[29]
Implicitly, at least, Landon Carter, Bland's associate in the
Virginia House of Burgesses, subscribed to the same general
argument when, in four separate essays against the Stamp
Act, he vigorously pressed the colonists' claim "of being
solely governed and taxed by Laws made with the Consent
of the Majority of their own Representatives, according to an
Englishman's inherent Birthright."[30]
Nor were these Virginians peculiar in explicitly arguing that the limitations on Parliament's colonial authority
extended to all of the internal affairs of the colonies, and not
just to taxation. "The general superintending Power of the
Parliament over the whole British Empire," four members of
the Massachusetts Assembly, including Samuel Adams and
James Otis, wrote to a London correspondent in December
1765, "is clearly admitted here, so far as in our Circumstances
is consistent with the Enjoyment of our essential Rights, as
Freemen, and British Subjects." As Adams emphasized, however, that "general superintending Power" did not extend to
the internal affairs of the colonies. Claiming "an exclusive
Right to make Laws for our own internal Government &

---

[29] Bland, *Inquiry*, in Van Schreeven and Scribner, eds., *Revolutionary Virginia*, 1: 38–9.
[30] Jack P. Greene, ed., "'Not to be Governed or Taxed, But By … Our Representatives': Four Essays in Opposition to the Stamp Act by Landon Carter," *Virginia Magazine of History and Biography* 76 (1968): 259–300.

Taxation," Adams argued that if the colonists were "indeed…
British Subjects, (& they never can brook to be thought any
thing less) it seems necessary that they should exercise this
Power within themselves; for they are not represented in the
British Parliam[en]t & their great Distance renders it imprac-
ticable." Only if each legislature within the empire had an
exclusive legislative authority within its own jurisdiction, the
Massachusetts Assembly declared in elaborating this point,
would it be possible to ensure "that equality [of rights and
status] which ought ever to subsist among all his Majesty's
subjects in his wide extended empire."[31]

Stephen Hopkins carried this point still farther. "In an
imperial state, which consists of many separate governments
each of which hath peculiar privileges and of which kind
it is evident that the empire of Great Britain is," Hopkins
observed, "no single part, though greater than another part,
is by that superiority entitled to make laws for or to tax such
lesser part." That was the reason, Hopkins believed, why each
of the colonies had to have "a legislature within itself to take
care of its interests and provide for its peace and internal government." Yet, like Bland and the Massachusetts representatives, he recognized that there were "many things of a more
general nature, quite out of the reach of these particular legislatures, which it is necessary should be regulated, ordered,
and governed." Among these "matters of a general nature,"
Hopkins included regulations concerning the commerce and
good order of "the whole British empire, taken collectively,"
including "those grand instruments of commerce," money
and paper credit. With regard to all such general matters, he
thought it "absolutely necessary" to have "a general power
to direct them, some supreme and overruling authority with
power to make laws and form regulations for the good of
all, and to compel their execution and observation." Within

[31] Massachusetts House to Bernard, Oct. 23, 1765; Samuel Adams to
Reverend G[eorge] W[hitfield], Nov. 11, 1765; James Otis et al., to
Dennys De Berdt, Dec. 20, 1765, in Cushing, ed., *Writings of Samuel
Adams*, 1: 20, 28–9, 67.

the British Empire, this general power, according to Hopkins, could be lodged only in the British Parliament.[32]

All of these writers thus agreed that, although Parliament had to have jurisdiction over what the New York pamphleteer William Hicks referred to as "all such general Regulations as could not be effected by the single Powers of any one Colony," the internal and purely provincial affairs of the colonies should remain under the exclusive authority of the assemblies. So long as Parliament confined its regulations to "restrictions on navigation, commerce, or other external regulations," they reasoned, the "legislatures of the colonies" would be "left entire" and "the internal government, powers of taxing for its support, an exemption from being taxed without consent, and [all] other immunities which legally belong[ed] to the subjects of each colony agreeable to their own particular constitutions" would thereby, according to the "general principles of the British constitution," remain "secure and untouched." To govern the colonies *"according to the principles of the national constitution,"* they thus insisted, required that they be *"vested with authority of legislation"* over all provincial matters *"and have right to be represented in their Assemblies, in whom [alone] that authority"* was *"lodged."*[33]

The underlying implications of the conception of the empire suggested by these writers were, perhaps, most clearly spelled out by one of the colonists' supporters in Britain. "Our Constitution is so tender of the Rights and Liberties of the Subject," wrote the anonymous author of *A Vindication of the Rights of the Americans* in 1765, "that the People of *England* have their Repr[esentative]s, the *Scotch* theirs, the *Welsh* theirs, the *Irish* theirs, [and] the *Americans* theirs, for they have Assemblies and Parliaments, each of which represent the Bulk of the People, of that Generality, or Division,

[32] Stephen Hopkins, *The Rights of the Colonies Examined* (Providence, 1765), in Bailyn, ed., *Pamphlets*, 512, 519.

[33] [William Hicks], *Considerations upon the Rights of the Colonies to the Privileges of British Subjects* (New York, 1765), 11; [Fitch], *Reasons Why*, in Bailyn, ed., *Pamphlets*; 395, 406.

for which such Assembly or Parliament is appointed to be held." The reason why it was "necessary to have so many Houses of Representatives in the several Departments of Government" was "obvious." "In extensive Territories not confined to one Island, or one Continent, but dispersed through a great Part of the Globe," he explained, "the Laws cannot be put into execution, nor the Rights of the People preserved, without their being arranged into several Classes" of coordinate legislatures, each, presumably, having exclusive jurisdiction over the internal affairs of the territory for which it was responsible.[34]

As Tucker and Hendrickson have remarked, the "distinction between imperial and provincial purposes, between general and local areas of concern, between external and internal objects – the appeal, in other words, to principles recognizably federal, came naturally to men on both sides of the Atlantic when forced, during the crisis brought on by the Stamp Act, to articulate the character of the imperial constitution." Such distinctions effectively described the pragmatic and customary distribution of authority and functions within the empire as it had developed over the past century and a half. The colonists could not deny that Parliament had, during that time, occasionally passed statutes that "by express words" extended to the colonies. Some writers attempted to explain those acts as measures submitted to at an early point in the history of the colonies when the settlers were "too much employ'd by their necessary Avocations, to examine much into the Minutiae of Government," and few had any doubt that such measures, though perhaps justified by "political reasons," were "in some measure an exception from the general rule by which British subjects (according to the constitution) are governed." Yet they had to admit that parliamentary restraints on colonial trade, commerce, and manufacturing were "what has been customary, and therefore chearfully submitted to." Historians have generally failed to realize that, according to British constitutional tradition, custom itself

[34] *A Vindication of the Rights of the Americans* (London, 1765), 10–11.

was a form of consent. But it was precisely because colonial submission to these general, external measures had been so long *customary* that they obviously could not, strictly speaking, be taken as violations of the fundamental principle of no legislation without consent.[35]

When Britain's American "Provinces [thus] claim[ed] an exclusive Power of making Laws for their internal Polity and Government," they were, then, simply asserting their right to what they had long enjoyed: as one writer phrased it as early as 1741, "a perfect *internal* Liberty, as to the Choice of their own Laws, and in all other Matters that are *purely* provincial; under a *Salvo* of their inviolable Allegiance [to the Crown], and Complyance with the Acts of Navigation."[36] Notwithstanding metropolitan efforts over the previous century and a half to limit the extent of local self-government in the colonies, "local provincial authority," as Bailyn has noted, "continued to characterize" colonial governance. In the exercise of metropolitan authority, Crown and Parliament had, in fact, usually "touched only the outer fringes of colonial life" and dealt only "with matters obviously beyond the competence of any lesser authority" and with "the final review of actions initiated and sustained by colonial authorities." As Bailyn has remarked, all other powers – the vast area of "residual authority" that both constituted "the 'internal police' of the community" and "included most of the substance of everyday life" – "were enjoyed, in fact if not in constitutional theory, by local, colonial organs of government."[37]

In view of this situation, the colonists could scarcely avoid concluding that, insofar as their respective internal affairs were concerned, there could be "no proper subordination of one part [of the empire] to another." "It has been a grand

[35] Tucker and Hendrickson, *Fall of the First British Empire*, 175–6; [Fitch], *Reasons Why*, in Bailyn, ed., *Pamphlets*, 390–1, 394–5; [Hicks], *Considerations*, 10–11; *Letter to G. G.*, 38–9.
[36] *A Letter to the Gentlemen of the Committee of London Merchants Trading to North America* (London, 1766), 9–10; "Remarks on the Maryland Government," *American Magazine* 1 (1741): 30.
[37] Bailyn, *Ideological Origins*, 203.

Error of the present Times to consider separate Governments as one," complained a Barbadian pamphleteer at the conclusion of the Stamp Act crisis. But there was "no natural Impediment," he added, "to my Imagination's suggesting to me a Form of Government in the People Abroad, as little connected with that of the English, as the Count[r]ies or Soils themselves which both People inhabit." Even though "Our Governments … are founded on similar Principles," he concluded, "this is no Reason that in all Points, whether similar or not, the Stronger must give Law."[38] On the contrary, "In a confederacy of states, independent of each other, yet united under one head, such as I conceive the British empire at present to be," declared an anonymous writer in the *Pennsylvania Journal* in March 1766, "all the powers of legislation may subsist full and compleat in each part, and their respective legislatures be absolutely independent of each other."[39]

Although this analysis treated the crisis of the imperial constitution largely as a problem of identifying the proper allocation of authority, colonial spokesmen did not entirely ignore the knotty issue of sovereignty. The reader will recall that Grenville and his supporters had from the beginning seen that issue as fundamental, and from the point of view of the metropolis it would always remain "the intractable core of the controversy."[40] At first, the colonists had some difficulty in dealing with the metropolitan charge that by challenging the authority of Parliament they were denying the authority of Britain. Indeed, many writers who denied Parliament's right to tax the colonies seemed to go out of their way to acknowledge its sovereign authority over the colonies. Eventually sensing the inherent contradictions in that position, however, a few writers explicitly denounced it. Thus, charged Philalethes in a New York newspaper in May 1766, those who had admitted "a sovereign jurisdiction in the Parliament over the Colonies, in all other respects but

[38] *Candid Observations*, 20.
[39] F. L., in *Pennsylvania Journal* (Philadelphia), Mar. 13, 1766, in Morgan, ed., *Prologue to Revolution*, 91.
[40] Tucker and Hendrickson, *Fall of the First British Empire*, 196.

that of imposing internal taxes, for the purposes of raising a revenue" had thereby "betrayed the liberties of America."[41]

Looking at the whole subject more closely, a few proponents of the colonies focused more directly upon the question of precisely in what sense *"the people of America"* were "dependant on the *people of Britain.*" They quickly concluded that, as Stephen Hopkins emphatically wrote, it would be "absurd to suppose that the common people of Great Britain have a sovereign and absolute authority over their fellow subjects in America, or [indeed] any sort of power whatsoever over them." And if it could not be shown that the inhabitants of the metropolis were sovereign over those in the colonies, it was "still more absurd to suppose," wrote Hopkins, that they could "give a power to their representatives which they have not themselves." If Parliament had "not receive[d] this authority from their constituents," Hopkins concluded, "it will be difficult to tell by what means" it "obtained it, except it be vested in them by mere superiority and power."[42]

But if Parliament was not sovereign over the colonies, what then was the connection between the colonies and Britain? Building on John Locke's notion of the natural right of people "to quit the Society of which they are Members, and to retire to another Country," Richard Bland worked out an elaborate answer to this question. "When Men exercise this Right, and withdraw themselves from their Country," Bland argued, "they recover their natural Freedom and Independence: The Jurisdiction and Sovereignty of the State they have quitted ceases; and if they unite, and by common Consent take Possession of a new Country, and form themselves into a political Society, they become a sovereign State, independent of the State from which they separated." Being "No Part of the Kingdom of *England*" and, at the time of settlement, still

[41] Philalethes, *New York Gazette & Post Boy*, May 8, 1766.
[42] A Letter from a Plain Yeoman, *Providence Gazette*, May 11, 1765, in Morgan, ed., *Prologue to Revolution*, 73; Hopkins, *Rights of the Colonies*, in Bailyn, ed., *Pamphlets*, 518–19; *New York Gazette*, July 25, 1765.

"possessed by a savage People, scattered through the Country, who were not subject to the *English* Dominion, nor owed Obedience to its Laws," America, Bland asserted, was thus an "independent Country ... settled by Englishmen at their own Expense" on the basis of a "Compact with the Sovereign of the Nation, to remove into a new Country, and to form a civil Establishment upon the Terms of the Compact." When he used the term "Sovereign of the Nation," Bland was pointedly referring to the king alone – and not to the king-in-Parliament.[43]

Bland was only one of many writers who thus suggested that the colonies had "no civil connection [with Britain], but by means of the King as the bond of union and the sovereign of both." As the person who had initially granted the colonists "License ... to remove into a new Country, and to settle therein," the king, and not Parliament, these writers concluded, was "*sovereign* and *supreme* over the Colonies." Again, this conclusion conformed with colonial experience. The colonies, as James Otis observed, had always been and still were "entirely subject to the Crown." No laws could be made without the Crown's consent "as sovereign," and, because he thus exercised "an actual supremacy ... in every Legislation," there seemed to be no need for "a supreme Legislature, to which all other Powers must be subordinate." From these conclusions, it followed that the "Kingdom of Great-Britain" could claim no "*sovereignty* or *supremacy* over the colonies."[44]

[43] Bland, *Inquiry*, in Van Schreeven and Scribner, eds., *Revolutionary Virginia*, 1: 35–8. Benjamin Franklin employed precisely the same argument in his essay "On the Tenure of the Manor of East Greenwich," Jan. 11, 1766, in Verner W. Crane, ed., *Benjamin Franklin's Letters to the Press* (Chapel Hill: University of North Carolina Press, 1950), 48.

[44] Philalethes, *New York Gazette*, May 8, 1766; Bland, *Inquiry*, in Van Schreeven and Scribner, eds., *Revolutionary Virginia*, 1: 38–9; Bland, *Colonel Dismounted*, and Otis, *Rights of the British Colonies*, in Bailyn, ed., *Pamphlets*, 318, 323, 458; Landon Carter to *Maryland Gazette* (Annapolis), May 8, 1766, in Greene, ed., "'Not to be Governed or Taxed,'" 272; Letter from a Plain Yeoman, *Providence Gazette*, May 11, 1765, in Morgan, ed., *Prologue to Revolution*, 73; *New York Gazette & Post Boy*, July 25, 1765.

A few writers pointed to the relationship between Hanover and Britain as a model for that between the colonies and the metropolis. Although the colonists "still remain[ed] under the most sacred tie, the subject[s] of the *King* of Great Britain," Britannus Americanus remarked in the *Boston Gazette* in the late winter of 1765, the "people of England could have no more political connection with them or power and jurisdiction over them, than they now have with or over the people of Hanover, who are also subjects of the same King."[45] Just as the Hanoverians "continued to be governed by their own Laws, under the general Superintendance and Controul of the supreme Magistrate in England, and his lawful Deputies and Officers abroad," declared another writer, so "with Respect to the Parliament, and the Power of imposing Taxes" should "all the Dominions of the Prince ... be on one and the same Footing." The colonists were thus "utterly unaccountable to, and uncontroulable by the people of Great-Britain, or any body of them whatever."[46] Because the king was the "sovereign of America, distinct from the power and authority of the parliament of Great-Britain," an anonymous New York pamphleteer asserted, also in 1765, "no body, or set of men, but your assemblies or parliament here ... can lay any tax, tallage or impositions whatsoever within this your dominion of America."[47]

Although, at the beginning of the Stamp Act crisis, the questions, in Franklin's words, of "how far, and in what particulars" the colonies were "*subordinate* and *subject* to the British parliament" were "points newly agitated [and] never yet ... throughly considered," that was no longer the case by the time of the repeal of the Stamp Act in the late winter of 1766.[48] Over the preceding two years, the colonists had slowly begun to construct what John Adams called "a formal,

[45] Britannus Americanus, *Boston Gazette*, Mar. 17, 1766, in Hyneman and Lutz, eds., *American Political Writings*, 1: 89–91.
[46] *Candid Observations*, 23–24.
[47] C. P., *A Letter to his Most Excellent Majesty, George the Third ...* (New York, 1765), 1.
[48] Franklin, "On the Tenure of the Manor of East Greenwich," Jan. 11, 1766, in Crane, ed., *Franklin's Letters to the Press*, 48.

logical, and technical definition" of the imperial constitution under which they lived. As a result of this "great inquiry," they had learned that, as Richard Bland put it, it was "in vain to search into the civil Constitution of *England* for Directions in fixing the proper Connexion between the Colonies and the Mother Kingdom."[49] The underlying principles of that constitution were certainly relevant to their inquiry, but the British Constitution was not, in and of itself, a suitable constitution for an "extended and diversified" empire.[50]

Instead, in their efforts to understand the nature of the relationship between Britain and the colonies, the colonists turned for guidance to the traditional rights of Englishmen and to their own experience with the actual pattern of customary relations within the empire as developed over the previous century and a half. They agreed with the Cambridge natural law theorist Thomas Rutherforth that the best "way of determining what form [of constitution] has been established in any particular nation" was to examine "the history and customs of that nation. A knowledge of its present customs will inform us what constitution of government obtains now," Rutherforth wrote, "and a knowledge of its history will inform us by what means this constitution was introduced or established."[51] Indeed, one of the central conclusions of their inquiry – and one of the arguments they pressed most vigorously in their claims against the intrusion of parliamentary authority in the colonies – was that, like Britain itself, both the individual colonies and the empire as a whole had long-standing constitutional traditions that, at least from the point of view of the colonies, seemed to supply legitimacy to their determined efforts to resist what Bland referred to as

---

[49] Earl of Clarendon [John Adams] to William Pym, Jan. 27, 1766, in Adams, ed., *Works of John Adams*, 3: 477; Bland, *Inquiry*, in Van Schreeven and Scribner, eds., *Revolutionary Virginia*, 1: 34.

[50] J. M., *The Legislative Authority of the British Parliament with respect to North America and the Privileges of the Assemblies there, briefly considered* (London, 1766), 11.

[51] Thomas Rutherforth, *Institutes of Natural Law*, 2d American ed. (Baltimore, 1832), 296.

this "new System of Placing *Great Britain* as the Centre of Attraction to the Colonies."[52]

In 1764–6, only the most advanced thinkers among the colonists were willing to argue that Parliament had no role in either the imperial or the several colonial constitutions, or to suggest that there was "no *dependence* or relation" between Britain and the colonies except "only that we are all the common subjects of the same King."[53] All colonial protests did, however, have in common a clear concern to fix the boundaries between the authority of the metropolis and that of the colonies, between the power of Parliament and that of the colonial assemblies. If Parliament had a constitutional role in the empire, that role, they were persuaded, had to be limited. They were virtually unanimous in agreeing that it did not include authority to tax the colonies for revenue, and a substantial body of sentiment also held that it did not include authority to legislate for the internal affairs of the colonies.

Whether they drew the jurisdictional boundaries between taxation and legislation or between internal and external spheres of authority, the attempt to draw them implied a conception of the empire in which authority was not concentrated in the center but was distributed among several distinct polities within the empire, much in the manner of the old English medieval empire and of the American federal system that would be contrived in 1787. An expression of an impulse, manifest in the colonies since the earliest days of English colonization, "to suffer as little interference by the metropolis as possible [in their internal affairs] while still remaining within the protective framework of the empire,"[54] this conception also strongly implied both the existence of a pragmatic distribution of authority among those polities and the need for some definition of how, exactly, those powers

[52] Bland, *Inquiry*, in Van Schreeven and Scribner, eds., *Revolutionary Virginia*, 1: 43.
[53] Letter from a Plain Yeoman, *Providence Gazette*, May 11, 1765, in Morgan, ed., *Prologue to Revolution*, 73.
[54] Tucker and Hendrickson, *Fall of the First British Empire*, 344.

were distributed and what, precisely, were the principles governing the distribution.

The colonial case against the Stamp Act got a mixed reception in Britain. Better than most later historians, several metropolitan commentators realized that some colonists had not just challenged Parliament's authority to tax but had carried their objections "so far, as to dispute in great measure, [its] ... Power of making any Law[s] whatever, that can be considered as affecting the Colonies internally." They also recognized that each assembly pretended "to an equality with the British parliament, and" allowed "no laws binding but those, which" were "imposed by itself." Few disputed "that the Colonists of any particular Province, have, in what Relates to their internal Police, a Right to make Laws, by their Representatives, on the same Principles, as the *British-Parliament*, provided" that they were "not repugnant to the Laws of their Mother-Country." Some writers were even willing to acknowledge that the assembly in each colony was a "better judge of its own province than" Parliament ever could be and should therefore enjoy "an exclusive legislative right" for "the conclusive regulating of their internal affairs." Moreover, in insisting that Parliament alone was competent to oversee and therefore had to maintain its authority to regulate "all general Affairs concerning the Colonies, as a *collective* Body, with Respect to *Trade* and *Commerce*, and all other Matters of a general Nature and Tendency," such people, in effect, also endorsed the colonial distinction between internal and external spheres of authority, with the former belonging to the colonial assemblies and the latter to Parliament.[55]

To people who thought in these terms, the relationship between the British and the Irish parliaments seemed to be an appropriate model for the connection between Parliament and the assemblies, an analogy that appeared to gain traction

---

[55] J. M., *Legislative Authority of the British Parliament*, 4, 6, 8–10, 13; *The Justice and Necessity of Taxing the American Colonies, Demonstrated* (London, 1766), 26–7, 32; F. J. Hinkhouse, *The Preliminaries of the American Revolution as Seen in the English Press, 1763–1775* (New York: Columbia University Press, 1926), 120.

because the constitutions of Ireland and the colonies were "not greatly dissimilar." To be sure, Parliament had "plainly asserted" its sovereignty over Ireland. But it had also been "very cautious in the exercise of it, particularly with respect to internal taxation." In fact, Parliament had "constantly left to" the Irish "legislature the power of imposing taxes and regulations for the defence and interior police of the country." What the Irish example seemed to suggest was thus that, though the "legislative authority of every country must, in the nature of things, be all-powerful," "justice and wisdom ought, and will restrain the exercise of that power," and metropolitan "controll should be exercised with due regard to all privileges, laws, and judicatures." In short, as one writer observed, it was "a presumptuous, as well as unpopular thing, to depart from the antient forms of a state, and to go out of the usual road of government; and, without absolute necessity, should never be done." Wherever possible, the example of Ireland seemed to indicate, government should "every where" be carried on "in the usual constitutional channel, without infringing or violating the rights and franchises of any part of the British subjects." In Ireland, as in America, the "usual constitutional channel" seemed to be to give the local legislature effective control over all internal affairs.[56]

But most people in Britain seem not to have understood that the colonists' challenge to parliamentary authority went beyond the realm of taxation, and even with regard to this more restricted conception of the colonial position, only a few men in Parliament agreed with the colonists that there were limits upon Parliament's colonial authority. Chief among them were William Pitt in the Commons and Lord Camden, former attorney general and then chief justice of common pleas, in the Lords. Although Camden admitted that "the sovereign authority, the omnipotence of the legislature," was "a favourable [favorite?] doctrine," he argued that there

[56] *The Late Occurrences in North America, and Policy of Great Britain Considered*(London, 1766), 5; *What should be Done: Or, Remarks on the Political State of Things* (London, 1766), 16–19; *Letter to G. G.*, 74, 84.

were "some things it cannot do." Specifically, he declared, it could not act "contrary to the fundamental laws of nature, contrary to the fundamental laws of this constitution." In this formulation, Camden implicitly distinguished between ordinary law and fundamental law. Deriving either "from the Law of Reason and of Nature" or "from [the] Custom and Usage [of] our own Constitution," fundamental law consisted of those "public laws" that "prescribe[d] the form, and establish[ed] the constitutional power of the legislative body of the society."[57] As Rutherforth had earlier remarked, such laws had been "usually understood to bind the legislative body itself, and not to be alterable by its authority."[58]

Among these fundamental laws, Camden, Pitt, and others of like mind argued, was the ancient British principle of no taxation without representation. Out of respect for this fundamental law, they contended, Parliament had "never levied Internal Taxes on any subject without their own consent." "The Commons of America, represented in their several assemblies, have ever been in possession of the exercise of this, their constitutional right, of giving and granting their own money," Pitt asserted. "At the same time," he noted, "this kingdom, as the supreme governing and legislative power, has always bound the colonies by her laws, by her regulations, and restrictions in trade, in navigation, in manufactures – in every thing, except that of taking their money out of their pockets without their consent." Although few colonists had explicitly distinguished between Parliament's authority to tax and its authority to legislate for the colonies, for Pitt and Camden the distinction was crucial. In Pitt's words, it was "essentially necessary to liberty."[59]

Although there was substantial support in the pamphlet literature for these and similar arguments against the exertion

---

[57] Camden's speeches, Feb. 6, Mar. 7, 1766; Beckford's speech, Feb. 3, 1766, in Simmons and Thomas, eds., *Proceedings and Debates*, 2: 127, 147, 320–22.

[58] Rutherforth, *Institutes of Natural Law*, 399.

[59] Camden's Speech, Mar. 7, 1766; Pitt's Speech, Jan. 14, 1766, in Simmons and Thomas, eds., *Proceedings and Debates*, 2: 81–92, 320–22.

of parliamentary power in the colonies,[60] few people in power found such arguments persuasive. They both rejected the colonists' contention that they were not represented in Parliament and dismissed the argument that charters and custom exempted the colonies from parliamentary taxation. They acknowledged that the Crown could grant charters that would protect the colonists "from violence or impositions, which might be attempted by authority of the prerogative of the Crown" and thereby secure the "colonies ... from the despotism of the Crown." But they emphatically denied that "the constitution of Great Britain" empowered the Crown to "grant an exemption to any subject of Great Britain, from the jurisdiction of Parliament." Because the constitution acknowledged "no authority superior to the legislature, consisting of king, lords, and commons," they argued, the Crown constituted "but a part of the British sovereignty." "Considered as the executive power," the Crown, by itself, obviously could neither "controul the legislature, nor dispense with its acts," much less put the colonies "out of the subjection to the *summum Imperium* of Great Britain." For that reason, it was evident both that "no Charter from the Crown" could "possibly supersede the Right of the whole Legislature" and that the king could not possibly "govern the Colonies, independent of his British parliament."[61]

Nor did custom seem to offer any more solid support for the colonial cause. At least some metropolitan commentators admitted that the "long uninterrupted *Custom* and *Usage* in the Colonies, of taxing themselves by Representatives of their own choosing; and also the Non-usage of the *British* Parliament in that particular," might appear to have become "a kind of possessory Right" that, in turn, "might naturally

---

[60] See, in this connection, [John Fothergill], *Considerations relative to the North American Colonies* (London, 1765); *Vindication of the Rights; Late Occurrences.*

[61] [Knox], *Claim of the Colonies*, 3–4, 8; *Late Occurrences*, 1–2; [Soame Jenyns], *The Objections to the Taxation of our American Colonies, by the Legislature of Great Britain, Briefly Consider'd* (London, 1765), 9; *Letter to G. G.*, 74; Northington's speech, Feb. 3, 1766, in Simmons and Thomas, eds., *Proceedings and Debates*, 2:129.

induce Persons, perhaps not thoroughly acquainted with the Nature and Constitution of our Parliament, to imagine the sole right of laying Taxes, belonged to themselves." From the perspective of the metropolis, however, the logic of the emerging constitution of parliamentary supremacy seemed to render absurd all suggestions of customary restraints upon the authority of Parliament. Any custom or usage to the contrary notwithstanding, "upon the principles of the Revolution," Parliament was "the only natural, constitutional Seat of compleat Jurisdiction in the Kingdom" and that jurisdiction necessarily extended not just throughout the home islands but "over the property and person of every inhabitant of a British colony" as well.[62]

In making these arguments, metropolitan supporters revealed considerable confusion over the ancient question of the precise legal status of the colonies. Most seem to have fallen back on the position traditionally taken by Crown officials in their recurring polemics with colonial assemblies over the previous century: That the colonies were equivalent merely to domestic corporations within Britain and as such could "have no ... Pretence" to any "legal or constitutional Existence which" might "entitle them to greater Privileges than ... the Corporations in this Kingdom enjoy[ed] by their respective Charters of Incorporation." According to this argument, "the mighty Powers of" the colonies' "little Assemblies" consisted of nothing more than a "Licence or Authority, flowing from the royal Prerogative of the Crown, to frame such Laws and Regulations, for the Management of their own domestick Concerns, as may best answer the Ends of their Institution." Such limited powers could not possibly justify the colonies even in claiming "an Exemption from ... parliamentary Authority," much less operate "to erect them into that State of Independency" that would justify their

---

[62] *The General Opposition of the Colonies to the Payment of the Stamp Duty* (London, 1766), 25–6; *A Letter to a Member of Parliament, Wherein the Power of the British Legislature, and the Case of the Colonists Are Briefly and Impartially Considered* (London, 1765), 21; [Knox], *Claim of the Colonies,* 2.

"placing their *Indulgencies* in Competition with *Privileges*, Or, in other Words, setting up their *Bye-Laws* in Opposition to *Acts of Parliament.*"[63]

Not everyone adhered to such a limited conception of the colonies. Thus, Sir William Blackstone, in his celebrated and widely read *Commentaries on the Law of England*, the first volume of which was published while the Stamp Act was under consideration, characterized the colonies, like Ireland, as "distinct, though dependent dominions."[64] Even those who thought of the colonies in this more expansive sense, however, tended to emphasize their dependence rather more than their distinctiveness. As Grenville declared in his speech introducing the Stamp Act, "all colonies" were "subject to the dominion of the mother country, whether they" were "a colony of the freest or the most absolute government." The very word *colony*, echoed Charles Townshend in the brief debate that followed, implied "subordination."[65]

Charles Yorke succinctly summarized the predominant argument in a House of Commons debate in 1766. "That the dominions of the Crown wherever they lie are bound by Act of Parliament of Great Britain, either expressly named or manifestly included," he declared was one of the central "maxims" that formed the basis for Britain's "mighty empire." "This universality of the legislative power," he exclaimed, "is the vital principle of the whole Empire, and it has been confirmed at the Revolution that wherever the sovereignty of the Crown extends, the legislative power extends likewise."[66] In the debate over the repeal of the Stamp Act in the House of Lords in February 1766, Lords Mansfield, Northington, and Lyttelton made the same point. In specific answer to Camden,

---

[63] [Jenyns], *Objections to the Taxation of our American Colonies*, 9–10; [Charles Jenkinson], Notes on the Right to Tax the Colonies, [1765], Additional Manuscripts 38339, ff. 133–5, British Library, London; *Letter to a Member of Parliament*, 12–13.

[64] Sir William Blackstone, *Commentaries on the Laws of England*, 4 vols. (London, 1822), 1: 50.

[65] Grenville's and Townshend's speeches, Feb. 6, 1765, in Simmons and Thomas, eds., *Proceedings and Debates*, 2: 9, 13.

[66] Charles Yorke, speech, February 3, 1766, in ibid., 2: 137.

Mansfield flatly declared that, "as to the power of making laws," Parliament represented "the whole British empire" and had "authority to bind every part and every subject without the least distinction" in matters of taxation as well as legislation. That the colonists, as a result of their physical situation, did not "have a right to vote" for members of Parliament, according to Mansfield, meant not that they were exempt from Parliament's authority but only that they were "more emphatically subjects of Great Britain than those without the realm."[67] "A free and extended empire," wrote an anonymous pamphleteer in making the same point, "are incompatible: to think they are not is a perfect solecism in politicks."[68]

From this point of view, colonial claims for exemption from parliamentary taxation seemed, as Grenville had defined them when he first proposed to levy stamp duties on the colonies, to be nothing less than a challenge to British sovereignty. As it had gradually developed over the previous century and a half, the conventional conception of sovereignty was that in all polities, including "an Empire, extended and diversified, like that of *Great-Britain*," there had to be, as Blackstone wrote, "a supreme, irresistible, absolute uncontrolled authority, in which the *jura summi imperii*, or the rights of sovereignty reside[d]" and, as another writer asserted, "to which all other *Powers* should be *subordinate[d]*."[69] Because, most contemporaries seem to have believed, the king-in-Parliament was sovereign in the British polity, it could accept no restrictions upon its authority without relinquishing the sovereignty of the nation over the colonies. By definition, there could be no limitation upon a supreme authority. It was either complete or nonexistent. For that reason, it seemed obvious that the king-in-Parliament had full authority over all matters relating to all Britons everywhere. And for the same reason, it also seemed evident that no clear line could be drawn between

[67] Mansfield's and Northington's speeches, Feb. 3, 1766, in ibid., 2:128–30.
[68] *Justice and Necessity of Taxing the American Colonies*, 21.
[69] J. M., *Legislative Authority of the British Parliament*, 11; Blackstone, *Commentaries on the Laws of England*, 1: 50–1, 178–80.

Parliament's power to legislate for the colonies and its power
to tax them. As Grenville noted early in the controversy, the
claim of the colonists "not to be taxed but by their representatives" applied with equal force "to all laws in general,"
and if Parliament could not legislate for the colonies, the
British nation no longer had any control over them.[70] As the
Connecticut agent Jared Ingersoll reported to his constituents
in February 1765, the metropolitan establishment regarded
the power to tax as "a necessary part of every Supreme
Legislative Authority" and believed that "if they have not
that Power over America, they have none, & then America is
at once a Kingdom of itself."[71]

In the metropolitan view, there was thus no distribution,
but rather a concentration of authority within the empire: "as
the sovereign of the whole," the king-in-Parliament had "control over the whole British empire." To most metropolitans,
in fact, the colonial position appeared incomprehensible
because it seemed to imply the existence of more than one
sovereign authority within a single state, and sovereignty,
according to conventional theory, could not be divided. An
"*Imperium in imperio*" – a sovereign authority within a sovereign authority – was a contradiction in terms. As Lyttelton
put it, the colonies were either "part of the dominions of the
Crown of Great Britain" and therefore "proper objects of our
legislature," or they were "small independent communities,"
each operating under its own sovereign authority. There was,
according to metropolitan theory, no middle ground between
these two extremes. Even those who, like Lord Egmont, held
that the supreme power in any polity could delegate "to other
subordinate powers a part of itself" and that, in such cases,
"time" would "give to these subordinate powers a right of
prescription" that could not be recalled "excepting only in

---

[70] Grenville's speech, Feb. 6, 1765, in Simmons and Thomas, eds.,
Proceedings and Debates, 2: 9.
[71] Ingersoll to Thomas Fitch, Feb. 11, 1765, in Morgan, ed., *Prologue
to Revolution*, 30. Bailyn, *Ideological Origins*, 198–202, provides an
excellent brief account of the development of the concept of sovereignty
in early modern Britain.

the utmost emergency," also believed that "when the exigencies of government required it," Parliament, by virtue of its "supreme, absolute and unlimited" power, could levy taxes "upon the People not by right of their having *representatives* but [by virtue of their] ... being *subjects* to the Government."[72]

The strength of colonial opposition to the Stamp Act forced Parliament to retract it, but repeal was accompanied by passage of the Declaratory Act, modeled on the Irish Declaratory Act of 1720 and asserting Parliament's authority "to bind the colonies and people of America ... in all cases whatsoever." But this fiat from the center by no means resolved the question of the distribution of authority within the empire. Even though the Declaratory Act stated that Parliament "retain[ed] the idea of right," people in the metropolis realized that "the circumstances of the repeal" stood as "convincing proof that ... parliament" could not "execute it" and made it possible for the colonists to interpret repeal as "a full renunciation of the right" that left the colonies "*at full liberty.*" At the same time, the Declaratory Act powerfully impressed upon the colonists that Parliament had kept the door open to some future attempt to force them to acknowledge "Parliament's Right to tax us ... or that in every other Respect but Taxation, they have an absolute Right to make Laws to bind us without our own Consent."[73]

As Colonel Isaac Barre announced in the House of Commons early in 1766, the Stamp Act crisis had thus provoked "the people of America to reason ... closely upon

[72] *Letter to G. G.*, 74; Lyttelton's and Egmont's speeches, Feb. 3, Mar. 7, 1766, in Simmons and Thomas, eds., *Proceedings and Debates*, 2: 126–7, 320–1; *Justice and Necessity of Taxing*, 21; *Protest against the Bill to Repeal the American Stamp Act* (Paris, 1766), 16; *The Rights of Parliament Vindicated, on the Occasion of the Late Stamp-Act* (London, 1766), 10–11. Several people, of course, charged that the colonists were aiming at independence. See, for instance, [Josiah Tucker], *A Letter from a Merchant in London to His Nephew in North America* (London, 1766), 42.

[73] *A New and Impartial Collection of Interesting Letters, from the Public Papers* (London, 1767), 138; *New York Gazette & Post-Boy*, May 22, 1766.

the relative rights of this country and that" the undefined and "loose texture" of Britain's "extended and diversified" empire had fostered the development of two widely divergent interpretations of how authority was distributed between the metropolis and the colonies. Whereas most people in the metropolis thought the empire a unitary state "organized on the principle of devolution," with "sovereignty ... vested in Parliament" and the authority of the colonies consisting "merely of privileges" that were always "subject to the discretion of Parliament and could, in extremis, be curtailed," most people in the colonies thought of the empire as being "predominantly federal in practice," with the authority of the center limited by the authority delegated to the colonies.[74]

In this situation, many people on both sides of the Atlantic called for a permanent resolution of the constitutional issues raised by the Stamp Act. At this early stage, few thought beyond the possibility of incorporating the colonies into the metropolitan polity through the extension of representation in Parliament. In the words of one anonymous writer, that seemed to be the only means both to insure an equality of rights within the empire and to unite Britons and Americans "as *Englishmen*, – as Freemen, equally bound to support and maintain the Laws and Liberties of this Kingdom." Nor did this author confine this privilege to Americans. "In whatever Part of the Globe they are established," he wrote in following out the logic of his proposal, "*Britons* ... will never be willingly obedient to Laws" to which "they have not in some manner ... consented."[75] A few observers went further and called for the creation of an intercolonial Parliament with full authority to tax and to attend to the general concerns of the colonies, while still others, with the example of the Stamp

[74] Barre's speech, Feb. 24, 1766, in Simmons and Thomas, eds., *Proceedings and Debates*, 2: 296; *The Political Balance, in which the Principles and Conduct of the Two Parties Are Weighed* (London, 1765), 45; J. M., *Legislative Authority of the British Parliament*, 11; Tucker and Hendrickson, *Fall of the First British Empire*, 175, 179.
[75] *General Opposition of the Colonies to the Payment of the Stamp Duty*, 31–2, 38.

Act Congress before them, feared the establishment of such "a dangerous federal union" among the colonies. However a closer union might be accomplished, the Stamp Act crisis had made it clear that metropolitan authorities needed to "discover such Means of perfect and stable Connection with the Colonies, as may secure a just Authority over them, and at the same Time, preserve inviolable, the Privileges and Immunities" of the colonies.[76]

In the meantime, having learned from the crisis that the metropolitan government was too weak to force the colonies to comply with measures the people there did not support, the colonists, as Francis Bernard reported from Boston in November 1765, "seem[ed] to be resolved that their Idea of their relation to Great Britain however extravagant various & inconsistent" should "be the standard of it."[77] At least in regard to the "new" questions posed by the Stamp Act, the crisis of the imperial constitution in 1764–6 had taught them, as a New York writer phrased it, that "the People of England" understood "them not a whit better that we do in America."[78]

---

[76] [Fothergill], *Considerations*, 46–7; [Joshua Steele], *An Account of a Late Conference on the Occurrences in America* (London, 1766), 24–7, 33–40; Robert M. Calhoon, ed., "William Smith Jr.'s Alternative to the American Revolution," *William and Mary Quarterly*, 3d ser., 22 (1965): 105–18; Speeches of Charles Yorke, Feb. 15, 1765, and Edmund Nugent and Welbore Ellis, Jan. 27, 1766, in Simmons and Thomas, eds., *Proceedings and Debates*, 2: 111.

[77] Bernard to Barrington, Nov. 23, 1765, in Channing and Coolidge, eds., *Barrington-Bernard Correspondence*, 95.

[78] *New York Gazette & Post-Boy*, May 22, 1766.

3

EMPIRE RECONSIDERED, 1767–1773

A NEW CHALLENGE FROM PARLIAMENT

If the Stamp Act crisis "first led the colonists into [systematic] Enquiries concerning the nature of their political situation," its resolution in early 1766 by no means put an end to those inquiries.[1] Indeed, Parliament's renewed efforts early in 1767 to tax the colonies through the Townshend Acts quickly reopened the question. For the next six years, people on both sides of the Atlantic further explored the difficult problem, in the words of Jonathan Shipley, Bishop of St. Asaph in 1773, of "by what bond of union shall be hold together members of this great empire, dispersed and scattered as they lie over the face of the earth?"[2] Agreement was widespread that this question was "as arduous and important ... as ever the English government was engaged in." But as they dug ever deeper into the subordinate questions of how far the authority of Parliament extended over the colonies and "how far, if

---

[1] William Hicks, *The Nature and Extent of Parliamentary Power Considered* (New York, 1768), in Merrill Jensen, ed., *Tracts of the American Revolution, 1763–1776* (Indianapolis: Bobbs Merrill, 1967), 177.

[2] Jonathan Shipley, *A Sermon Preached before the Incorporated Society for the Propagation of the Gospel in Foreign Parts* (London, 1773), in Paul H. Smith, comp., *English Defenders of American Freedoms, 1774–1778* (Washington: Library of Congress, 1972), 25.

at all," the colonies were "subject to the controul of the parent state," people of all persuasions revealed a fundamental ambivalence about the implications of their findings. On the one hand, they desperately hoped that, once it was "better understood," the "political relation between the colonists and the mother country" would be settled to the mutual satisfaction of all parties.[3] On the other, they were deeply afraid that the continued exploration of that relationship would produce results that would be detrimental to the very "continuance of the structure of the empire."[4]

During the crisis over the Townshend Acts, these fears helped to account for a considerable amount of pragmatic flexibility that was manifested, on both sides, by a pronounced concern to contain the dispute within a narrow compass. At the same time, however, the length and intensity of the dispute pushed some analysts on the colonial side to think through the nature of the connection between Britain and the colonies more thoroughly than anyone had ever done before. Although these thinkers regarded their conclusions as no more than an articulation of long-standing practice, they represented a radical challenge to the metropolitan belief in Parliament's supremacy over the entire empire, a belief that, for most members of the metropolitan political nation, continued to be nonnegotiable.

Notwithstanding a palpable crystallization of informed colonial opinion around this emerging and, from the

[3] *An Inquiry into the Nature and Causes of the Present Disputes between the British Colonies in America and Their Mother Country: And Their Reciprocal Claims and Just Rights Impartially Examined and Fairly Stated* (London, 1769), 46; "Valerius Poplicola" [Samuel Adams] to *Boston Gazette*, Oct. 28, 1771, in Henry Alonzo Cushing, ed., *The Writings of Samuel Adams*, 4 vols. (New York: G. P. Putnam's 1904–8), 2: 257; Benjamin Franklin to Thomas Crowley, Oct. 21, 1768, and to Thomas Cushing, Feb. 5, 1771, in Leonard W. Labaree et al., eds., *The Papers of Benjamin Franklin*, 30 vols. (New Haven: Yale University Press, 1959), 15: 241, 18: 28.

[4] Thomas Pownall's speech, May 8, 1770, in R. C. Simmons and P. D. G. Thomas, eds., *Proceedings and Debates of the British Parliament Respecting North America, 1754–1783*, 5 vols. to date (New York: Kraus, 1982–87), 3: 284.

perspective of the center, radical view of the constitutional organization of the empire, the spirit of conciliation ran so deep that constituted authorities in no colony officially endorsed it during the Townshend Act crisis. Indeed, Parliament's repeal of most of the Townshend duties in 1770 and the rapid subsidence of overt colonial opposition to Parliament over the next three years provided dramatic testimony to the depth of that spirit. Yet those same years were also marked by a revival of the much older controversy over the scope of the Crown's prerogative powers in the colonies. This revival underlined the fundamental problem of the distribution of authority within the empire as a major continuing source of tension between metropolis and colonies.

Throughout the first phase of this controversy, the vast majority of people in the metropolitan establishment, in both Britain and the colonies, adhered strictly to the position articulated by Grenville and his supporters during the Stamp Act crisis. To be sure, some people thought it unwise for Parliament to "endeavour to enforce novel measures and regulate old established regulations"[5] in ways that would seem to be "innovating upon what" the colonists "thought their usages, and customs."[6] Still others, mostly members of the minority Rockingham party that had engineered the settlement of 1766, insisted that it was possible "to maintain the due authority of the mother country, and yet satisfy the demands of the Americans" merely by adhering to the spirit of that settlement.[7] Thus, as Edmund Burke argued in May 1770, Parliament had no need to tax the colonies because the Declaratory Act already "sufficiently establish[ed] the sovereignty of this country over its plantations and colonies."[8] However, although a few people, like the Rockinghams, consistently argued for lenient measures on grounds of expediency, virtually no one in the British establishment was willing,

[5] Henry Seymour Conway's speech, Feb. 8, 1769, in Ibid., 3: 98

[6] Richard Hussey's speech, Jan. 26, 1768, in Ibid., 3: 69.

[7] Rockingham's speech, May 18, 1770, in Ibid., 3: 338.

[8] Edmund Burke's speech, May 9, 1770, in ibid., 3: 323.

as the Connecticut agent William Samuel Johnson reported
to his constituents in the fall of 1768, to discuss "the principle
of right, it being almost universally" believed to have been
"completely settled by the late Declaratory Act."[9] "Our right
of legislation over the Americans," agreed a writer who was
not entirely unsympathetic to the colonial argument in 1769,
was "asserted by most, doubted of by some, and wholly dis-
claimed [only] by a few."[10]

Franklin's friend Stephen Sayre was one of the very few
disclaimers. Challenging the prevailing assumptions that
Britain had expended great sums in settling the colonies and
that colonies derived their political authority from metropolitan grants, Sayre pointed out that all of the colonies, except
Georgia and Nova Scotia, had "settled themselves, without
any expence to their mother-country" and initially "under
no civil government but what they formed themselves." Only
"after they had established their several settlements," he
argued, did they, "out of regard to their mother-country,"
send "home their several agents, to tender their new acqui-
sitions to their mother-country, on certain conditions then
agreed on by the several parties, and ratified by their respective charters." "Without such a surrender, therefore, Great
Britain," he claimed, "could have no pretence to authority
over any of the" colonies. Although Britain's colonial authority was thus "founded in compact," he reasoned, that "same
compact that" gave Britain "any rightful authority over
them" also secured to the colonists "the privileges stipulated
in that contract; which is, the *sole right of taxing themselves,*

[9] William Samuel Johnson to William Pitkin, Nov. 10, 1768, in "The
Trumbull Papers," Massachusetts Historical Society, *Collections,* 5th
ser., 9 (Boston, 1885): 13.
[10] *An Inquiry into the Nature and Causes of the Present Dispute* (London,
1769), 39. The Jamaican William Beckford was almost the only MP after
1766 even to suggest that there might be constitutional limitations upon
Parliament's colonial authority. See his remark in a speech of December
7, 1768, that "Acts of Parliament are not like the laws of the Medes and
Persians. An Act of Parliament against common right is a nullity, so says
Lord Coke." (Simmons and Thomas, eds., *Proceedings and Debates,*
3: 32).

by their own representatives." Looking upon these compacts "as sacred ... like our *Magna Charta*," he concluded, it was no wonder that the colonists had resisted ministerial efforts to violate "their *Magna Charta*" and deprive "them of the privileges of Englishmen."[11]

Running strongly against the current of opinion, however, such arguments had limited appeal within the metropolitan political nation. Interpreting all suggestions for any limitations upon Parliament's colonial authority as a challenge to the British constitution of parliamentary supremacy and to the sovereignty of the metropolis over the colonies, the vast majority of that group continued to insist, as they had throughout the Stamp Act crisis, that sovereignty was indivisible. "*Sovereignty*," declared Allan Ramsay, a polemicist with connections to George III, in 1768, "admits of no degrees, it is always *supreme*, and to level it, is, in effect, to destroy it."[12] In every community, wrote Richard Phelps, an undersecretary of state, there had to be both "an unlimited authority lodged somewhere ... and an unreserved obedience to that authority required of every individual." Without such a sovereign authority, Phelps believed, a polity would lack that essential "attracting power" by which "both those who rule[d] and those who obey[ed]" were drawn "to the same common centre."[13] William Knox spelled out the full implications of this line of reasoning in his influential *The Controversy Between Great Britain and Her Colonies Reviewed*, published in 1769. "If the authority of the legislature be not in one instance equally supreme over the Colonies as it is over the people of England," Knox wrote, "then are not the Colonies of the same community with the people of England. All distinctions," he continued, "destroy this union;

[11] Stephen Sayre, *The Englishman Deceived: A Political Piece, Wherein Some Very Important Secrets of State Are Briefly Recited, and Offered to the Consideration of the Public* (London, 1768), 38–40.
[12] Allan Ramsay, *Thoughts on the Origin and Nature of Government* (London, 1768), 53.
[13] [Richard Phelps], *The Rights of the Colonies, and the Extent of the Legislative Authority of Great-Britain* (London, 1769), 3–4.

and if it can be shown in any particular to be dissolved, it must be so in all instances whatever."[14]

From this emerging metropolitan perspective, both the distinction between taxation and legislation made by Chatham and Camden during the Stamp Act crisis and the colonial argument that compacts made with the Crown exempted them from parliamentary taxation seemed thoroughly untenable. "Legislation and taxation," Lord Hillsborough, secretary of state for the colonies, declared in 1768 in a typical remark, "were essentially connected and would stand and fall together."[15] The king, "being a limited monarch," asserted Richard Hussey in the House of Commons in 1769, could not "for a moment release" the colonies "from the sovereign power of this country."[16] One of "the great fundamental principles of the Government of Great Britain," the Crown's incapacity to grant any "dispensation from the laws of the land, and the authority of parliament" without the concurrence of the other two branches of the legislature, could not be violated, an anonymous pamphleteer insisted, without dissolving the constitution and annihilating the most important foundation of British liberty.[17] In Hillsborough's words, the colonial contention that the Crown had granted the colonies a "power of absolute legislation ... tended to the absurdity of introducing [an] *imperium in imperio*, and to create" within the empire a series of "independent state[s]," an arrangement he roundly condemned as nothing less than a "polytheism in politics."[18]

[14] [William Knox], *The Controversy Between Great Britain and Her Colonies Reviewed* (London, 1769), 50–1.
[15] Hillsborough's speech, Dec. 15, 1768, in Simmons and Thomas, eds., *Proceedings and Debates*, 3: 48.
[16] Hussey's speech, Jan. 26, 1769, in ibid., 3: 70.
[17] Ramsay, *Thoughts*, 29, 52; *The Constitutional Right of the Legislature of Great Britain, to Tax the British Colonies in America, Impartially Stated* (London, 1768), 11.
[18] William Samuel Johnson to William Pitkin, Feb. 13, 1768, in "The Trumbull Papers," Massachusetts Historical Society, *Collections*, 5th ser., 9 (Boston, 1885): 257. Hillsborough's speech, Dec. 15, 1768, in Simmons and Thomas, eds., *Proceedings and Debates*, 3: 48.

Maintaining "the supremacy and legislative authority of Parliament" in its fullest extent over the colonies thus continued to be viewed by most members of the metropolitan establishment as "essential to the existence of the empire."[19] If this "great constitutional point" were ever given up,[20] if Britain should ever permit the colonists, who were "already proprietors of the soil," to "govern themselves in the same manner that she is governed," if their assemblies were ever allowed to enjoy all "rights of national legislation," they would "be, then, necessarily, possessed of every qualification of sovereignty; and in every respect ... free and independent of Great Britain." For the colonists to deny Parliament's authority to tax them was thus also "to deny her sovereignty," and to deny her sovereignty was "to change their political existence: and in place of sons and provinces of their mother country, to become aliens: and to form themselves into a mother country, and an independent nation."[21] In Knox's words, there was "no alternative: either the colonies are a part of the community of Great Britain, or they are in a state of nature with respect to her, and in no case can be subject to the jurisdiction of that legislative power which represents her community, which is the British parliament."[22] The colonies, added Phelps, "must either acknowledge the legislative power of Great Britain in its full extent, or set themselves up as independent states."[23]

Indeed, from the vantage point of London, colonial opposition to the Townshend measures seemed to betray nothing less than a "high and imperious ambition of being themselves, a nation of independent states."[24] Their resolves against parliamentary taxation looked little short of a series of colonial "Declaratory Act[s] ... against the Declaratory Act of Great

---

[19] Hillsborough's speech, Dec. 15, 1768, in Simmons and Thomas, eds., *Proceedings and Debates*, 3: 48.
[20] Hillsborough's speech, May 18, 1770, in ibid., 3: 334.
[21] *Constitutional Right of the Legislature*, 6–7, 12.
[22] [Knox], *Controversy*, 50–1.
[23] [Phelps], *Rights of the Colonies*, 11.
[24] *Constitutional Right of the Legislature*, 27–8.

Britain,"[25] and their economic sanctions against the metropolis suggested that the colonists already thought of Britain
and the colonies as "independent nations at war with each
other."[26] Such behavior, one writer charged, could only be
the product of a deep-seated "desire of managing their own
affairs more to their own advantage, than what they think
can be accomplished, under the government ... of Great
Britain."[27]

Such alarming impulses unleashed a demand within the
metropolitan establishment to determine, in the words of
Hans Stanley in a House of Commons debate in November
1768, precisely "what we were, what the Americans were,"
and there was a surprisingly narrow range of opinion on this
subject.[28] As Allan Ramsay pointed out, the colonists strongly
preferred to use "the word *Colony*" to refer to their polities
because, he charged, it carried connotations of "a degree of
independency." But most people seem to have agreed with
Ramsay that, strictly speaking, those polities were "not
properly *colonies* either in word or deed. Their most ancient
English and legal name," Ramsay contended, was "*plantations*, and they have always been, in fact, *provinces*, governed
by a lieutenant or governor, sent by the King of Great Britain,
and recalled by him at pleasure." Although people recognized
that metropolitan failure to establish "any system of government, natural and proper to their situation and condition, as
provinces" was the reason why the colonists had by "uninterrupted habit ... come to think their corporation assemblies
to be no less than parliaments" and been "emboldened ...
to grasp at national and independent legislation and government," few had any doubt that, as Ramsay declared, the
"plain truth" was "that those countries, let them be called
plantations, settlements, colonies, or by what other name

[25] Lord North's speech, Dec. 7, 1768, in Simmons and Thomas, eds.,
Proceedings and Debates, 3: 32.
[26] Hans Stanley's speech, Nov. 8, 1768, in ibid., 3: 4.
[27] *Constitutional Right of the Legislature,* 27–8.
[28] Stanley's speech, Nov. 8, 1768, in Simmons and Thomas, eds.,
Proceedings and Debates, 3: 3.

they will," were "from their nature and situation, only subordinate parts of the empire of Britain."[29] They were, in short, *provinces*, and, wrote Matthew Wheelock in early 1770, it was "the essential quality of a province to depend on that state which formed and supported it."[30]

The anonymous author of *The Constitutional Right of the British Legislature to Tax the British Colonies*, the fullest exploration of this subject by an administration writer before the mid-1770s, carried this discussion still further. Declaring that "not adverting to the natural and necessary difference between national, and provincial legislation and government" had "been the principle cause of the difference in opinion, about the rights of British legislation in America," he heralded the "high humour of the North Americans" in resisting Parliamentary authority "as one of the happiest incidents that could have fallen out" because it had "opened the eyes of the nation" to this problem and provided "an opportunity to the legislature, while it is not yet too late, to new model the government of North America, upon a plan of liberty suitable to the nature of colonies, and the dominion of the mother country." In pursuit of this objective, the author offered "the rough outlines of a provincial system," the central objective of which was to "Fix the nature, power, and extent of the colony assemblies, so, that they may never be mistaken, hereafter, for parliaments: but known and acknowledged as corporate bodies only, having power to propose laws for the internal police of the colony, to be approved or rejected by his Majesty in Council, as usual; and always subject to the revisal and alteration of parliament." The author did not deny that, as "the offspring of Britain" and as the owners "of property, the efficient cause of power and dominion," the Americans were "morally and naturally intitled to all the liberty, rights, and privileges of Britons; and of consequence ... ought ... to have

---

[29] Ramsay, *Thoughts*, 60–2; *Constitutional Right of the Legislature*, 2–3.
[30] [Matthew Wheelock], *Reflections Moral and Political on Great Britain and Her Colonies* (London, 1770), 52.

their property ... taxed with their own consent." But colonial liberty, he insisted, was limited by the provincial status of the colonies, and colonial residents could only "enjoy as much freedom, liberty, and independency, as their situation will admit of, as subjects of Great Britain." In short, both because the "interest of a part" always had "to give way to the interest of the whole" and because, within the extended British Empire, Great Britain was itself "that whole; and her colonies ... but that part," it followed that "North America must be governed as a province, if Great Britain be inclined to govern her at all."[31]

From this perspective, the British Empire seemed to be a unicentric polity in which, as Thomas Pownall put it, "the realm ... [and] government of Great Britain [w]as the Sovereign, and the Colonies ... the subject, without full participation in the Constitution" and "bound implicitly to obey the orders of the [metropolitan] government." In view of the "inherent pre-eminence" of the parent state in this arrangement and the colonies' status as nothing more than "so many appendages or factories to this kingdom, devoted solely to the emprovement of its particular interest, wealth, and power, and without any rights or privileges which" were "not perfectly consistent with the attainment of those desired objects," any suggestion that "each petty colony" might actually have a "right to be [Britain's] ... equal" seemed ludicrous.[32]

Notwithstanding this tendency to define the controversy in extreme terms, metropolitan authorities resisted the impulse to take sweeping coercive measures against the colonies during the crisis over the Townshend Acts. Sensing the expediency of Pownall's declaration that "*You may exert power over, but you can never govern an unwilling people,*" they instead took in 1770 what they regarded as a conciliatory approach. At the same time that they indicated that they would seek no new parliamentary taxes and guided through Parliament a repeal of most of the Townshend duties, they

---

[31] *Constitutional Right of the Legislature,* 12–13, 20–1, 27, 49, 53, 57.
[32] Ibid.

retained the tax on tea to stand as a symbol of Parliament's colonial authority.[33]

If anything, the urge toward conciliation during the crisis over the Townshend Acts was even more powerful in the colonies. On both sides of the Atlantic, John Dickinson's *Letters from a Farmer in Pennsylvania*, published in 1767, was certainly the most widely circulated expression of colonial opinion. "By no means fond of inflammatory measures," Dickinson had chaired the committee of the Pennsylvania Assembly that had drafted the Pennsylvania resolves against the Stamp Act in September 1765, the first set of resolutions by any colonial assembly that did not explicitly couple taxation and internal polity as areas over which the colonial legislatures had exclusive jurisdiction. The following month, Dickinson also took a prominent role in drafting the Declaration of the Stamp Act Congress, which made similarly limited claims. With his *Letters*, as well as with these earlier documents, Dickinson obviously intended to confine the controversy within the narrowest possible bounds.[34]

To that end, he addressed his pamphlet exclusively to the issue of the moment – Parliament's right to tax the colonies for revenue – and did not consider the wider problems of the relationship between metropolis and colonies, the extent and nature of metropolitan sovereignty over the colonies, or the distribution of authority within the empire. Thus, although he denounced all parliamentary attempts to tax the colonies for revenue as unwarranted efforts "to erect a new Sovereignty over the Colonies with Power inconsistent with Liberty or Freedom" and warned that colonial submission to those efforts would eventually reduce "these colonies ... into [the] 'COMMON CORPORATIONS'" that "their enemies, in the debates concerning the repeal of the *Stamp Act*, [had] *strenuously insisted they were*," Dickinson was careful to separate

[33] Pownall's speech, Apr. 19, 1769, in Simmons and Thomas, eds., *Proceedings and Debates*, 3: 156.

[34] John Dickinson, *Letters from a Farmer in Pennsylvania to the Inhabitants of the British Colonies* (Philadelphia, 1768), in Forrest McDonald, ed., *Empire and Nation* (Englewood Cliffs, N.J.: Prentice Hall, 1962), 6.

himself from those colonists who during the Stamp Act crisis had seemed to suggest that the colonies were separate states. "He who considers these provinces as states distinct from the *British Empire*," he declared, "has very slender notions of *justice*, or of their *interests*. We are but parts of a *whole*; and therefore there must exist a power somewhere, to preside, and preserve the connection in due order. This power," he acknowledged, "is lodged in the parliament."[35]

Of course, in granting Parliament this general presiding power, Dickinson also took pains to point out that the colonists could only be "as much dependent on *Great Britain*, as a perfectly free people can be on another." Neither the maintenance of Parliament's "legal power to make laws for preserving" the dependence of the colonies nor "the relation between a mother country and her colonies," Dickinson insisted, required that "she should raise money on them without their consent." Contrary to what many historians have assumed, however, he did not explicitly admit Parliament's authority over all matters except taxation for revenue. Rather, he specifically restricted Parliament's presiding authority to those areas in which it had customarily exerted colonial jurisdiction: to measures intended "to regulate trade, and preserve or promote a mutually beneficial intercourse between the several constituent parts of the empire." At the same time, he maintained a discreet silence on the question of whether Parliament might legislate for the internal affairs of the colonies.[36]

Nevertheless, by focusing debate so closely upon the narrow question of taxation, Dickinson helped to de-escalate the controversy. The widespread acceptance of his definition of the situation seems both to have inhibited free and wide-ranging discussion of the nature of the metropolitan-colonial relationship such as had occurred during the Stamp Act crisis and to have been in no small part responsible for confining all

---

[35] Ibid., 7, 67; John Dickinson, An Address Read at a Meeting of Merchants to Consider Non-Importation, Apr. 25, 1768, in Paul Leicester Ford, ed., *The Writings of John Dickinson*, (Philadelphia, 1895), 413.

[36] Dickinson, *Letters*, in McDonald, ed., *Empire and Nation*, 7–8, 27.

but a few official colonial challenges to parliamentary authority during the late 1760s and very early 1770s to the single issue of taxation for revenue. Indeed, the Virginia legislature was one of the few colonial assemblies that explicitly continued to assert its exclusive authority over matters of internal polity as well as taxation.[37]

Although during the crisis over the Townshend Acts, most colonial assemblies, as the Massachusetts legislator Thomas Cushing later observed, "Acquiesced in the distinction between Taxation and Legislation and were disposed to Confine the dispute to that of Taxation only and entirely to wave the other as a subject of too delicate a Nature,"[38] a number of thinkers in both the colonies and Britain took a much deeper look at the controversy and concluded, as Benjamin Franklin wrote his son in March 1768, that, although "Something might be made of either of the extremes; that Parliament has a power to make *all laws* for us, or that it has a power to make *no laws* for us," "no middle doctrine" of the kind proposed by Dickinson could successfully be maintained.[39] Worried about the long-term effects of the "spirit of compliance and moderation" represented by the mainstream colonial response to the Townshend Acts, such people developed an interpretation of the relationship between Britain and the colonies that was much closer to the arguments set forth by Richard Bland, Stephen Hopkins, and other advanced thinkers in the mid-1760s than to the conciliatory views of Dickinson.[40]

In this inquiry into the problem of state organization within the British Empire, these analysts produced an interpretation of the structure of the empire that proceeded from three underlying assumptions. The first was that Parliament's claims to colonial jurisdiction had to be proved and could

[37] Virginia legislature to George III, Apr. 16, 1768, in William J. Van Schreeven and Robert L. Scribner, eds., *Revolutionary Virginia: The Road to Independence*, 4 vols. (Charlottesville, 1973), 1: 55.

[38] Cushing to Franklin, May 6, 1773, in Labaree et al., eds., *Franklin Papers*, 20: 204.

[39] Franklin to William Franklin, Mar. 13, 1768, in ibid., 15: 75–6.

[40] Hicks, *Nature and Extent of Parliamentary Power*, in Jensen, ed., *Tracts*, 12.

"not [simply be] take[n] ... for granted" or permitted to rest on "the monstrous idea of a *Virtual Representation*." The second was that the "civil constitution" of Britain "by no means" determined "the connection which ought to be established between the parent country and her colonies, nor the duties reciprocally incumbent on each other." The third was that the history of the colonies and of their relationship to the metropolis was the most authoritative guide to the exact nature of that connection.[41]

In examining the history of the colonies, these writers were specifically concerned to refute the metropolitan contention that the Crown in its executive capacity had no authority to grant any of its subjects an exemption from parliamentary authority. Elaborating on points that had been widely canvassed during the Stamp Act crisis, they pointed out that, with the exception of Jamaica and New York, both of which had subsequently been accorded English privileges, and those areas in Canada, Florida, and the Caribbean that had been acquired as a result of the Seven Years' War, the colonies were not conquered territories but settlements of "free People" who, with the consent of the Crown, had merely exercised their natural and "just Right to" emigrate and "separate themselves" from their old society.[42]

These writers had no doubt that the Crown had acted legally in giving its consent to these undertakings. "From the earliest times, down to the present," declared Gervase Parker Bushe, a metropolitan sympathetic with the colonists, "the disposition of foreign territory belonging to Great Britain" had "always been vested in the Executive." If, as it

[41] [Gervase Parker Bushe], *The Case of Great Britain and America* (London, 1768), 27; [George Canning], *A Letter to The Right Honourable Wills Earl of Hillsborough, on the Connection Between Great Britain and Her American Colonies* (London, 1768), 9–10; *A Letter to the Right Honourable The Earl of H - -b - - h* (London, 1769), 2–3.

[42] Franklin to Lord Kames, Feb. 25, 1767, in Labaree et al., eds., *Franklin Papers*, 14: 68; [Thomas Hollis], *The True Sentiments of America* (London, 1768), 16; Edward Bancroft, *Remarks on the Review of the Controversy Between Great Britain and Her Colonies* (London, 1769), 44–45.

had repeatedly done, the Crown could legally cede territory to foreign powers, why, Bushe asked rhetorically, could it not also fix "the terms, on which its present and future inhabitants should continue the subjects of Great Britain? Where it could have relinquished all the authority possessed by Great Britain," he contended, "certainly it could relinquish a *part* of that authority. Where it could make a *total alienation*, to enemies, even, surely it could make a *modified grant*, to subjects."⁴³

Because the Crown thus had "a Constitutional Right" both to grant the colonists "an accession of foreign Territory, which he had a legal Right to alienate from the Crown and Realm," and to "permit them to enter into a second Community," it also followed that it had authority to enter into formal constitutional compacts with them. By these instruments, as Franklin put it, the colonists "voluntarily engaged to remain the King's Subjects, though in a foreign Country," in return for the Crown's recognition of their traditional rights as Englishmen, including especially the right to have "a Share in the Power of making those Laws which they are to be governed by." With these compacts, each group of colonists became in effect a separate "body politic" with "power to make all laws and ordinances for the well governing of the people." Because their "distant situation" made "it impossible for" them either "to be represented in the [metropolitan] parliament ... or to be governed from thence," these new polities had to have "a distinct intire Civil Government, of like Powers, Pre-eminence, and Jurisdictions, (conforming to the like Rights, Privileges, Immunities, Franchises, and Civil Liberties), as" were "established in the British Government, respecting the British Subject within the Realm." To this end, the "formation of legislatures" with "full and absolute powers" of "legislation and taxation" became "the first object of attention in the colonies."⁴⁴

---

⁴³ [Bushe], *Case of Great Britain and America*, 3–4.
⁴⁴ Bancroft, *Remarks*, 44–5; Franklin to Lord Kames, Feb. 25, 1767, in Labaree et al., eds., *Franklin Papers*, 14: 68; [Thomas Pownall], *State of the Constitution of the Colonies* [London, 1769], 2; William Samuel

At no point in this process had Parliament taken any role. As Franklin noted, the first two Stuarts "Governed their Colonies, as they Governed their Dominions in France, without the Participation of Parliament." Having "had no hand in their Settlement," Parliament, Franklin insisted, "was never so much as consulted about their Constitution ... took no kind of Notice of them till many Years after they were established," and "never attempted to meddle with the Government of them, till that Period [the Civil War and Interregnum] when it destroy'd the Constitution of all Parts of the Empire, and usurp'd a Power over Scotland, Ireland, Lords and King."[45] Throughout this early period, before "that revolution in provincial policy, which produced the act of navigation," added an anonymous Briton who claimed to have resided in the colonies for more than two decades, the colonies "not only considered themselves, but were considered by the king, parliament, and people of England, as free distinct states, not depending on the parliament of this kingdom, though owing allegiance to its sovereign, and intitled to a free unrestrained trade to all nations, with a positive exemption from every species of taxation, by any authority but that of their own assemblies."[46]

The early history of the colonies thus seemed to confirm the view that the act of emigration and the establishment of a new polity had effectively "annihilate[d] the sovereignty and jurisdiction of the abandoned society," that Parliament's "Jurisdiction did not extend out of the Realm," and that the colonists were, therefore, exempted from its authority "as soon as they landed out of its Jurisdiction." So long as the colonists had resided within the realm of England "as a collective

Johnson to William Pitkin, Feb. 13, 1768, and Pitkin to Johnson, June 10, 1768, in "Trumbull Papers," 259, 286–7; Silas Downer, *A Discourse at the Dedication of the Tree of Liberty* (Providence, 1768), in Charles S. Hyneman and Donald S. Lutz, eds., *American Political Writings during the Founding Era, 1760–1805*, 2 vols. (Indianapolis: Liberty Fund, 1983), 1: 100.

[45] Franklin to Lord Kames, Feb. 25, 1767, and to William Strahan, Nov. 29, 1769, in Labaree et al., eds., *Franklin Papers*, 14: 68, 16: 244.

[46] *Letter to H - -b - - h*, 12–13, 57, 99.

Part of its Inhabitants, and received Protection from its Laws
and Government, no Power whatever could possibly exempt
them from Obedience to its Legislative Authority." But, they
argued, "this Obligation to Obedience ... naturally ceased
on their Separation from" the realm. They willingly admitted
that the king's prerogative extended "indiscriminately, to all
States owing him Allegiance." Yet they contended that the
legislative power, being derived entirely from the inhabitants
of the state over which it presided, was "necessarily confined
within the State itself." A "Subjection to Acts of Parliament"
was thus, as Franklin declared, "no part" of the colonies'
"original Constitution[s]."[47]

Nor had subsequent events changed this situation to any
important extent. "By the act of navigation, and several subsequent ... regulations" during and after the Restoration,
Parliament had indeed circumscribed the "commerce of the
colonies with foreign nations." "From the area of their settlement to the last war," however, it had never made "any
attempt ... to regulate their internal policy or legislation, or
impose taxes upon them." As a result, even those colonies
founded after the Restoration had been "undertaken in full
confidence and expectation of being perfectly independant of
the parliament of this kingdom, except in commercial regulations only."[48] Indeed, in Franklin's view, Parliament's failure in the wake of the Glorious Revolution to act in a more
extensive sphere with regard to the colonies, itself constituted
sufficient refutation of the metropolitan contention that the
early histories of the colonies were irrelevant because the
revolution had established Parliament's authority over "all
parts of the British dominions." Just as the revolution had
"made no alteration in the nature of the union then subsisting between England and Scotland," Franklin wrote to the

[47] *Letter to H – -b – – h*, 15–16; Franklin's Marginalia to [Tucker], *Letter
from a Merchant in London*, and to Matthew Wheelock, *Reflections
Moral and Political on Great Britain and Her Colonies* (London, 1770),
in Labaree et al., eds., *Franklin Papers*, 17: 353, 396; Bancroft, *Remarks*,
44–5; Franklin to William Strahan, Nov. 29, 1769, in Labaree et al.,
eds., *Franklin Papers*,16: 244.
[48] *Letter to H – -b – – h*, 13, 99.

London Chronicle, so it had not changed the relationship "between England and her colonies; for after that period, there was not any attempt made to alter their internal governments: but that their legislative power and administration of justice remained unaltered." What, according to Franklin, "very strongly" continued to mark "the independence of the Americans on the British Parliament" was "that it has never been thought of, to make the House of Lords the ultimate resort in their appeals in law, as is the case from Ireland, the King in council remaining to this day sole arbiter."[49]

Even if the Crown did not initially have authority to grant the colonies independence from parliamentary authority, moreover, the fact that Parliament, "for more than a century," had both "constantly recognized and assented to the King's Prerogative Right of permitting his subjects to withdraw themselves from the Realm, and the Jurisdiction of its Laws" and permitted the colonists "a long uninterrupted enjoyment" of "the privileges originally granted by charter" seemed, as one writer asserted in reminding metropolitan readers of the importance of custom in English constitutional law, "alone sufficient to render all their claims valid, agreeable to the laws of this kingdom." "Is there not a term," asked Bushe in invoking the same tradition, "after which uninterrupted possession confers a right? Have not the Colonists possessed their charters, much longer than that term? Have they not dedicated their lives and fortunes to the improvement of that country, from a dependance upon the validity of their title? Have not the British Parliament seen and acquiesced in their doing so?" According to this line of reasoning, Parliament, through its inaction, had at once "confirmed *sub silentia*" the rights originally granted by charter and strengthened those rights by according them both "a Parliamentary sanction, as well as a title by prescription."[50]

[49] Franklin to *London Chronicle*, Oct. 18–20, 1768, in Labaree et al., eds., *Franklin Papers*, 15: 234–5.
[50] William Samuel Johnson to William Pitkin, Feb. 13, 1768, in "Trumbull Papers," 258; Bancroft, *Remarks*, 44–5; [Bushe], *Case of Great Britain and America*, 3–4; *Letter to H - -b - - h*, 13.

History and usage thus seemed to make clear that the colonies had never been "incorporated with Great Britain in a legislative capacity." This being the case, it seemed equally obvious that the colonies could not suddenly be treated as a mere collection of individual emigrants from Britain. Rather, reasoned William Hicks, they ought to "be considered as so many different countries of the same kingdom, the nature of whose situation prevents them joining in the general council, and reduces them to a necessity of applying to their Prince for the establishment of such a partial polity as may be the best adapted to their particular circumstances." In effect, said Samuel Adams, each colony was "a separate body politick" whose inhabitants had "a right equal to that of the people of Great Britain to make laws for themselves, and are no more than they, subject to the controul of any legislature but their own." As "Separate states (all self-governing communities)," it appeared evident both that the colonies "must be considered as independent of the legal parliamentary power of Great Britain" and that the metropolitan Parliament had no authority to "make laws for their internal government."[51]

According to this line of argument, Great Britain and the British Empire were distinct political entities. As the Georgia minister Johan Joachim Zubly explained, the British Empire was a far "more extensive word, and should not be confounded with the kingdom of Great Britain." Rather, it was a "confederal" polity that consisted of both the home islands and a number of "extrinsic Dominions," including "several islands and other distant countries, asunder in different parts of the globe." As the "head of this great body," England was "called the mother country" and "all the settled inhabitants of this vast empire" were "called Englishmen." But those

[51] *Letter to H--b--h*, 109; Wm. Pitkin to Richard Jackson, June 1, 1768, in "Trumbull Papers," 286–7; Hicks, *Nature and Extent of Parliamentary Power*, in Jensen, ed., *Tracts*, 171; "Valerius Poplicola" [Samuel Adams] to *Boston Gazette*, Oct. 28, 1771, in Cushing, ed., *Writings of Samuel Adams*, 2: 261; "Massachusettensis" [Daniel Leonard] to "All Nations of Men," *Massachusetts Spy*, Nov. 18, 1773, in Hyneman and Lutz, eds., *American Political Writings*, 1: 210.

phrases by no means implied that the empire was "a single state." Rather, each of its many separate entities had a "legislative power ... within itself," and "the several legislative bodies of Great-Britain, Ireland and the British Colonies" were "perfectly distinct, and entirely independent upon each other."[52]

If, however, the British Empire was not a unitary state, and if legislative power within it was both distributed among *"a number of self-governing states"* and, within each of those states, confined within its territorial limits, its several constituent parts were nevertheless, in Franklin's words, *"all united in allegiance to one Prince,* and to the *common law."* If they were "absolutely free from any obedience to the *power of the British Legislature,"* they were bound "to the Power of the Crown." If they did "not [have] the same legislatures," they did "have the same king." Moreover, if, as this developing position suggested, the several polities of the empire were "only connected, as England and Scotland were before the Union, by having one common Sovereign," then it followed that the colonies and other parts of the king's "extended dominions" were *"not* part of the Dominions of *England."* As nothing more than "a Dominion itself," England could not, in fact, have dominions. Nor could "Subjects of one Part of the King's Dominions" possibly have any legitimate claim to be "Sovereigns over the King's Subjects in another Part of his Dominions."[53]

[52] "Mucius Scevola" [Joseph Greenleaf] to *Boston Gazette and Country Journal,* Mar. 4, 1771; John Joachim Zubly, *An Humble Enquiry Into the Nature of the Dependency of the American Colonies upon the Parliament of Great-Britain* (Charleston, 1769), in Randall M. Miller, ed., *"A Warm & Zealous Spirit": John J. Zubly and the American Revolution, A Selection of His Writings* (Macon, Ga.: Mercer University Press, 1982), 57; Franklin, "Subjects of Subjects," Jan. 1768, Franklin to Jacques Barbeu-Duborg, Oct. 2, 1770, and Franklin, Marginalia to *An Inquiry into the Nature and Causes of the Present Disputes* (London, 1769), in Labaree et al., eds., *Franklin Papers,* 15: 36–7, 17: 233, 320.

[53] "Massachusettensis" [Daniel Leonard] to "All Nations of Men," *Massachusetts Spy,* Nov. 18, 1773, in Hyneman and Lutz, eds., *American Political Writings,* 1: 212; Franklin, Marginalia in *Protests of the Lords against Repeal of the Stamp Act,* Mar. 11, 1766, Franklin, "Subjects of Subjects," Jan. 1768, Franklin to *London Chronicle,* Oct. 18–20,

Such an analysis disturbed those who preferred to think of the entire British world as a single "compacted empire." "Disuniting the subjects of the Crown, and splitting the widely-extended territories" of the "empire into so many distinct and separate states, independent of, and co-ordinate with, each other, and connected together by no other tie but that of owing allegiance to the same Sovereign," decried one writer, was to put the colonies and Ireland in precisely the same "relation in which Hanover has stood to Great-Britain ever since the accession of the present royal family."[54] But its exponents strongly denied that there was anything new in their view of the organization of the empire. "Our Kings," Franklin declared in 1769, "have ever had Dominions not subject to the English Parliament," and he cited a long list of precedents from the French provinces under the Norman monarchs to contemporary Hanover.[55]

In the view of its proponents, however, the real virtue of this emerging conception lay not in its foundations in past practice but in its appropriateness for the governance of an extended polity. The "Excellency of the Invention of Colony Government, by separate independent Legislatures," Franklin wrote in 1769, was that it permitted "the remotest Parts of a great Empire" to be "as well governed as the Center." By guaranteeing maximum autonomy to peripheral states and thereby helping to prevent wholesale "Misrule, Oppressions of Proconsuls, and Discontents and Rebellions" in those areas, the authority of the British monarch seemed to be infinitely expandable, capable, in Franklin's words, of being "extended

---

1768, Franklin to Samuel Cooper, June 8, 1770, Franklin to Barbeu-Duborg, Oct. 2, 1770, Franklin, Marginalia to *An Inquiry*, 1769, and Franklin, Marginalia to Wheelock, *Reflections*, 1770, in Labaree et al., eds., *Franklin Papers*, 13: 219, 15: 36–7, 233–4, 17: 162–3, 233, 325, 333, 388; Massachusetts House of Representative to Dennys De Berdt, Jan. 11, 1768, in Cushing, ed., *Writings of Samuel Adams*, 1: 134.

[54] [Francis Maseres], *Considerations on the Expediency of Admitting Representatives from the American Colonies into the British House of Commons* (London, 1770), 5.

[55] Franklin, Marginalia to *An Inquiry*, 1770, in Labaree et al., eds., *Franklin Papers*, 17: 320.

without Inconvenience over Territories of any Dimensions how great soever." From the vantage point of the peripheral states, an important additional benefit of this constitutional organization was that, whenever the several parts of the polity had "different and opposite Ideas of Justice or Propriety," they could each follow the course dictated by "their own Opinions" and interests so long as they did "not interfere with the common Good." Nor did there seem to be much danger that the centrifugal impulses inherent in such a system would get out of hand. With "the restraining power [securely] lodged in" its hands, the Crown would, Hicks declared, always be in a position to ensure that no part would act against "the general welfare of the whole."[56]

This conception of the British Empire as consisting, in Benjamin Prescott's words, "of a great and glorious King, with a Number of distinct Governments, alike subjected to his royal Scepter, and each governed by its own Laws" also seemed to its proponents to offer a solution to the problem of the indivisibility of sovereignty. Posed by metropolitan protagonists during the earliest days of the Stamp Act controversy, the logical dilemma of "an *imperium in imperio*" had remained at the heart of metropolitan resistance to colonial claims for exemption from parliamentary authority. According to the emerging conception of empire among the most advanced defenders of the colonies, however, sovereignty within the extended polity of the British Empire resided not in Britain and not in the king-in-Parliament but in the institution of the monarchy alone. In the imperial realm, according to these writers, the theory of coordination, of the legal sovereignty of the king-in-Parliament, did not apply.[57]

---

[56] Franklin to William Strahan, Nov. 29, 1769, and Franklin, Marginalia to *An Inquiry*, 1770, in Labaree et al., eds., *Franklin Papers*, 16: 246, 17: 322; Hicks, *Nature and Extent of Parliamentary Power*, in Jensen, ed., *Tracts*, 171.

[57] Benjamin Prescott, *A Free and Calm Consideration of the Unhappy Misunderstandings and Debates* ... (Salem, 1774), 30; Franklin to *London Chronicle*, Oct. 18–20, 1768, in Labaree et al., eds., *Franklin Papers*, 15: 233. Though not published until 1774, the Prescott pamphlet was written in 1768.

Franklin was an early and insistent exponent of this view. "All of the Colonies," he explained to the Scottish philosopher Lord Kames in February 1767, "acknowledge the King as their Sovereign: His Governors there represent his Person. Laws are made by their Assemblies or little Parliaments, with the Governor's Assent, subject to the King's Pleasure to confirm or annul them." "The Sovereignty of the King," Franklin observed, was "therefore easily understood." Because the colonies "totally disclaim[ed] all subordination to, and dependence upon, the two inferior estates of their mother country," however, notions like the *"Sovereignty of Parliament*, and the *Sovereignty of this Nation* over the Colonies" appeared to people like Franklin to be both without any clear legal foundations and unnecessary.[58] "The freemen settled in *America*," Hicks declared, "may preserve themselves absolutely independant of their fellow subjects who more immediately surround the throne, and yet discharge, with the strictest fidelity, all their duties to their sovereign" monarch.[59]

To its proponents, this view of the empire as "many states under one Sovereign" seemed thoroughly defensible on the basis both of the terms of the colonial charters and the customary constitutional arrangements that had grown up since the establishment of the colonies. No country, declared Edward Bancroft, had "a better Title to its Constitution, than ... the Colonies." Thus, when Grenville and his supporters "artfully endeavoured to confound the original distinctions which the colonies derived from their charters; and [to] contract them within the limits of this kingdom, and consequently within the extent of parliamentary jurisdiction," they were claiming for Parliament an authority to "make Laws relating to Persons and Societies of Men" who simply were "not within their Jurisdiction." By thus attempting to "arrogate to themselves" a "jurisdiction so infinitely extensive, and so

---

[58] Franklin to Kames, Feb. 25, 1767, Franklin to *London Chronicle*, Oct. 18–20, 1768, and Franklin, Marginalia to *An Inquiry*, 1769, in Labaree et al., eds., *Franklin Papers*, 14: 68–9, 15: 233, 17: 321.

[59] Hicks, *Nature and Extent of Parliamentary Power*, in Jensen, ed., *Tracts*, 170–1.

little capable of limitation," these would-be "sovereigns of the new-discovered world" had at once invaded the rights of both the people in the colonies and the king and thereby tried fundamentally to alter the constitution of the empire.[60]

To prove that such acts were indeed unconstitutional, colonial advocates, as they had done during the Stamp Act crisis, invoked the hallowed British doctrine of consent. Because the mutual "consent *of* [all] ... *the contracting parties*" was required to change the terms of any constitutional contract and because each of the colonies was founded on the basis of a "compact between the King and the people of the colony who were *out of the realm* of Great Britain," wrote Franklin, "there existed nowhere on earth a power to alter it" without the colonists' "formal and express Consent, which," as Edward Bancroft insisted, had "never been given." "In a Dispute between two Partys about Rights," declared Franklin, the mere "Declaration of one Party can never be suppos'd to bind the other."[61]

The explicit assumption behind this position was that, far from having authority to change the constitution of any part of the British world, Parliament was "limited and circumscribed by the constitution that formed it, and from whence it derives its authority." Ridiculing the modern metropolitan idea "that an act of parliament when once passed ... becomes a part of the constitution," colonial proponents quoted the Swiss natural law theorist Emmerich de Vattel to prove that "the supreme legislative [power] cannot change the constitution." Great Britain, declared the Georgia minister Johan Joachim Zubly in 1769, had "not only a Parliament, which is the supreme legislature, but also a constitution," and "the

[60] Franklin, Marginalia to Wheelock, *Reflections*, 1770, in Labaree et al., eds., *Franklin Papers*, 17: 385; Bancroft, *Remarks*, 6–7; *Letter to H - -b - - h*, 26–27; Prescott, *Free and Calm Consideration*, 11; Hicks, *Nature and Extent of Parliamentary Power*, in Jensen, ed., *Tracts*, 175–6; Downer, *Discourse*, in Hyneman and Lutz, eds., *American Political Writings*, 1: 102.

[61] Franklin to Thomas Cushing, Dec. 24, 1770, and to William Franklin, Sept. 1, 1773, in Labaree et al., eds., *Franklin Papers*, 17: 308, 20: 386; Bancroft, *Remarks*, 75.

now Parliament," Zubly insisted, derived "its authority and power from the constitution, and not the constitution from Parliament." Whatever authority Parliament might possess over either the metropolis or the overseas components of the British Empire therefore necessarily had to be "agreeable to the constitution."[62]

Although the colonists could thus make a strong case that for over a century and a half they had without interruption "been trusted in a good measure with the entire management of their affairs," the doctrine of usage on which their developing conception of the empire rested so heavily cut two ways. Although Parliament had no role whatever in their early history and subsequently had not customarily interfered in their internal affairs, they could not deny that from the mid-seventeenth century on, Parliament had "exercised its Authority in the Colonies, for regulating their Trade, and afterwards for directing their exterior Policy." Furthermore, they had to admit that even though Parliament's authority had "in some Instances been executed with great Partiality to Britain and Prejudice to the Colonies," they had "nevertheless always submitted to it" and thereby "consented to consider themselves as united to Great Britain in a commercial capacity, and to have their trade governed by its parliament."[63]

Such an arrangement not only had the sanction of custom but seemed to be dictated by "the circumstances of the times, and complications of the British Empire." As the Irish peer Sir Hercules Langrishe put it, the extended character of the empire rendered it "in some measure ... necessary,

---

[62] William Pitkin to William Samuel Johnson, June 6, 1768, "Trumbull Papers," 280; Massachusetts House of Representatives to Dennys De Berdt, Jan. 12, 1768, to Shelburne, Jan. 15, 1768, and to the king, Jan. 20, 1768, Alfred [Samuel Adams] to *Boston Gazette*, Oct. 2, 1769, Candidus [Samuel Adams] to *Boston Gazette*, Jan. 27, 1772, in Cushing, ed., *Writings of Samuel Adams*, 1: 134, 156, 164, 390, 2: 325–26; Zubly, *An Humble Enquiry*, in Miller,ed., "A Warm & Zealous Spirit," 58.

[63] Shipley, *Sermon*, in Smith, comp., *English Defenders of American Freedoms*, 22; Franklin to William Strahan, Nov. 29, 1769, in Labaree et al., eds., *Franklin Papers*, 16: 244; Bancroft, *Remarks*, 76; *Letter to H – -b – – h*, 29, 104.

that a general superintending power should be somewhere deposited, for the arbitration of commerce, and for directing, restraining, and regulating the external relations between the different members of the empire," and few disputed the contention that that power could not "reside any where with such propriety, as in the British legislature." But they insisted that although this general regulating power was "indeed a great power" that enabled Parliament to "restrain the external operations of the whole" extended British polity, they denied that it could be used to "abridge the internal liberty of a single man," much less that of an entire colony. Whatever the general superintending authority of Parliament, the Massachusetts House of Representatives wrote George III in 1768, it could not violate "the fundamental Rights of Nature & the Constitution to which your Majesty[']s happy Subjects in all parts of your Empire conceive they have a just & equitable Claim."[64]

Derived from a century and a half of experience, custom thus seemed to prescribe a clear allocation of authority within the broad, extended polity of the early modern British Empire, an allocation precisely along the lines identified by Bland and other colonial writers during the Stamp Act crisis. The many provincial governments, Ireland in the near-periphery and the several American colonies in the far periphery, had full jurisdiction over their own particular local and internal affairs, while the metropolitan government at the center had authority over all general matters, including the external relations of the several provincial governments. As Pownall noted, this division of authority seemed to have been "established by invariable prescription from the [colonies'] first establishment."[65]

---

[64] [Sir Hercules Langrishe], *Considerations on the Dependencies of Great Britain* (London, 1769), 52–3; Franklin to Lord Kames, Feb. 25, 1767, in Labaree et al., eds., *Franklin Papers*, 14: 69; Massachusetts House to King, Jan. 20, 1768, in Cushing, ed., *Writings of Samuel Adams*, 1: 164.

[65] Pownall's speech, Feb. 8, 1769, in Simmons and Thomas, eds., *Proceedings and Debates*, 3: 109.

From the point of view of the colonies, the logic of this pragmatic and long-established division of authority seemed to leave no doubt that, though "the authority of parliament in its proper extent" was indeed "justly supreme," the "same ought to be said of the general assemblies of the colonies." That is, as Governor William Pitkin of Connecticut declared in 1768, no "superintending supreme power in the British Parliament to regulate and direct the general affairs of the empire" could deprive the colonists of the "essential privileges" of their constitutions as defined by charters, inheritance, and custom. In both Britain and the colonies, declared an anonymous metropolitan writer who was sympathetic to the colonial argument, "the king has his prerogative and the subjects their rights, and in both the people as their supreme privilege, have the exclusive right of granting their own property" and otherwise governing themselves in all matters relating to their own internal concerns. In "an empire of freemen, no power," declared Zubly, was "absolute but that of the laws, and," he noted in an important addendum, the only laws that carried such absolute authority were those "to which they that are bound by them have consented."[66]

Notwithstanding the antiquity of the colonists' acquiescence in the exertion of parliamentary authority over their external affairs, however, the logic of the doctrine of no legislation without representation led a few people to question that authority as well. Such people did not deny that Parliament could "propose regulations for the trade, and restrictions for the manufactures of those by whom they were appointed" in Britain. But they questioned how, in the words of the New York writer William Hicks, "they can, with any face of equity[,] resolve to extend those regulations to those from whom they have received no *delegated power*." Other writers agreed. So long as they were unrepresented in Parliament, an anonymous metropolitan pamphleteer argued in 1769,

[66] *Letter to H – -b – – h*, 80; Pitkin to William Samuel Johnson, June 6, 1768, in "Trumbull Papers," 280; Zubly, *An Humble Enquiry*, in Miller, ed., *"A Warm & Zealous Spirit,"* 66.

the colonists could, "with equal justice and propriety, dispute" Parliament's "right of legislation in general." "Perfect political liberty," observed Gervase Parker Bushe, consisted "in not being subject to any laws, but such as we have consented to, by ourselves, or by our representatives." "The very spirit of the constitution," said both the Rhode Islander Silas Downer and the New Yorker William Hicks, required that the colonists should not be subject "to any laws, but those which they themselves have made, by regular agreement with the deputy of the Crown, properly authorized for that purpose." In short, as Franklin asserted as early as 1766 in paraphrasing and parodying the Declaratory Act, Parliament had "never had, and of Right never can have without our Consent, given either before or after[,] Power to make Laws of sufficient Force to bind the Subjects of America in any Case, whatever."[67]

If, as the logic of the developing colonial argument thus seemed to indicate, the colonies were wholly independent of Parliament, there existed no properly constituted authority either to legislate on matters relating to the general affairs of the empire or to settle disputes among its component entities. To resolve this problem, a number of people called for some formal legislative union among Britain, Ireland, and the colonies. Though Franklin later changed his mind about the desirability of such a union, during the crisis over the Townshend Acts he joined Thomas Pownall and Francis Maseres in calling for a full "consolidating Union, by a fair and equal Representation of all the Parts of this Empire in Parliament." Others, including William Hicks, more cautiously advocated only a limited legislative union, with the colonies having "representation in parliament for the purposes of commerce [or

[67] Hicks, *Nature and Extent of Parliamentary Power*, in Jensen, ed., *Tracts*, xiv, 170; *An Inquiry into the Nature and Causes of the Present Disputes*, 29; [Bushe], *Case of Great Britain and America*, 15–16; Downer, *Discourse*, in Hyneman and Lutz, eds., *American Political Writings*, 1: 101; Hicks, ibid., 170; Franklin, Marginalia in Protests of the Lords, Mar. 11, 1766, in Labaree et al., eds., *Franklin Papers*, 13: 232.

other matters of general concern] only." According to these proposals, most fully articulated by an anonymous writer in New York in 1768, local legislatures in every part of the empire would continue to have authority over all "their own provincial legislation," while "*One Central Parliament* representing the Whole" would be responsible for all "Matters of *national* Concern (Such as Protection, Defence, Regulation of Trade and naval Concerns, [and] all such Matters as may properly be deemed *national*, or such as concern the Benefit and Welfare of the Whole)."[68]

But such schemes had little support on either side of the controversy. Insisting that Parliament already had full legislative authority over the colonies, most members of the metropolitan establishment thought them unnecessary. Worried that limited representation in such a distant institution would only lend legitimacy to metropolitan efforts to curtail autonomy in the colonies, most colonials thought them unwise. The latter continued to believe that it was absolutely "necessary to settle a Constitution for the Colonies" and to advocate an explicit settlement that would, by determining the nature of the colonies' connection to the metropolis and "ascertaining the relative Rights and Duties of each," fix the constitution of the empire upon "an equitable and permanent Basis," and the former continued to resist any suggestion for constitutional change that would in any way limit the omnipotence of Parliament.[69]

In the absence of any impartial tribunal to settle constitutional disputes between the metropolis and the colonies, there was, as Pownall lamented in 1768, "no means of deciding

[68] Franklin to Kames, Feb. 25, 1767, in Labaree et al., eds., *Franklin Papers*, 14: 65; Pownall, *Administration of the Colonies*, 4th ed., 164–75; *An Inquiry into the Nature and Causes of the Present Disputes*, 23; [Maseres], *Considerations*, 9–15; Hicks, *Nature and Extent of Parliamentary Power*, in Jensen, ed., *Tracts*, 14; *Observations and Propositions for an Accommodation between Great-Britain and her Colonies* ([New York], 1768).

[69] Franklin, Marginalia in *Protests of the Lords*, Mar. 11, 1766, Franklin to Joseph Galloway, Jan. 11, 1770, in Labaree et al., eds., *Franklin Papers*, 13: 224, 17: 24; Bancroft, *Remarks*, 115.

the controversy" by law. "Every act you have taken," Burke pointed out to his colleagues in Parliament in May 1770, "has got a contrary act," and the resulting constitutional impasse left metropolitan leaders with no fully satisfactory course of action. Unwilling to give in, they were, as yet, also unwilling to resort to force. They still understood the power of the political axiom that, in the words of Burke, there was "no such thing as governing the whole body of the people contrary to their inclinations," and, as Lord John Cavendish told Parliament, "dominion without the affection of the governed" was "not worth having." Such considerations were behind Parliament's decision in the spring of 1770 to repeal all the Townshend duties except the tax on tea. This essentially political resolution of the crisis in effect went back to the settlement adopted by the Rockingham party in 1766. That is, it left the issue of the extent of Parliament's colonial authority to rest on the Declaratory Act and token taxes on sugar products and tea, with an implicit understanding that, as in the case of Ireland, Parliament would not thenceforth levy any further taxes on the colonies.[70]

Like the Stamp Act crisis, the controversy over the Townshend Acts had helped to illuminate still further the ancient question of how, within the extended polity of the British Empire, authority was distributed between metropolis and the colonies. To be sure, it produced little change in the metropolitan position as it had been articulated in 1764–6, and the conciliatory thrust of both Dickinson's *Letters from a Pennsylvania Farmer* and most of the official colonial protests helped to obscure the radical drift of sentiment among spokesmen in both America and Britain who supported the colonial side. Pursuing the logic of the customary constitutional arrangements that had obtained in the empire over the previous century, a great many writers between 1767 and 1770 had worked out detailed arguments to prove what a few colonial thinkers had already implied in 1764–6: that the

[70] Burke's speeches, Nov. 8, 1768, May 9, 1770; Cavendish's speech, Dec. 7, 1768; Pownall's speech, Apr. 19, 1769, in Simmons and Thomas, eds., *Proceedings and Debates*, 3: 7, 38, 154, 303.

British Empire was a loose association of distinct political entities under a common king, each of which had its own legislature with exclusive jurisdiction over its own internal affairs. A few writers during these years even challenged Parliament's competence to legislate on matters relating to the general affairs of the empire. As in 1764–6, a major constitutional crisis had thus functioned to intensify, rather than to resolve, differences in interpretations of the constitutional organization of the empire.

CROWN PREROGATIVE AND COLONIAL RIGHTS

Nevertheless, repeal of the Townshend Acts brought a temporary respite from the turmoil that had beset metropolitan-colonial relations over the previous six years. For the next three and a half years, debate over the respective jurisdictions of Parliament and the peripheral legislatures in Ireland and the American colonies fell into temporary abeyance. Yet throughout the early 1770s, constitutional relations within the empire remained troubled. Beginning with the Stamp Act crisis, the long-standing conflicts over the relative balance between prerogative power and colonial rights, conflicts that had been an endemic feature of metropolitan-colonial relations ever since the middle of the seventeenth century, had been subordinated to the new and more pressing debate over the extent of Parliament's colonial authority. To be sure, the older conflict had never fully disappeared. Indeed, not since the late 1740s had there been so many serious controversies between metropolitan authorities and local legislatures as there were in the years just before and during the Stamp Act crisis.

During the early 1760s, there were several major confrontations over the extent of the king's prerogative in the colonies. Though they were often intensely fought, most of these, like the altercation that occurred in Massachusetts in the fall of 1762 over Governor Francis Bernard's attempts to expend public funds without legislative authorization, were soon over.[71]

[71] James Otis, *A Vindication of the Conduct of the House of Representatives of the Province of Massachusetts-Bay* (Boston, 1762).

In a few instances, however, these disputes lasted for years and seriously disrupted provincial political life. Such was the case in New York, where, thoughout the early 1760s, a debilitating battle occurred between Lieutenant Governor Cadwallader Colden and local leaders over two related issues. First was the question of whether the Crown should appoint judges during good behavior, as it had done in Britain since the Revolution Settlement, or, as metropolitan authorities insisted, only during the Crown's pleasure. Second was the issue of whether the governor and council could, on appeal, overrule jury decisions.[72]

Similarly prolonged and even more intense disputes left both South Carolina and Jamaica without operative legislatures for long periods and were resolved only by the resignation or removal of the royal governors. In the former, government was virtually halted for more than nineteen months beginning in the spring of 1762 when Governor Thomas Boone attempted to interfere with what the Commons regarded as its exclusive right to judge the legitimacy of the elections of its own members.[73] In the latter, Governor William Henry Lyttelton's efforts to restrict the customary parliamentary privilege that exempted assembly members from suits at law during legislative sessions produced a profound deadlock that lasted from December 1764 through the summer of 1766.[74] That deadlock was the primary reason why the Jamaica Assembly failed to enter a formal protest against the Stamp Act.[75]

---

[72] Milton M. Klein, "Prelude to Revolution in New York: Jury Trials and Judicial Tenure," *William and Mary Quarterly*, 3d ser., 17 (1960): 439–62. For a recent assessment of the legal implications of this dispute, see Daniel J. Hulsebosch, *Constituting Empire: New York and the Transformation of Constitutionalism in the Atlantic World, 1664–1830* (Chapel Hill: University of North Carolina Press, 2005), 114–22.

[73] Jack P. Greene, "The Gadsden Election Controversy and the Revolutionary Movement in South Carolina," *Mississippi Valley Historical Review* 46 (1959): 469–92.

[74] Jack P. Greene, "The Jamaica Privilege Controversy, 1754–1766: An Episode in the Process of Constitutional Definition in the Early Modern British Empire," *Journal of Imperial and Commonwealth History*, 22 (1994): 16–53.

[75] But see Charles Price et al. to Stephen Fuller, Dec. 1764, Lyttelton Papers BA 5806/12 (iii), Worcester Record Office for the expression by the

Underlining the persistence of the long-standing tensions
between metropolitan authorities and the colonial legislatures, these battles all revolved around the familiar issues
of the previous century: whether the royal prerogative in
the colonies should be placed under the same restraints it
had been subjected to in Britain in the wake of the Glorious
Revolution, whether royal instructions had constitutional
standing, whether the rights of British people in the colonies
were civilly equal to those who continued to reside in the
home islands, whether colonial legislatures were entitled to
the same privileges and powers enjoyed by the metropolitan
House of Commons, and whether usage had the same constitutional authority in the colonies as it had traditionally had
in Britain. Underlying these battles, moreover, were the same
old fears. Metropolitan authorities worried that the continual grasping after power by these distant colonial legislatures
would eventually erode all control from the center; colonial
leaders were anxious lest the Crown's continuing efforts to
extend the "prerogative beyond all bounds" would sooner or
later cheat the colonists "out of their liberties" and thereby
degrade them "from the rank of Englishmen" to "a condition
of slavery."[76]

Throughout the second half of the 1760s, this ancient
contest between prerogative and liberty was superseded
or at least pushed into the background by the debate over
Parliament's relationship to the colonies. Coincident with
the repeal of most of the Townshend duties, however, a new
series of quarrels arose over the scope of the Crown's colonial
authority, quarrels that punctuated the so-called period of

Jamaican Committee of Correspondence, fourteen of the fifteen members who were Jamaican legislators, regarding a powerful attack on the
constitutionality of the Stamp Act.

[76] Otis, *Vindication of the House of Representatives*, 51; [Nicholas Bourke],
*The Privileges of the Island of Jamaica Vindicated with an Impartial
Narrative of the Late Dispute between the Governor and House of
Representatives* (London, 1766), 47, 64; John Dickinson, *A Speech
Delivered in the House of Assembly of the Province of Pennsylvania,
May 24th, 1764* (Philadelphia, 1764), in Paul Leicester Ford, ed., *The
Writings of John Dickinson*, (Philadelphia, 1895), 40.

quiet during the early 1770s and revealed that the extent of
the Crown's prerogative in the colonies was still hotly contested. Major controversies developed in Georgia, Maryland,
and North Carolina, respectively, over the governor's right to
reject the Georgia Commons' choice as speaker, the governor's authority to set the fees of public officers without legislative approval, and the North Carolina Assembly's authority
to give its constituents the right to attach the property of non-
residents in suits for debts. Much more serious were quarrels in Massachusetts over the governor's right to transfer the
meetings of the legislature from the traditional site at Boston
to Cambridge and in South Carolina over the Commons'
authority to issue money from the treasury without executive
approval. With the former lasting for over two years and the
latter for five, both of these contests resulted in long interrup-
tions in the legislative process and, like the more limited controversies in Georgia and North Carolina, revolved around
metropolitan efforts to use royal instructions to curb the
power of local assemblies.[77]

In one sense, these controversies were simply the latest
rounds in the long contest between central prerogative power
and local colonial rights as championed by provincial assemblies. From the 1670s on and more systematically since the
late 1740s, the "Governing of Colonies by Instructions," as
Franklin observed in January 1772, had "long been a favou-
rite Point with Ministers" in the metropolis.[78] Ministers had
indeed made so many "daring and injurious attempt[s] to

---

[77] Jack P. Greene, *The Quest for Power: The Lower Houses of Assembly
in the Southern Royal Colonies, 1689–1763* (Chapel Hill: University
of North Carolina Press, 1963), 420–4, 433–6; Peter S. Onuf, ed.,
Maryland and the Empire, 1773: The Antilon-First Citizen Letters
(Baltimore: Johns Hopkins University Press, 1974); Donald C. Lord
and Robert M. Calhoon, "The Removal of the Massachusetts General
Court from Boston, 1769–1772," *Journal of American History* 55
(1969): 735–55; Jack P. Greene, "Bridge to Revolution: The Wilkes
Fund Controversy in South Carolina, 1769–1775," *Journal of Southern
History* 29 (1963): 19–52.

[78] Franklin to James Bowdoin, Jan. 13, 1772, in Labaree et al., eds.,
Franklin Papers, 19: 11.

raise and establish a despotic power over them"[79] that, as the Maryland lawyer Charles Carroll of Carrollton remarked during the fee controversy in Maryland in May 1773, it had long since become "a common observation confirmed by general experience" that any "claim in the colony governments of an extraordinary power as ... part of the prerogative" was "sure to meet with the encouragement and support of the ministry in Great-Britain."[80]

From the perspective of the crises over the Stamp and Townshend Acts and the debate over Parliament's new pretensions to authority over the internal affairs of the colonies, however, these old questions about the Crown's relationship acquired a new and heightened urgency in the colonies. Because, as an impressive number of colonial spokesmen had begun to argue during the late 1760s, sovereignty within the empire rested not in the Crown-in-Parliament but in the Crown alone, it became especially important for the colonists to establish the boundaries not just of parliamentary but also of royal authority in the colonies. For that reason, colonial defenders in all of the battles of the early 1770s revealed a pronounced tendency to build upon their own particular local constitutional heritages to argue, as their predecessors in earlier generations had often done, that, no less than in Britain itself, the Crown's authority – the freedom of its "will" – in the colonies had been effectively limited over the previous century by specific idiosyncratic constitutional developments in each of the colonies. Again just as in Britain, these developments had led, colonial leaders believed, irreversibly in the direction of increasing authority in the hands of the local legislatures and greater restrictions on the prerogatives of the Crown. By this process, they argued, the rights of the inhabitants in the colonies had gradually been secured against the power of the metropolis.[81]

[79] William Bollan, *The Free Britons Memorial* (London, 1769), 25.
[80] First Citizen's Third Letter, May 6, 1773, in Onuf, ed., *Maryland and the Empire*, 149.
[81] See Jack P. Greene, ed., *The Nature of Colony Constitutions: Two Pamphlets on the Wilkes Fund Controversy by Sir Egerton Leigh and*

As refined and elaborated during the contests of the early 1770s, this view of colonial constitutional history powerfully helped to reinforce traditional views of the colonial legislatures as both the primary guardians of the local rights of the corporate entities over which they presided and, like Parliament in Britain, as the dynamic forces in shaping the colonial constitutions. Insofar as the constitution of the empire was concerned, this emphasis upon the peculiarity and integrity of the several colonial constitutions certainly constituted a vigorous defense of constitutional multiplicity that had profound implications for the ongoing debate over the nature of sovereignty within the empire.[82] For, together with the emerging conviction that Parliament had no authority over the colonies, the renewed contention that the Crown's authority in the colonies was also limited by local constitutions, which had emerged not just from the colonists' inherited rights as Englishmen and their charters but also from local usage and custom, pushed the colonists still further in the direction of a wholly new conception of sovereignty in an extended polity such as the early modern British Empire. That conception implied that ultimate constitutional authority – sovereignty – lay not in any institution or collection of institutions at the center of the empire but in the separate constitutions of the many separate political entities of which the empire was composed.

CONDITIONS OF LAW IN THE COLONIES

Explicit in these formulations was an underlying preference for a system of authority in which local law, institutions, officials, and populations had ultimate authority over local and provincial matters, and this preference was not confined to the lawyers, opinion leaders, and other members of provincial and local political establishments who produced the essays and pamphlets that laid out the emerging colonial

---

Arthur Lee (Columbia, S.C.: University of South Carolina Press, 1970), 49–55.
[82] See Onuf, ed., *Maryland and the Empire*, 29.

case. Repeatedly, beginning with the Stamp Act crisis, many crowds, denominated *mobs* by metropolitan representatives and their supporters, used force and intimidation to prevent the enforcement of metropolitan laws contrary to local customs and interests. These popular gatherings, commonly a broad cross section of the free population, sometimes wreaked considerable damage upon the property and persons of people associated with those laws. The sacking and burning of Stamp Collector Andrew Oliver's and Lieutenant Governor Thomas Hutchinson's houses in Boston on August 14, 1765, were only the most dramatic and destructive of the popular protests that occurred in opposition to the Stamp Act. For a decade thereafter, similar crowds acted as an adjunct to local officials in resisting the efforts of metropolitan officers to enforce metropolitan law when it seemed antagonistic to local interests or at variance with local law.

Such actions occurred in every major colonial city on the mainland and even in rural Virginia, but they were particularly prevalent in Boston and in eastern New England, where crowds acting in defense of local interests often interfered with the enforcement of customs regulations and sometimes brawled with British soldiers. The "rescue" of the cargo of the merchant Job Smith's sloop *Polly* from custom officials in Dighton, Massachusetts, on April 7, 1765[83]; the prevention of a customs search of Captain Daniel Malcolm's house in Boston on September 24, 1766[84]; the riot over the new customs commissioners' seizure of John Hancock's sloop, *Liberty*, on June 10, 1768[85]; the confrontation with British troops at the so-called Boston Massacre on March 5, 1770[86]; the burning in Narragansett Bay of the grounded royal naval

[83] Edmund S. Morgan and Helen M. Morgan, *The Stamp Act Crisis: Prologue to Revolution* (Chapel Hill: University of North Carolina Press, 1953), 40–52.

[84] John Phillip Reid, *In a Rebellious Spirit: The Argument of Facts, the Liberty Riot, and the Coming of the American Revolution* (University Park: Pennyslvania State University Press, 1979), 11–19.

[85] Ibid., 86–120.

[86] Hiller B. Zobel, *The Boston Massacre* (New York: W. W. Norton, 1970), is the fullest account, but it is set in an anachronistic framework.

schooner, the *Gaspee*, by Rhode Islanders on June 10, 1772[87], and the Boston Tea Party of December 16, 1773,[88] were the most prominent of these incidents.

Traditionally, historians have depicted these and similar incidents as evidence of mounting disorder and lawlessness in which the rule of law was steadily supplanted by the rule of the mob. More recently, however, legal historians have shown that such characterizations have been based upon an anachronistic conception of the law as sovereign command, a modern conception that derives from a positive jurisprudence that was only just coming into vogue during the last half of the eighteenth century and would not gain full ascendancy until the nineteenth and twentieth centuries. For Britons on either side of the Atlantic during the pre-Revolutionary crisis, by contrast, law did not always mean command or will, and legal theorists, judges, and lawyers did not necessarily associate law with sovereignty. Rather, in the context of British and British–American legal traditions, law in the 1760s and 1770s was still thought of as being as much custom and community consensus as sovereign command. As a result, eighteenth-century law throughout the British world was considerably less coercive and considerably more dependent for its enforcement upon community support than most earlier historians have recognized.[89]

An important case study of the legal limitations upon government in late colonial Massachusetts has demonstrated that the restraint of governmental power and the security of individuals in their lives, liberties, and property were among the most intense concerns of free colonial British Americans of all social classes and that in Massachusetts they managed,

---

[87] For a short account, see William R. Leslie, "The *Gaspee* Affair: A Study of its Constitutional Significance," *Mississippi Valley Historical Review*, 39 (1952): 233–56.

[88] Benjamin Woods Labaree, *The Boston Tea Party* (New York: Oxford University Press, 1964), 126–46.

[89] John Phillip Reid, *In a Defiant Stance: The Conditions of Law in Massachusetts Bay, the Irish Comparison, and the Coming of the American Revolution* (University Park: Pennsylvania State University Press, 1981), 193–227.

to an extraordinary degree, to construct a polity that thoroughly reflected these concerns. Because Massachusetts, like the other colonies, had no permanent police force and only a tiny bureaucracy, the provincial courts were the only governmental institution with much coercive power. Because they wanted to be ruled by law, not by judges possessing vast discretionary powers that could be turned to the service of arbitrary rulers, however, legislators were careful to limit judicial discretion. In part, legislators were aided in this task by long-standing custom, according to which courts never went against precedent. As in England itself, precedent, usage, or custom both had the force of law and were invariably used to fill the interstices in statute and common law. But legislators also gave juries wide jurisdiction in both civil and criminal cases and, even more important, vast authority to find both the law and the facts in cases in those areas. The virtually unlimited power of juries to find law in effect meant both that judges had little law-making power and that representatives of local communities assembled as jurors generally possessed effective power to control the content of substantive law in the localities.[90]

Other officials, both provincial and metropolitan, had even less power than judges. Almost entirely without coercive power of their own, they were, in fact, subject to common law actions for damages whenever they committed a "wrong" in the exercise of their duties. In effect, then, officials were unable to exercise their powers without the consent of local communities. Even the sheriffs and constables responsible for enforcing court judgments could do so only when local communities were willing to allow the judgments to be carried out. Colonial Massachusetts was thus a standing example of one of early modern British political theorists' favorite maxims, that all government depended on opinion. No less than in Britain itself, Massachusetts, and presumably all the other British-American colonies, thus functioned within the venerable Anglo-American tradition of a government whose

[90] Ibid., 27–84.

limited law enforcement personnel relied upon the public to assist them in implementing the law.[91]

The implications of these findings for understanding the origins of the American Revolution in Massachusetts and elsewhere are profound. They mean that law was bicentric, not unicentric. Generated by Parliament and royal officials and judges in London, *metropolitan law* was anemic. With no effective legal institutions at their command, Massachusetts officials charged with its enforcement were helpless without the support of the local community. Already weak before the Revolutionary crisis, metropolitan law became even more so over time, as local opinion increasingly came to perceive it as in large part a series of arbitrary measures intended to undermine their traditional constitutional rights and their economic and political autonomy.

But the decline in respect for metropolitan law, the new legal historians have demonstrated, did not lead to a breakdown in respect for law in general. On the contrary, at the same time that metropolitan law was becoming steadily weaker, *local law* – those provincial statutes, judicial precedents, and customs that were upheld by the courts, grand juries, traverse juries, magistrates, and other institutions that comprised the colony's effective legal system – retained its full vigor. The two essential features of that law were that it was a reflection of community consensus and that it was under local, not metropolitan, control.[92]

No less than metropolitan law, local law lacked strong formal instruments of coercion and depended upon public support for its enforcement. Throughout Britain's American colonies during the eighteenth century, popular uprisings had repeatedly acted to defend the urgent interests of communities, both to enforce the will of local magistrates and to compensate for the inability of constituted authorities to act on their own. In this regard, the colonies were not all that different from contemporary Britain, where it was a well-established

[91] Reid, *In a Rebellious Spirit*, and *In a Defiant Stance*, passim.
[92] Ibid.

tradition for people to take matters into their own hands in two different types of situation: first, when they had no other means to nullify arbitrary, unconstitutional measures, and, second, when ordinary legal processes failed to function or did not exist.

So long as popular uprisings served a public function and confined their actions to harassing those charged with enforcing unconstitutional statutes of Parliament, they were thus perfectly in accord with British legal traditions as expressed in the contemporary doctrine that it was legal to resist unlawful government power. So far from being outside the bounds of law, then, recent legal historians have found, the popular uprisings described by earlier historians as expressions of lawless violence actually functioned as the police unit, the *posse comitatus*, of local law.[93] No wonder that throughout the colonies between 1765 and 1776 the institutions of provincial and local government almost always supported such uprisings. No wonder that provincial political establishments everywhere depended upon informal bodies such as the sons of liberty that sprang up during the Stamp Act crisis or, beginning in 1774, public associations and popularly elected committees of safety to enforce nonimportation agreements and other sanctions designed to nullify metropolitan laws and regulations.

Of course, customs and other metropolitan officials and supporters who were the victims of public uprisings or patriot committees saw them as open violations of law. But their perspective was not that of the majority. Far from being illegal, resistance to metropolitan law was actually undertaken in defense of local law. American crowds thus served largely as an auxiliary enforcement agency for locally dominated legal institutions. Acting in concert and with overwhelming popular support, the formal instruments of law – juries and magistrates – and the informal instrument – the crowd – managed

---

[93] The classic article on this subject is Pauline Maier, "Popular Uprisings and Civil Authority in Eighteenth-Century America," *William and Mary Quarterly*, 3rd ser., 27 (1970): 1–35.

in one incident after another after 1765 to nullify those many parliamentary statutes and metropolitan regulations that were deemed both arbitrary and contrary to the vital interests of the colonies. In the process, they effectively underlined the impotence of metropolitan agents to enforce any measure opposed by locals.

The rescue of the contents of the sloop *Polly* provides a case in point. When Collector of Customs John Robinson in Newport decided in April 1765 that the master of the sloop *Polly* had probably underreported the number of hogsheads of sugar imported from Surinam, he chased it up Narragansett Bay, overtook it at Dighton, searched it, and, after finding twice the reported amount of sugar, seized it along with the undeclared part of its cargo for the king. But no local mariners would agree to take the ship back to Newport where it was to be condemned in court, and Robinson had to leave the vessel in the hands of two of his subordinates. No sooner had those subordinates left the *Polly* to refresh themselves at a shore-side tavern than locals stole their boat and proceeded to unload the entire cargo, divest the sloop of its sails, rigging, cables, anchors, and other marine equipment, and, by boring holes in the hull, render it wholly unseaworthy. When Robinson heard what had happened, he returned to Dighton with a party of royal marines and sought to obtain a writ of assistance to enable him to search for the missing cargo. But local magistrates refused his request on the grounds that only the Massachusetts Supreme Court could issue such a writ. Nor could the few marines with him prevent his arrest upon a legal action brought by the *Polly*'s owner, Job Smith, who sued Robinson for £3,000 in damages for the loss of his ship and cargo, and Robinson spent three days in the Taunton jail before his Boston superior could send money to bail him out. Robinson subsequently found and seized eight of Smith's more than 120 hogsheads of sugar, refloated the *Polly*, and succeeded in having it condemned in Newport. But this incident revealed the limited extent of metropolitan authority in the colonies and the ways in which local populations mobilized and functioned as auxiliaries to local officials in resisting metropolitan efforts to enforce regulations from London.[94]

Nor was the force of metropolitan law in New England in any way strengthened by the stationing of British troops in Boston after 1768: That event did not lead to arrests and executions of resistance leaders. Never empowered to act as a police force, the army remained subject to civilian control. The result was that it could not be used as an instrument of coercion and was easily neutralized by the same agencies of local law that had already – by *legal* means – rendered metropolitan law a dead letter in the colony. The neutralization of metropolitan power after 1765 thus occurred not, as so many earlier historians have suggested, because metropolitan representatives were restrained or timid in their use of power, but because they were so rapidly and fully immobilized by local law.[95]

Although they usually acted in cooperation with or even under the direction of provincial political leaders and rarely veered out of control, the participants in these crowd actions clearly had opinions, interests, and objectives of their own that sometimes diverged from those of provincial or local figures of authority. Thus, in several such actions, the fear of being impressed into the British naval service dramatically swelled the size of crowds. No matter how great the divergence in interests, opinions, and goals between the leadership and the other participants, these crowds demonstrated a remarkable solidarity with provincial leaders on the desirability of preventing the enforcement of metropolitan law whenever it conflicted with local law and opinion and of retaining local control over all matters affecting local interests.

How far colonials were willing to go to express their objections to metropolitan interference in provincial affairs was vividly illustrated by the *Gaspee* Affair. The capture and

---

[94] Morgan and Morgan, *Stamp Act Crisis*, 40–52.
[95] John Phillip Reid, *In Defiance of the Law: The Standing Army Controversy, the Two Constitutions, and the Coming of the American Revolution* (Chapel Hill: University of North Carolina Press, 1981), 192–227.

burning of the vessel and the wounding of its commander, Lieutenant William Dudingston, on June 9–10, 1772, marked the culmination of a long battle between Rhode Island watermen and royal and naval customs officials over the latter's efforts to enforce regulations prescribed by the American Plantations Duty Act of 1764 and its later modifications. In 1764, Rhode Islanders had fired on a British man-of-war and in 1769 had burned the *Liberty*, one of the king's sloops, in Newport, without repercussions from either British or Rhode Island authorities. Regarding Dudingston's operations as piratical because he had refused to take the customary oaths before Rhode Island authorities, in disregard of long-established Rhode Island law regarding vessel seizures, the vigilante crowd that acted in the *Gaspee* Affair did so in the name of law enforcement. When Governor Joseph Wanton moved too slowly to identify the perpetrators and bring them to justice, Dudingston's superior, Admiral John Montagu, opened an independent investigation and presented a state of the case to London authorities.

Deeply incensed by this defiance of their authority, metropolitan officials appointed a commission, headed by Governor Wanton, to investigate the case, proposing to bring the ringleaders to Britain for trial. Although the commission was only a fact-finding body without prosecutorial powers, Rhode Islanders regarded it as an unconstitutional infringement of provincial authority and a violation of the ancient English legal principle that the accused should be tried before a jury of peers in the locality in which the offense was committed. The commission failed to identity any of those responsible for the incident, and London's designs were frustrated. Even before the commission had started its work, the Rhode Island press circulated the ideas that the burning of the *Gaspee* was an act in defense of Rhode Island law and that it was Dudingston's efforts to enforce a contradictory metropolitan law, using procedures unsanctioned by the provincial constitution, that were illegal. Theorizing the existence of "two separate and distinct juridical areas," one in Rhode Island and the other in Britain, "to which the respective laws of each were confined and outside of which [they] were to have no force and effect," colonial analysts argued that "only the civil authority in Rhode Island … had the legal right to inquire into the *Gaspee* affair." This argument fully complemented the arguments that Franklin and other advanced colonial thinkers had developed in response to the Townshend Act crisis about the distribution of legislative authority in the British Empire and the exclusive jurisdiction of colonial legislatures over the domestic affairs of their respective colonies.[96]

[96] Leslie, "*Gaspee Affair*, 233–56. The quotations are from pp. 251–2.

4

EMPIRE SHATTERED, 1774–1776

When Parliament's passage of the Tea Act in May 1773 revived the dispute over its colonial authority, colonial resistance to that measure provoked the crisis that would, in a mere two and a half years, lead to the secession of a significant part of the early modern British Empire. At no time during this crisis did either side show much disposition to compromise. As each quickly took a determined stand on the position marked out by its most extreme proponents during the previous crises, the spirit of conciliation that had marked the crisis over the Townshend Acts rapidly gave way to complete intransigence. While the metropolitan political nation refused to back down from its insistence that the king-in-Parliament was the supreme sovereign of the empire, the colonial assemblies and the First and Second Continental Congresses, composed of delegates from the thirteen colonies from New Hampshire south to Georgia, gave official sanction to views that had previously been held only by private individuals, views developed by Franklin and others during the late 1760s and early 1770s that called for complete colonial autonomy over internal affairs. By 1776, what had begun as yet another crisis over Parliament's right to tax the colonies had become a crisis over whether the colonies would become independent, and the empire foundered over the inability of Britain and the colonies to agree on a formula for governance that would give Britons overseas the same legal and constitutional rights and the same control over their domestic affairs as Britons at home.

In both Britain and the colonies, supporters of Parliament's right to legislate for the colonies insisted, as they had ever since the beginning of the controversy during the Stamp Act crisis, that the British Empire, consisting of Great Britain *and* all its territories, was a single state composed of "ONE people, ruled by ONE constitution, and governed by ONE King." Arguing that the early Stuarts, no less than the postrevolutionary Hanoverians, had always been "under the control of the other parts of the legislative power" and therefore had no authority to exempt the colonists from Parliament's jurisdiction, they held that the colonists were "subjects of the Kings of England, not as the inhabitants of Guyenne formerly were, or as those of Hanover now are, but subjects of an English parliamentary King." As such, like all other Englishmen, they necessarily owed obedience to parliamentary statutes.[1]

Reiterating the same central contentions that had underlain their argument from the beginning, most metropolitans continued to interpret the controversy as a dispute over sovereignty. Dismissing the doctrine of no legislation without representation as "an obsolete maxim" that had no applicability to the distant parts of an extended polity like the British Empire, they persisted in asserting that "No maxim of policy" was "more universally admitted, than that a supreme and uncontroulable power must exist somewhere in every state." In the British Empire, they insisted, that power was vested "in King, Lords, and Commons, under the collective appellation of the Legislature," which, as James Macpherson phrased it, was merely "another name for the Constitution of State," was, "in fact, the State itself."[2]

---

[1] *Colonising, or Plain Investigation of That Subject* (London, 1774), 8; [Jonathan Boucher], *A Letter from a Virginian to the Members of the Congress* (Boston, 1774), 17–19.
[2] [James Macpherson], *The Rights of Great Britain Asserted Against the Claims of America* (London, 1776), 3–5, 11.

Thus, if the colonists refused obedience to Parliament, they were "no longer Subjects, but rebels" who, by arrogating "to themselves all the functions of Sovereignty," were obviously endeavoring to put themselves "on the footing of a Sovereign State." "The question between them and Great Britain," then, as Macpherson gravely noted in summarizing the dominant position within the metropolitan political nation, was nothing less than "dependence or independence, connection or no connection." With "no common Principle to rest upon, no common Medium to appeal to," wrote Josiah Tucker, the dispute seemed to have no middle ground. To admit any qualification in "the controuling right of the British legislature over the colonies," its proponents devoutly believed, would mean nothing less than the abandonment of "the whole of our authority over the Americans."[3]

Underlying the administration argument was the assumption that the colonies were merely subordinate extensions of the metropolitan state. Colonials and their metropolitan supporters might talk about the colonies, as did one anonymous writer in 1774, as "constituent parts of the British Empire," thereby implying "an idea of perfect equality, so far as interest is concerned," between them and the metropolis and suggesting that "every province" should "form a little empire within itself, subject to its own laws." But in the administration view such formulations merely represented an ineffective effort to ignore the fact that the very word *colony* implied "a subjection to the power, and ... a subserviency to the interest of the ruling state."[4]

Administration apologists did not deny that the colonies had been treated liberally and allowed a large measure of

---

[3] [Macpherson], *Rights of Great Britain*, 3, 11; Nathaniel George Rice's speech, Mar. 7, 1774, and Charles Cornwall's speech, Apr. 19, 1774, in William Cobbett and T. C. Hansard, eds., *The Parliamentary History of England from the Earliest Period to 1803*, 36 vols. (London, 1806–20), 17: 1149, 1214; Josiah Tucker, Tract V, *The Respective Pleas and Arguments of the Mother Country, and of the Colonies, Distinctly Set Forth* (Gloucester, 1775), 38.

[4] *A Letter to Doctor Tucker on his Proposal of Separation between Great Britain and Her American Colonies* (London, 1774), 6–7.

self-government. "Ever since they could be called a People," wrote Adam Serle in 1775, "they have enjoyed … all the Advantages and Immunities of *Britons*. Not the nearest Subjects to the Throne in *England*, nor the remotest Members of the State in *Asia*," he observed, "have had a wider Field of Freedom to range in, than the once happy Sons of high-ly-favored and indulged *America*."[5] Even Samuel Johnson, the lexicographer, political writer, and unrelenting critic of colonial resistance, agreed that "an English Colony has very liberal powers of regulating its own manners and adjusting its own affairs."[6] In the administration view, however, this experience did not exempt the colonies from metropolitan authority, and, as Johnson wrote in a 1774 pamphlet, it seemed absurd to "suppose that by sending out a colony, the nation established an independent power."[7] Because the colonies and their inhabitants were "intitled to all the rights of Englishmen," were "governed by English laws, [and] entitled to English dignities," he declared, they were also "regulated by English counsels, and protected by English arms; and it seems to follow by consequence not easily avoided, that they are subject to English government, and chargeable by English taxation," and he denounced those who would try "to deprive the nation of its natural and lawful authority over its own colonies."[8]

In the emerging political atmosphere of the 1760s and 1770s, it was easy for writers to conflate the nation's authority with parliamentary authority. The Glorious Revolution had laid the groundwork for the slow development of the idea of Parliament, composed of the Crown and the two houses, as the locus of British sovereignty, a view that the constitutional debate with the colonies helped to enshrine, and in this

[5] [Ambrose Serle], *Americans against Liberty: or An Essay on the Nature and Principles of True Freedom, Shewing that the Designs and Conduct of the Americans Tend Only to Tyranny and Slavery* (London, 1775), 27.

[6] Samuel Johnson, *Taxation no Tyranny: An Answer to the Resolutions and Address of the American Congress* (London, 1775), 24.

[7] [Samuel Johnson], *The Patriot* (London, 1774), 22–3.

[8] Ibid., 22; Johnson, *Taxation no Tyranny*, 29.

atmosphere it was easy to assume, contrary to actual fact, that "the legislature," and not merely the Crown, had been an active participant in the formation of the colonies, even in the granting of "charters for their security and protection in trade." What could be more outrageous, administration spokesmen asked, than for colonies so "entirely dependent" on the British legislature in their origins and so recently benefited by British arms in the removal of the French from North America now to offer such profound resistance to metropolitan measures and even to "aim at independency, and endeavour to form an internal government among themselves, to the prejudice of the state to whom they owed their very being."[9]

As colonial resistance intensified in the wake of the Coercive Acts of 1774, many metropolitan defenders traced it not just to incipient colonial desires for independence but specifically to the repeal of the Stamp Act in 1766. "Great Britain and her Colonies derive their present dispute, and its consequent misfortunes from the PATRIOTISM of the motley Junto who formed the appearance of an Administration, in the end of 1765 and beginning of 1766," and who pushed through the repeal of the Stamp Act, Macpherson lamented in early 1776. "From that moment," he complained, "may be dated ... the commencement of ... an Aera of Public Ruin."[10] "So unreasonable in itself and so disgraceful to authority," said another writer in the previous year, "the absurd and impolitic repeal of the stamp act ... was a concession repugnant to the idea of government, and, at the same time, such a sacrifice of power and revenue that has operated very much against that subordination which every state reasonably requires, and which every component part of a Nation owes to the supreme authority."[11] By emphasizing short-term commercial considerations over the long-term objective of

---

[9] *A Full and Circumstantial Account of the Disputes Between Great Britain and America* (Glasgow, 1775), 2.
[10] [Macpherson], *Rights of Great Britain*, 21.
[11] Americanus, *The False Alarm; or the Americans Mistaken* (London, 1775), 11–12.

keeping the colonies tightly under the thumb of the metropolis, such concessions, they were persuaded, undermined the very foundations of empire.

To maintain Britain's superiority over the colonies, it appeared to administration supporters in 1774–6, required a firm hand. They pointed out that the New-York Restraining Act of 1767, suspending the New York Assembly until it complied with an act requiring assemblies to provide for the costs of quartering British troops stationed in their colonies, had worked, the New York Assembly having "recovered the just sense of" its "duty" so that it could be "restored to [its] ... authority."[12] Colonial resistance to the Tea Act of 1773 and the subsequent Coercive Acts now rendered beyond "a single doubt," asserted an anonymous writer in December 1774, that "the loose situation of things in our American Colonies requires a speedy reformation, and demands the full exertion of the Legislature of this Kingdom to remedy subsisting evils before they grow rooted and confirmed, by bringing the Colonies into so good and sound a state, that every part of those distant territories may enjoy its due proportion of nutriment, and be fitted and disposed to promote the interest, honour, and dignity of Great Britain, their Head, Mother, and Protectress."[13]

A few advocates of a hard-line response even proposed a massive reconstruction of Britain's mode of colonial governance. Declaring that it would be "Happy ... for the government of our colonies" if the government eliminated assemblies altogether, one government supporter in 1774 expressed the opinion that the colonies "would have experienced a much greater degree of felicity, had their government consisted only of a governor and council, with a board of trade and other inferior officers and magistrates to enforce the police ...,instead of their assemblies, where the most important affairs of state are cavilled in a manner that would disgrace the

[12] *Full and Circumstantial Account*, 7.
[13] *A Letter to a Member of Parliament on the Present Unhappy Dispute Between Great-Britain and Her Colonies, Wherein the Supremacy of the Former Is Asserted and Proved* (London, 1774), 43–4.

most illiterate assembly, and the dignity of government and magistracy excited to ridicule under the mask of patriotism." "Without any of those pompous ideas of popular governments, which our countrymen are elated with," he predicted, the colonies would become models of "harmony, industry, and virtue," instead of "disorder and anarchy." "Respecting the management of their colonies," he added in expressing a widely shared opinion, nations had no choice but to formulate "certain principles of policy" and then "strictly" adhere to them.[14]

Nor, added another writer in November 1775, did the fact that the colonies had enjoyed a large measure of British liberty over the previous century and a half present any obstacle to such a reformation. For a colony to "*claim* its own laws, and choose its own mode of raising a revenue" seemed to him absolutely "contrary to the principles of [imperial] government, and acting in open defiance of that state from whence the colony derived its being." Because those principles dictated that colonies could always "be controuled by such laws as a parent-state judges most conducive to the joint interest of both," however, it followed that "Right ... to a particular form of government," no matter how long established, could not "be pleaded by any colonies. Expedience may, but of that expedience the legislature of the parent-state must judge." When it came to colonial governance, he suggested, British libertarian traditions and decades of practice counted for nothing in comparison with considerations of state as defined by the metropolis.[15]

Not everyone in Britain viewed the situation in such dire terms. Jonathan Shipley and Edmund Burke, for example, thought that no drastic remedies were required. Arguing that it was "unnecessary to lay down the limits of sovereignty and obedience," they believed that imperial harmony could yet be restored simply by a return to "lenient and conciliating

[14] *Thoughts on the Act for Making more Effectual Provision for the Government of the Province of QUEBEC* (London, 1774), 13–15, 29.
[15] *A Plain State of the Argument Between Great-Britain and Her Colonies* (London, 1775), 9–11.

measures."[16] But others saw the crisis as an opportunity for constitutional reform, which, by explicitly incorporating the traditional British principle of consent into the constitutional structure of the empire, would serve as a via media between "absolute obedience in the colonies to be taxed by parliament, and their total independence on the parent state from which they are descended."[17]

"The question now depending before both Houses of Parliament," declared one writer in the spring of 1774, was whether "*Great-Britain* shall, by pursuing the maxims of a sound and upright policy with respect to the Colonies, *forever* establish a permanent and solid foundation for a just constitutional Union between both countries." If, another critic of government policy declared in a pamphlet published in the same month, Britons had "succeeded pretty well ... in procuring a constitution for Britain, what we now want is ... a constitution for the British Empire." This task, he said while essentially endorsing traditional colonial conceptions of the way the empire worked, would present no great difficulty because it offered "itself to the plainest understanding; it is nothing more ... than taking the constitution of Britain, and applying it to" the empire so that "every province would form a little empire within itself, subject to its own laws, and obedient to its own regulations," while revolving around "one common centre, where Great Britain is placed with power and dignity to controul the whole."[18]

There were two quite different approaches to this task. The first, which had been widely canvassed during previous crises,

[16] Jonathan Shipley, *A Sermon Preached before the Incorporated Society for the Propagation of the Gospel in Foreign Parts* (London, 1773), in Paul H. Smith, comp., *English Defenders of American Freedom, 1774–1778* (Washington: Library of Congress, 1972), 30.

[17] *An Argument in Defence of the Exclusive Right Claimed by the Colonies to Tax Themselves* (London, 1774), 5–6.

[18] *A Friend to Both Countries [Charles Garth], America Vindicated from the High Charge of Ingratitude and Rebellion; with a Plan of Legislation, Proposed to the Consideration of Both Houses, for Establishing a Permanent and Solid Foundation for a Just Constitutional Union, Between Great Britain and Her Colonies* (Devizes, 1774), 5–6; *Letter to Dr. Tucker*, 8, 13–14.

was that no major innovations were necessary. Its advocates believed that a medium could be found either in the example of the customary relationship between Britain and Ireland or in the explicit codification of existing divisions of authority. Either way, this approach involved the establishment of what Thomas Pownall called "A LINE OF PACIFICATION" based on the by now familiar distinction between internal and external spheres of authority. According to this formulation, the colonies, with respect to their "interior rights, within the bounds of their corporation[s]," would have the same "absolute and sovereign" authority "as the government of the mother country hath within its realm," and the metropolitan government would retain "supreme sovereign power" over all matters involving the external affairs of the empire. As Pownall explained in elaborating on the views he had set forth at the time of the controversy over the Townshend Acts, this arrangement was far from new. Rather, it merely gave explicit sanction to the very *"line of the administration of the government of England, towards the Colonies, and of their obedience towards its supreme empire, for near a century and a half."* Furthermore, another writer declared, such long and successful usage made it clear that acknowledging the internal autonomy of the colonies would "no more" lead "to their independency, than the possession of those [same] privileges" had led "to the independency of Ireland."[19]

What was new in this formulation was Pownall's perception that the new European colonies of the early modern era represented a new species of political entity that, through usage, had developed a distinctive form of government, which Pownall referred to as "a mixed or COLONIAL GOVERNMENT." Neither, as many colonists now contended, *"states sui juris"* with "external as well as internal sovereign jurisdiction" nor, as most people in the metropolitan political nation seemed to

---

[19] Matthew Robinson-Morris, Baron Rokeby, *Considerations on the Measures Carrying on with Respect to the British Colonies in North America* (London, 1774), in Smith, comp., *English Defenders of American Freedom*, 56, 65; Thomas Pownall, *The Administration of the British Colonies*, 5th ed., 2 vols. (London, 1774), 2: 37–8, 78.

agree, merely *"communities within the state* of Great Britain," colonial governments, in Pownall's view, were something in between. Less free than national and more free than provincial governments, this new species of polity had gradually emerged to meet the specific conditions of governance in a wide, extended polity.[20]

A second approach to constitutional reform involved more sweeping measures. Believing that the metropolitan establishment had so far "evade[d] a fair discussion of *the question of right*," its advocates held that the long and increasingly acrimonious conflict made it clear that "the constitution of the Colonies must be [wholly] newmodelled." As one anonymous writer of this persuasion declared, the "question should be, not what the constitution was, or is, but what present circumstances considered, it ought to be." According to this view, which had support among conservative Americans as well as liberal metropolitans, the most effective way to make sure that the doctrine of consent obtained in the extremities as well as at the center of the empire was to create a central American Parliament that, while leaving the specifically local affairs of the colonies in the hands of their *"little Parliaments,"* would have jurisdiction over such matters of general concern as defense expenditures.[21]

Following Parliament's passage of the Coercive Acts in the spring of 1774, most opinion leaders in America certainly agreed with those metropolitan writers who thought that the time had come for constitutional reform. "For nine successive

<hr/>

[20] Pownall, *Administration of the Colonies*, 5th ed., 2: 36–7, 100; *An Argument in Defence of the Exclusive Right*, 131.
[21] John Cartwright, *American Independence, the Interest and Glory of Great Britain* (Philadelphia, 1776), in Smith, comp., *English Defenders of American Freedom*, 169; *America Vindicated from the High Charge of Ingratitude and Rebellion*, 6, 40–1. For American expressions of similar views, see [Joseph Galloway], *A Candid Examination of the Mutual Claims ...* (New York, 1775), 53, and William Henry Drayton, *A Letter from "Freeman" of South Carolina to the Deputies of North America, Assembled in the High Court of Congress at Philadelphia* (Charleston, 1774), in Robert W. Gibbes, ed., *Documentary History of the American Revolution* (New York, 1855), 18–19.

years," one metropolitan writer complained in 1774, the
colonists had "been impoliticly kept in a state of continual
training." In quick succession, the Stamp and Townshend
Acts had forced them to examine their constitutional "situation more closely and critically than they had ever done"
before. In the process, they conducted a "thorough examination" of questions that had not previously been so intensively
and "accurately canvassed," fundamental questions concerning those important points relating to "the bounds of power
and of obedience" within the empire that, as Baron Rokeby
remarked, were "in all governments" better left "unsettled
and undetermined."[22]

As a result of "their eager researches after that information
which was so essentially necessary to the preservation of their
liberties," the colonists had gradually acquired, during the
years of crisis beginning in 1764, a far "better understanding" of the "nature of their political situation." By 1770, in
fact, they had as individual thinkers and writers worked out
an elaborate and fully formed body of theory designed to
secure colonial rights against metropolitan power. In 1774,
during the early stages of what would become the crisis of
independence, that body of theory needed only the sanction
of constituted authority to make it the official position of the
several colonies. That sanction was supplied by the actions
of the First and Second Continental Congresses in 1774–5
and endorsement by the local legislative bodies of the thirteen
protesting colonies.[23]

[22] *A Letter to a Member of Parliament on the Unhappy Dispute Between
Great Britain and Her Colonies* (London, 1774), 6; James Iredell, "The
Principles of an American Whig," [1775–6?], and "Causes of the American
Revolution," June 1776, in Don Higginbotham, ed., *The Papers of
James Iredell*, 1 vol. (Raleigh: North Carolina Department of Archives
and History, 1976), 1: 333, 375; Cartwright, *American Independence*,
in Smith, comp., *English Defenders of American Freedom*, 157; Rokeby,
Considerations on the Measures, in ibid., 58; *A Further Examination of
Our Present American Measures* (London, 1776), 115.
[23] William Hicks, *The Nature and Extent of Parliamentary Power
Considered*, in Merrill Jensen, ed., *Tracts of the American Revolution,
1763–1776* (Indianapolis: Bobbs Merrill, 1967), 177; Drayton, Letter
from "Freeman," in Gibbes, ed., *Documentary History*, 1: 32.

The colonial position, as it was enunciated in mid-1774 and elaborated over the next two years, was founded on a complete rejection of the prevailing metropolitan theory of an omnipotent Parliament, a theory that was "evidently of [such] a modern structure" that it was not "even now an established idea on either side of the Atlantic." By ignoring the vital and traditional British constitutional principle of consent, of no legislation without representation, this "dreadful novelty," supporters of the colonial position declared, was at total variance with both "the ancient rights of the people" and "the settled, notorious, invariable practice of" imperial governance within the empire over the previous century and a half.[24]

No less important, when applied to distant and unrepresented colonies, this "modern doctrine," it seemed to the colonists, obviously also represented "a total contradiction to every principle laid down at the time of the [Glorious] Revolution, as the rules by which the rights and privileges of every branch of our legislature were to be governed for ever." Indeed, by its insistence on exerting a "supreme jurisdiction" over the colonies, Parliament seemed, not merely to be violating the most essential principles of the Glorious Revolution, but actually to be assuming and acting on precisely the same "high prerogative doctrine[s]" against which that revolution had been undertaken. Thus, the colonists believed, if by resisting Parliament they had become rebels, they were "rebels in the same way, and for the same reasons that the people of Britain were rebels, for supporting the Revolution." That is, they were merely acting to defend rights that they had "possessed for about two hundred years."[25]

[24] *An Answer to a Pamphlet, Entitled Taxation no Tyranny* (London, 1775), 6; John Dickinson, *An Essay on the Constitutional Power of Great Britain over the Colonies in America* (Philadelphia, 1774), in Samuel Hazard et al., eds., *Pennsylvania Archives*, 138 vols. to date (Philadelphia and Harrisburg, 1852–), 2d ser., 3: 601; *An Argument in Defence of the Exclusive Right*, 104; [Arthur Lee], *An Appeal to the Justice and Interests of the People of Great Britain* (London, 1774), 20–1.

[25] Dickinson, *Essay on the Constitutional Power*, in Hazard et al., eds., *Pennsylvania Archives*, 2d ser., 3: 565; *An Argument in Defence of the*

If, as the colonists and many people in the metropolis believed, the most important legacy of the Glorious Revolution was freedom from arbitrary government, then the experience of the past ten years had taught them that their right to share in that legacy could never be secure unless they enjoyed full autonomy over their own internal affairs. As their metropolitan advocate John Cartwright remarked, they were simply "too far removed to be governed on ... [revolutionary] principles of freedom by the mother country." Indeed, they could now see clearly that it was precisely "because no man thought at that time that the *English* Parliament" could possibly be "a constitutional or adequate Legislature in ordinary, for Dominions beyond Sea" that the Crown had initially granted "*Ireland* ... a Parliament of her own" and then established assemblies in each of the colonies. Having from the beginning been "considered as being out of the jurisdiction of parliament," the king's many external dominions in America and Ireland had thus had to have their own legislatures, each of which necessarily enjoyed "supreme power of legislation" over its respective territory. There was no other way either "to supply the want of ... [a legislative] jurisdiction" or to guarantee that Englishmen in distant countries would continue to enjoy English liberties.[26]

By 1774, few people in America thus any longer doubted that, over the previous decade, it had "been clearly and fully proved that the Assemblies or Parliaments of the *British* Colonies in *America*" had "an exclusive right, not only of taxation, but of legislation also; and that the *British* Parliament, so far from having a right to make laws binding upon those

Exclusive Right, 104; "An Apology for the Late Conduct of America," *London Gazetteer*, Apr. 7, 1774, in Peter Force, ed., *American Archives*, 9 vols. (Washington, 1837–53), 4th ser., 1: 242; "To the Freemen of America," May 18, 1774, in ibid., 336; [Hugh Baillie], *Some Observations on a Pamphlet Lately Published* (London, 1776), 2–3.

[26] Cartwright, *American Independence*, in Smith, comp., *English Defenders of American Freedom*, 159–60; *An Answer to a Pamphlet, Entitled Taxation no Tyranny*, in Force, ed., *American Archives*, 4th ser., 1: 1455. Moses Mather, *America's Appeal to the Impartial World* (Hartford, 1774), 34.

Colonies in all cases whatsoever," had "really no just right to make any laws at all binding upon the Colonies." Far from being subject to the "supreme" authority of Parliament, most American leaders now believed, the colonies had "always enjoyed a supreme Legislature of their own, and ... always claimed an exemption from the jurisdiction of a British Parliament." Not the king-in-Parliament, wrote the Virginian Thomson Mason, but the "King, at the head of his respective American Assemblies," constituted "the Supreme Legislature of the Colonies." Parliament's claim in the Declaratory Act "to regulate our internal police, give, take away, change, and infringe, our Constitutions and Charters," one speaker told a general meeting at Lewes, Delaware, in July 1774, was nothing more than a "lawless usurpation."[27]

Whether Parliament had any authority even over the external affairs of the colonies was now a point of contention among colonial resistance leaders. Already during the Townshend Acts crisis, some colonial supporters, as Sir John Dalrymple correctly charged, had begun to advance "the extravagant doctrines that" the colonies were "not bound by the Navigation Laws, and that" they were "even independent of Parliament altogether."[28] By 1774, many of the most influential tracts, including those written by James Wilson of Pennsylvania and Thomas Jefferson of Virginia, unequivocally took this position. The legislative authority of each of the many independent legislatures within the empire, including Parliament, wrote Wilson, was necessarily "confined within ... local bounds" and could not be imposed on any of the other areas of the empire without their consent.[29]

[27] [Thomson Mason], "The British American," nos. VI–VII, July 7, 14, 1774; "A Brief Examination of American Grievances," July 28, 1774; "To the Inhabitants of New-York," Oct. 6, 1774, in Force, ed., *American Archives*, 4th ser., 1: 522, 541, 658, 821.

[28] [Sir John Dalrymple], *The Address of the People of Great Britain to the Inhabitants of America* (London, 1775), in Force, ed., *American Archives*, 4th ser., 1:1423.

[29] James Wilson, *Considerations on the Nature and Extent of the Legislative Authority of the British Parliament* (Philadelphia, 1774), in Robert Green McCloskey, ed., *The Works of James Wilson*, 2 vols. (Cambridge, Mass.: Harvard University Press, 1967), 2: 741, 745–6;

During the early stages of the crisis of independence, however, most American leaders seemed still to have believed that Parliament did have authority over external affairs and, as both Alexander Hamilton and John Adams pointed out, that that authority derived from the "long usage and uninterrupted acquiescence" by which the colonists, since the middle of the seventeenth century, had given their "implied consent" to the navigation acts and other trade regulations.[30]

But although few of their protagonists yet claimed for the colonists "external as well as internal sovereign jurisdiction" as "independent nations," virtually everyone now agreed with those people who had begun to argue during the late 1760s that "all the different members of the British Empire" were "distinct states, independent of each other, but connected together under the same sovereign." On close examination, they had discovered that, as an entity "composed of extensive and dispersed Dominions," the empire was "in some degree a new case" in political history that had to "be governed ... more by its own circumstances, and by the genius of our peculiar Constitution, than by abstract notions of government." Separated by vast distances, "inhabited by different people, [living] under distinct constitutions of government, with different customs, laws and interests," its several constituent elements could not possibly be considered as a single civil state. Rather, each part had to be "considered as a [distinct] people, not a set of individuals." Presided over by its own legislature, each of these corporate entities was a separate realm that was entirely independent of all the others. According to this line of thought, no part of the empire was subordinate to any other part. As Franklin had remarked in 1770, there was thus

Thomas Jefferson, *A Summary View of the Rights of British-America* (Williamsburg, 1774), in Julian P. Boyd, ed., *The Papers of Thomas Jefferson*, 35 vols. to date (Princeton: Princeton University Press, 1950), 1: 125.

[30] Alexander Hamilton, *The Farmer Refuted* (New York, 1775), in Harold C. Syrett and Jacob E. Cooke, eds., *The Papers of Alexander Hamilton*, 26 vols. (New York: Columbia University Press, 1961-79), 1:1 22; John Adams, "Novanglus," 1775, in Charles F. Adams, ed., *The Works of John Adams*, 10 vols. (Boston, 1856), 4: 113-14.

no dependence among the several parts of the empire, "only a *Connection*, of which the King is the common Link."[31]

Indeed, to the colonists' few defenders in Britain, this dispersion of authority seemed not to be a defect but a necessary and viable solution to the problem of governance in an extended polity. Recognizing that it had "always been a most arduous task to govern distant provinces, with even a tolerable appearance of justice," they agreed with John Dickinson, who quoted the Italian political thinker Cesare Beccaria to the effect that "an over grown republic" like the British Empire could "only be saved from despotism by sub-dividing it into a number of confederate republics." "If an empire be too large, and its parts too widely separated by immense oceans, or other impediments, to admit of being governed on the principles essentially belonging to all free governments," argued John Cartwright, it was "an overgrown empire, and ought to be divided before it falls into pieces." As in all "large bodies," the "immutable condition, the eternal law, of extensive and detached empire," Burke declared in expanding on this theme, was that "the circulation of power must be less vigorous at the extremes." Even a despot like the sultan of Turkey, Burke explained, understood that "the force and vigor of his authority in his centre ... derived from a prudent relaxation in all his borders" and therefore governed his distant provinces "with a loose rein," in order that he might "govern [them] at all."[32]

---

[31] Pownall, *Administration of the Colonies*, 5th ed., 2: 100; Cartwright, *American Independence*, in *English Defenders of American Freedom*, 138; Wilson, *Considerations*, in McCloskey, ed., *Works of Wilson*, 2: 745; *An Answer to a Pamphlet, Entitled Taxation no Tyranny*, 8; Mather, *America's Appeal*, 47; Iredell, "To the Inhabitants of Great Britain," Sept. 1774, in Higginbotham, ed., *Papers of Iredell*, 1: 264; John Adams, "Novanglus," in Adams, ed., *Works of John Adams*, 4:123; Franklin, Marginalia to Wheelock, *Reflections Moral and Political*, 1770, in Leonard Labaree et al., eds., *The Papers of Benjamin Franklin*, 30 vols. to date (New Haven: Yale University Press, 1959), 17: 393

[32] Jonathan Shipley, *A Speech Intended to Have Been Spoken by the Bishop of St. Asaph*, in Smith, comp., *English Defenders of American Freedom*, 31; Cartwright, *American Independence*, in ibid., 144; Dickinson, *Essay on the Constitutional Power*, in Hazard et al., eds., *Pennsylvania*

George Johnstone, former governor of West Florida, took this theme even farther in several speeches in Parliament. Arguing that the British colonies had "flourished more than others" precisely because Britain had "found out the secret of carrying freedom to the distant parts of the empire," Johnstone asked his fellow MPs to "consider that the very first principles of good government in this wide-extended dominion, consist in subdividing the empire into many parts, and giving to each individual an immediate interest, that the community to which he belongs should be well-regulated. This is the principle," Johnstone declared, "upon which our ancestors established those different colonies or communities; this is the principle upon which they have flourished so long and so prosperously; this is the principle on which alone they can be well governed at such a distance from the seat of the empire." Before they tried to run "the different privileges belonging to the various parts of the empire into one common mass of power," therefore, Johnstone urged his listeners to recall that "the great maxim to be learned from the history of our colonization" was to "let men manage their own affairs; they will do it better on the spot," he contended, "than those at a distance ... can possibly do it for them."[33]

In view of the success of the empire, in view of the "riches and power, men and money," and "credit and honour in the world," which "the detached parts of its dominions" contributed to "the centre of government," both Americans and their supporters in Britain regarded it as absurd for the metropolis to risk so many palpable advantages in pursuit of what increasingly appeared to them to be nothing more than an academic and irrelevant political abstraction. To the vast majority of the metropolitan political nation, the "grand" question in dispute might very well appear to be "Whether

Archives, 2d ser., 3: 578; Edmund Burke, *Speech on Conciliation with America* (New York: D. C. Heath, 1907), 25–6.

[33] *Gov. Johnston's Speech on American Affairs on the Address in Answer to the King's Speech* (Edinburgh, 1776), 7–8; Johnstone's speeches, June 6, 8, 1774, in Sir Henry Cavendish, *Debates on the House of Commons in the Year 1774, on the Bill for Making More Effectual Provision for the Government of the Province of Quebec* (London, 1839), 187, 242.

or not the British parliament ... hath the right of sovereignty over North America." Throughout the debates between 1764 and 1776, however, most colonial leaders had resisted such reductionism and had endeavored, unsuccessfully, to focus debate on the seemingly more tractable and certainly less abstract problem of how power was or should be allocated in a polity composed of several related but nonetheless distinct corporate entities. For the colonists, resolution of their dispute with the metropolis had never seemed to require much more than the rationalization of existing political arrangements within the empire.[34]

For them, the "great solecism of an *imperium in imperio*" seemed, as James Iredell declared, to be little more than "a narrow and pedantic ... point of speculation," a "scholastic and trifling refinement," that had no relevance to the situation at hand. The claim "that two independent legislatures cannot exist in the community," George Johnstone observed, demonstrated "a perfect ignorance of the history of civil society" and a complete misunderstanding of the workings of the empire. "Mankind are constantly quoting some trite maxim, and appealing to their limited theory in politics, while they reject established facts," he complained. For colonial supporters, however, "custom and continual usage" were invariably, in Iredell's phrase, "of a much more unequivocal nature than speculation and refined principles." Notwithstanding the fact that it had been "so vainly and confidently relied on" by their antagonists, that "beautiful theory in political discourses – the necessity of an absolute power residing somewhere in every state" – seemed, as Iredell wrote, to be wholly inapplicable to a situation involving "several distinct and independent legislatures, each engaged in a separate scale, and employed about different objects."[35]

---

[34] Rokeby, *Considerations on the Measures*, in Smith, comp., *English Defenders of American Freedom*, 103; Cartwright, *American Independence*, in ibid., 134.

[35] Iredell, "To the Inhabitants of Great Britain," Sept. 1774, and "The Principles of an American Whig," [1775–6], in Higginbotham, ed., *Papers of Iredell* 1: 254, 264–7, 332; *Gov. Johnston's Speech*, 5–7.

Indeed, if the *imperium in imperio* argument had any relevance to the existing debate, the colonists had no doubt that it worked in favor of their argument in at least two senses. First, as Moses Mather noted in taking obvious delight in turning the conventional metropolitan argument on its head, because, in conjunction with the king, each of the "multiplicity of legislatures" in the empire already had full authority over its own jurisdiction, it was impossible to subject the colonies "at the same time to the legislative power of parliament" without introducing "an *imperium in imperio*, one supreme power within another," which, he mockingly remarked in parroting his opponents, was obviously "the height of political absurdity." Second, and more seriously, as the Earl of Abingdon pointed out, the most blatant "solecism" in the contemporary debate was the assertion "that in a limited government [like that of Britain], there can be an unlimited power." No less than the executive authority of the Crown, the "legislative power of Great Britain" was, they asserted in terms they had been using from the beginning of the debate, necessarily "limited to, and circumscribed by the constitution of the kingdom, and the fundamental laws thereof."[36]

Once the extent of colonial resistance to the Coercive Acts was known in Britain, several government opponents in early 1775 challenged the emerging doctrine of parliamentary supremacy and stressed the constitutional restrictions on Parliament's authority. "No Englishman," declared a writer in early 1775, would "deny the Supremacy of Parliament, however extended, within the Bounds of Reason: but Bounds it has," and only when "kept within those Bounds," he added, was "whatever it does ... right." "The true supremacy in our system," observed another writer, "is the *salus populi*; this is

---

[36] Mather, *America's Appeal*, 44; Hamilton, *Farmer Refuted*, in Syrett and Cooke, eds., *Hamilton Papers*, 1: 164; *An Answer to a Pamphlet, Entitled Taxation no Tyranny*, 8; Willoughby Bertie, Earl of Abingdon, *Thoughts on the Letter of Edmund Burke, Esq., to the Sheriffs of Bristol, on the Affairs of America* (Oxford, 1778), in Smith, comp., *English Defenders of American Freedom*, 219–20; *Resistance No Rebellion* (London, 1775), 46–7; Granville Sharp, *A Declaration of the People's Natural Right to a Share in the Legislature* (London, 1774), 233, 238–9.

our *suprema lex*, which controuls Parliaments, and to which
dictates their legislation ought to conform. The edicts of this
supreme law," he declared, "are the rules and principles of
our British constitution." "By this means," he added, "We
trace ... the *supremacy* to its true seat, and find it reposed in
the Constitution or fundamental laws: those *Palladia* of our
public freedom, and regulators of Parliamentary power." "In
extreme cases," warned another, "there is a controll in the
hands of the whole people, with whom *alone* the supreme
power *unlimited* of any community can reside, and with
whom it *always* does reside, though in common course they
delegate a portion of authority sufficient for legislation to
others, but so, as that they are not to subvert the constitution under which they act; nor to convert Government to
the misery and ruin of the people, for whose happiness and
prosperity it was formed." Thus, argued yet another British
writer two months later, Parliament was supreme over the
whole empire only *"as far as is requisite for the constitutional*
exercise of their dominion – but ... a government *whose basis*
is freedom, must govern *by the spirit of the constitution*,"
and in making regulations "for the welfare of the Empire,"
it was *"supreme to do justice, but not arbitrary to enslave.*
Where there are regular, constitutional assemblies – immediately *intended at their first appointment* to raise *their own*
internal taxes – the British Parliament," he wrote, "could not
infringe on their right, without violating the Constitution
which it is their duty to support."[37]

With Jonathan Shipley, bishop of St. Asaph, colonial leaders called on the metropolitan government to abandon its
pursuit of the "vain phantom of unlimited sovereignty, which

[37] *Three Letters to a Member of Parliament, on the Subject of the Present*
Dispute with Our American Colonies (London, 1775), 68–9; *An*
Address to the Right Honourable L–d M–sf–d in which the Measures of
Government Respecting America and Considered in a New Light; with
a View to his Lordship's Interposition Therein (London, 1775), 16–17.
An Answer to a Pamphlet, Entitled Taxation no Tyranny, Addressed
to the Author, 11; *The Pamphlet, Entitlerd, 'Taxation No Tyranny,'*
Candidly Considered, and Its Arguments, and Pernicious Doctrines,
Exposed and Refuted (London, 1775), 50.

was not made for man," and content itself with "the solid advantages of a moderate, useful and intelligible authority." As long as all members of the empire adhered to the customary arrangements that had developed over the previous century and a half, as long as the king was the "supreme head of every legislature in the British dominions," he would always have it in his power to "guide the vast and complicated machine of government, to the reciprocal advantage of all his dominions" and, by his authority to veto laws, would on any occasion be able to "prevent the actual injury to the whole of any positive law in any part of the empire." As long as "the power of every distinct branch [of the empire was] ... limited to itself," and the king, "the only sovereign of the empire," was "acknowledged, by every member" to have "Sovereign" authority "over the whole," Alexander Hamilton contended, there was absolutely no danger in having many legislatures in the same polity and no possibility that there would ever "be two sovereign powers, in the same state."[38]

That this entire line of argument applied to the relationship between Britain and all of its associated polities its proponents had no doubt. Every colony had within itself "the rights and the actual powers of legislation." The "West India islands, as well as the continental colonies," declared Cartwright, were exempt from Parliament's authority and "certainly have a right to their [legislative] independency, whenever they shall think proper to demand it." Parliament's authority, he contended, was "confined to the British Isles, and to the various *settlements and factories of our trade* in the different parts of the world, including *the government of Newfoundland*; together with the garrisons of *Gibralter* and *Minorca*" – those few British territories that did not "contain within themselves every necessary of legislation." Within the term *British Isles*, Cartwright meant to include Ireland, which, because of its proximity he thought was "naturally a

38 Shipley, *Sermon*, in Smith, comp., *English Defenders of American Freedom*, 38; Hamilton, *Farmer Refuted*, in Syrett and Cooke, eds., *Hamilton Papers*, 1: 99; Iredell, "To the Inhabitants of Great Britain," Sept. 1774, in Higginbotham, ed., *Papers of Iredell*, 1: 266.

dependent upon Great-Britain," albeit he did advocate a parliamentary union of the kind that had already been formed
between England and Scotland. Others strongly disagreed.
"The Representative Body of Ireland," wrote Rokeby, might
be "called a Parliament; that of America, an Assembly. The
term of kingdom" might obtain "in one country, and that of
colony in the other," but, he asked rhetorically, "Is there any
charm in the sound of these words, which makes a difference?" "By their own circumstances," Hamilton confidently
predicted, "the Irish ... will be taught to sympathise with us
and commend our conduct."[39]

Other than the thirteen dissident colonies, however, the
only overseas territory to align itself officially with the colonial
point of view was Jamaica, where, ever since the Stamp Act
crisis, there had been considerable support for the American
cause. In December 1774, just a few weeks after the adjourn-
ment of the First Continental Congress, the Jamaica Assembly
adopted a petition and memorial to the king that constituted
a ringing endorsement of the emerging colonial view of the
distribution of authority within the empire. Although this
document began by pointing out that Jamaica's extensive
slave population prevented it from offering any overt physical
resistance to British authority, it subscribed to the argument
that Parliament's legislative authority was confined to Britain.
Following the example of the North American Congress, the
Assembly "freely consent[ed] to the operation of all such Acts
of the *British* Parliament, as are limited to the regulation of
our external commerce only, and the sole object of which is
the mutual advantage of *Great Britain* and her Colonies,"
obviously intending thereby to give the navigation acts constitutional standing in Jamaica. "By the principles of our
Constitution, as it has arisen from colonization," however,
the Assembly denied that its constituents or, for that matter,

---

[39] Cartwright, *American Independence*, in Smith, comp., *English Defenders of American Freedom*, 149–52; Rokeby, *Considerations on the Measures*, in ibid., 65; Hamilton, *A Full Vindication of the Measures of the Congress* (New York, 1774) in Syrett and Cooke, eds., *Hamilton Papers*, 1: 60.

any other group of colonists, could be "bound by any other laws than such as they have themselves assented to, and are not disallowed by your Majesty" and prayed "that no laws shall be made and attempted to be forced upon them, injurious to their rights as Colonists, *Englishmen*, or *Britons*."[40]

The lack of formal endorsement from other colonies does not, however, mean an absence of extensive support for the American position. To be sure, in the fall of 1775, the Irish Parliament approved an address condemning the Americans as rebels. But it was vigorously opposed by the so-called Patriots, who throughout the previous decade of constitutional controversy had been sympathetic to the Americans and had emphasized the extent to which, as Henry Flood wrote to the colonists in 1768, "your circumstances and ours" were "exactly the same." Praising Americans for being the true heirs of William Molyneux, the great exponent of Irish home rule at the end of the previous century, Patriot speakers predicted that if Parliament succeeded in forcing the colonies to acknowledge its taxing power over them, it would next turn its attention to Ireland. Similarly, when in early 1776 the Irish Parliament voted, again with strong Patriot opposition, to send four thousand troops from Ireland to the colonies, a group of dissenting lords denounced the action and declared that Parliament's claim to tax any part of the empire other than Britain was "not inherent in the general constitution of the empire." For the first time since 1749, a new Irish edition of Molyneux's *Case of Ireland* was published in 1776 with a preface calling on Irishmen to "despise all authority which is not founded in justice and ... to defend with their fortunes and their lives those constitutional rights which they inherit from their ancestors."[41]

[40] Jamaica Assembly's Petition to King, Dec. 28, 1774, in Force, ed., *American Archives*, 4th ser., 1: 1072–4; George Metcalf, *Royal Government and Political Conflict in Jamaica, 1729–1783* (London: Longmans, 1965), 167–91; Richard B. Sheridan, "The Jamaican Slave Insurrection Scare of 1776 and the American Revolution," *Journal of Negro History*, 61 (1976): 299–301.

[41] The best existing published account of the Irish response to the American revolutionary argument is J. G. Simms, *Colonial Nationalism*,

In their efforts to explain – and to rationalize – existing constitutional relationships within the empire, colonial protagonists, between 1764 and 1776, had discovered that the locus of authority necessarily resided in each of the separate corporate entities that composed the empire. Contrary to metropolitan theory as it had developed following the Glorious Revolution, and more especially after 1740, authority, they now clearly understood, had never been concentrated in a sovereign institution at the center. Rather, it had always been dispersed among the several parliaments that routinely had been established to preside over – and express the collective will of – each new polity within the empire. Indeed, this proliferation of legislatures was the only way that those traditional English rights that had been confirmed to the inhabitants of the metropolis by the revolutionary settlement – especially that most fundamental right of no legislation without representation – could be extended to people in the outer reaches of a large, extended polity like the early modern British Empire. For the inhabitants of those – by then – quite ancient corporate entities, English liberty and their specific local corporate rights were identical.

1698–1776 (Cork: Mercier Press, 1976), 48–71. But see also Maurice R. O'Connell, *Irish Politics and Social Conflict in the Age of the American Revolution* (New Yprk: Oxford University Press, 1965), 25–36; Francis G. James, *Ireland in the Empire, 1688–1770* (Cambridge, Mass.: Harvard University Press, 1973), 307–12; and David N. Doyle, *Ireland, Irishmen and Revolutionary America* (Cork: Mercier Press, 1981), 152–61. The quotations are from Simms, *Colonial Nationalism*, 69, 71, and James, *Ireland in the Empire*, 311. In Barbados, a section of the assembly also endeavored, albeit unsuccessfully, to address the king in support of the Americans. See Agnes M. Whitson, "The Outlook of the Continental American Colonies on the British West Indies, 1760–1775," *Political Science Quarterly*, 45 (1930): 83–4, and S. H. H. Carrington, "West Indian Opposition to British Policy: Barbadian Politics, 1774–82," *Journal of Caribbean History*, 17 (1982): 30. The assembly of Nova Scotia, one of the weakest, least developed, and most dependent colonies, used the occasion of an address to the Crown not to deny parliamentary authority but to secure Crown recognition of local rights against prerogative power in the colony. See J. Bartlett Brebner, "Nova Scotia's Remedy for the American Revolution," *Canadian Historical Review* 15 (1934): 171–81, and *An Essay on the Present State of the Province of Nova Scotia* [Halifax, 1774] for an exploration of many of the issues that lay behind the assembly's petition.

Just as it had been throughout the colonial era, the integrity of those rights and of the constitutions and assemblies that embodied and protected them was thus, not surprisingly, the central theme of colonial constitutional protest during the 1760s and 1770s.

As Peter S. Onuf has pointed out, this insistence on the "autonomy and integrity" of the several colonial constitutions was a "defense of constitutional multiplicity" within the empire,[42] and the ancient and continuing association of its several separate polities clearly implied the existence of a larger imperial constitution. Though this constitution was obviously based on and expressed the same fundamental principles, it was emphatically not identical to the British constitution. By the 1760s the British constitution had become the constitution of parliamentary supremacy. But the emerging imperial constitution, like the separate constitutions of Britain's many overseas dominions, remained a customary constitution in which, according to the colonial point of view, sovereignty resided not in an all-powerful Parliament but in the Crown, the power of which had been considerably reduced over the previous century by the specific "gains made over the years in the direction of self-determination" by each representative body within the empire.[43]

When in 1774–5 colonial protagonists demanded the establishment of a new "Constitutional Charter" for the empire, what they had in mind was thus one in which these gains would be "recogniz'd and establish'd" on a secure foundation. Determined to be no longer governed "without known and stipulated rules," they were insistent that the "Extent of Power and Right" between metropolis and colonies be "explicitly stipulated" in such a way that, in Hamilton's words, "an *exact equality of constitutional rights*, among all His Majesty's subjects, in the several parts of the empire" would "be uniformly and invariably maintained and

---

[42] Peter S. Onuf, ed., *Maryland and the Empire, 1773: The Antilon-First Citizen Letters* (Baltimore: Johns Hopkins University Press, 1974), 29.

[43] Barbara A. Black, "The Constitution of the Empire: The Case for the Colonists," *University of Pennsylvania Law Review* 124 (1976): 1203.

supported." If, by their constitutions, the colonies had long been enjoined "to make no law[s] repugnant to the law of England," thenceforth England would be "bound ... to make no laws repugnant to the laws and rights of America." And such a parity of rights, they were persuaded, required local autonomy throughout the empire.[44]

To that end, they thought it necessary that Parliament repeal not simply all tax measures but the Declaratory Act and all measures, such as the Massachusetts Government Act and the Quebec Act, by which it had sought to alter the established constitutions of the colonies – measures that would signify both that Parliament had abandoned all pretensions to authority over the colonies and that the several "provincial legislatures" were "the only supreme authorities in our colonies." Moreover, they insisted that the new imperial constitution could not be established by the unilateral action of Parliament, which, having "no true authority for that purpose," would, as John Adams succinctly announced, never be "allow[ed] ... any authority to alter their constitutions at all."[45]

No one in a position of authority in Britain could take these demands seriously. The few "friends of America" in Parliament counseled conciliation and urged the abandonment of all measures that called attention to "the unlimited and illimitable nature of supreme sovereignty." By insisting on establishing what William Dowdeswell called "a most ridiculous superiority," Parliament, they argued, had effectively forced the colonists "to call that sovereignty itself in question" and thereby inadvertently "sophisticate[d] and poison[ed] the very source of government." The colonies, declared Charles James Fox, could only "be governed by ...

[44] Massachusetts Committee of Correspondence to Franklin, Mar. 31, 1774, Franklin to Thomas Cushing, Sept. 3, 1774, and to Joseph Galloway, Feb. 25, 1775, in Labaree et al., eds., *Franklin Papers*, 21: 166–7, 280, 509–10; Hamilton, *Farmer Refuted*, in Syrett and Cooke, eds., *Hamilton Papers*, 1: 163; [John Allen], *The American Alarm, Or the Bostonian's Plea, For the Rights, and Liberties, of the People* (Boston, 1773), 5.

[45] Adams, "Novanglus," in Adams, ed., *Works of John Adams*, 4: 105, 118; "To the Inhabitants of New York," Oct. 6, 1774, in Force, ed., *American Archives*, 4th ser., 1: 826.

affection and interest," and, he warned, no people could be expected to "love laws, by which their rights and liberties are not protected." Only by "rendering it reciprocally and equally advantageous," such people suggested, could "the connection between Great Britain and the colonies be perpetuated."[46]

Repeating the truism that all government was "founded on Opinion, and a Sense of Duty," an earlier analyst had quoted David Hume to the same effect: "Wherever the supreme Power by a Law, or positive Prescription, shocks *an Opinion regarded as fundamental*," Hume had written, "*the Principle is subverted by which Power is established, and Obedience can be no longer hoped for*." "The *first* law of every government," the "*supreme law* of every society," such colonial writers as James Wilson and Alexander Hamilton had declared in applying to the imperial crisis one of the central tenets of the new Scottish common-sense philosophy, was "its own happiness." Burke, building on the same theme, told Parliament, that, if "sovereignty and freedom" could not "be reconciled" in such a way as to make the colonists happy, they would not long hesitate to "cast your sovereignty in your face." The metropolis would then have to resort to arms to enforce parliamentary sovereignty. But the idea of governing such populous and extensive territories by force struck many metropolitan observers as entirely "visionary and chimerical." "That Country which is kept by power," said one MP, was "in danger of being lost every day," and Isaac Barre predicted that Parliament would never be able to "reduce to practice" the rights that it fancied it held "in theory."[47]

---

[46] Burke's speech, Apr. 19, 1774, Dowdeswell's speech, Apr. 15, 1774, in Cobbett and Hansard, eds., *Parliamentary History*, 17: 1198, 1265; Fox's speeches, May 26, June 8, 1774, in Cavendish, *Debates on the House of Commons in the Year 1774*, 62, 246; *A Letter to the Right Honourable The Earl of H - -b - - h* (London, 1769), 111.

[47] *Candid Observations on Two Pamphlets Lately Published* (Barbados, 1766), 33–4; Burke's speech, Apr. 19, 1774, Cavendish's speech, Mar. 14, 1774, in Cobbett and Hansard, eds., *Parliamentary History*, 17: 1169, 1265; Barre's speech, May 31, 1774, in Cavendish, *Debates on the House of Commons in the Year 1774*, 89; Shipley, *Sermon*, in Smith, comp., *English Defenders of American Freedom*, 36; Hamilton, *Farmer Refuted*, in Syrett and Cooke, eds., *Hamilton Papers*, 1: 90; Wilson, *Considerations*, in McCloskey, ed., *Works of Wilson*, 2: 723.

Regarding any diminution of parliamentary sovereignty as a prelude to the eventual loss of control of the colonies that seemed to be so intimately associated with Britain's rise to world power, the vast majority of the metropolitan political nation found it impossible to heed such warnings. Besides, from the perspective of Britain's own internal constitutional development during the previous century, colonial theories about the organization of the empire seemed dangerously retrograde. By placing the resources of Ireland and the colonies directly in the hands of the Crown and beyond the reach of Parliament, those theories appeared to strike directly at the root of the legislative supremacy that, for them, was the primary legacy of the Glorious Revolution.

In 1774, the Coercive Acts, which Johnstone denounced in Parliament as that "species of political phrenzy," had produced an astonishing union among the colonies. Though they were "divided in customs, manners, climate, and communication," the colonies were so alarmed that those measures would deprive them of "every essential privilege" that, as the Massachusetts Committee of Correspondence wrote Franklin in the spring of 1774, "the whole Continent" was united "in Sentiment and ... Measures." Already, in the initial response to those acts, a few writers, notably Thomas Jefferson and William Henry Drayton, had pointed out that many of the most egregious colonial grievances were attributable directly to the Crown. By thus raising the old question of the extent of the king's authority in the colonies, a question that had been given new force by the many local controversies of the early 1770s, they thereby both issued a new challenge to the Crown's claim for "more extensive [prerogative] in America, than it" was "by law limited [to] in England" and, implicitly at least, questioned the wisdom of the emerging argument that a continuing connection with Britain through the Crown would provide an adequate basis for the security of colonial rights.[48]

[48] *Gov. Johnston's Speech*, 8; Massachusetts Committee of Correspondence to Franklin, Mar. 31, 1774, in Labaree et al., eds., *Franklin Papers*, 21: 165–6; Jefferson, *Summary View*, in Boyd, ed., *Jefferson Papers*, 1: 129–35; Drayton, *Letter from "Freeman,"* in Gibbes, ed., *Documentary History*, 1: 17.

As it became increasingly clear in 1775–6 that Parliament would not abandon its "idle ideas of superiority" and that George III was every bit as committed to the idea of parliamentary sovereignty as was the rest of the metropolitan political nation, more colonials began to think of a new course of political action that included both independence from Britain and the creation of "an AMERICAN COMMONWEALTH." Notwithstanding the old conviction that every colony was "so fond of" its own "peculiarities" that they could "never unite into one state," they more and more came to the conclusion that there was no other way that was "likely to answer the great purpose of preserving our liberties." Whether independence would be the first step toward the establishment of a viable union that would enable them to resolve the problem that had brought the British Empire to grief, the problem of how in an extended polity authority should be distributed between metropolis and colonies was still an open question when they opted for independence in July 1776.[49]

Since the mid-1970s, several legal historians, including especially Barbara Black, John Phillip Reid, and Thomas C. Grey, have examined the legitimacy of the colonial case in the constitutional debates of the 1760s and 1770s. As Black has pointed out, "twentieth century scholarship" has been "virtually unanimous in holding that," in this debate, "Americans … were 'wrong on the law,'" that, in Reid's words, "American constitutional pretensions" should not be "tak[en] seriously because the constitution was what Parliament declared it to be." But Reid, Black, Grey, and others offer a powerful case against this conventional view. They argue that, so far from being right, that view is "really an incorrect conclusion of law."[50]

[49] Cavendish's speech, Mar. 14, 1774, in Cobbett and Hansard, eds., *Parliamentary History*, 17: 1169; "Z," in *Providence Gazette*, Oct. 16, 1773; Wm. Pitkin to William Samuel Johnson, June 6, 1768, in "The Trumbull Papers," Massachusetts Historical Society, *Collections*, 5th ser., 9 (Boston, 1885): 283.

[50] Black, "Constitution of Empire," 1157; John Phillip Reid, *In Defiance of the Law: The Standing Army Controversy, the Two Constitutions, and the Coming of the American Revolution* (Chapel Hill: University of North Carolina Press, 1981), 168–9, and "The Irrelevance of the Declaration," in Hendrik B. Hartog, ed., *Law in the American Revolution and the*

These scholars do not deny that London authorities thought "of the governance of their empire in terms of [a] ... unicentric power applying one law laid down by parliament." But they do contend, as has been argued in this work, that the "imperial constitution of eighteenth-century British North America was not [nearly] as precise as today's historians insist [that] it must have been" and that it by no means "furnish[ed] definitive answers" about the scope of Parliament's authority within the empire. The doctrine of parliamentary supremacy, they argue, was still sufficiently new as not yet to be fully understood or accepted even within England itself, and the "old idea of a ... fixed constitution standing above and limiting the working institutions of government ... [still] remained a respectable idea in England in the 1760s." In fact, as Reid remarks, the very concept of the constitution was still so imprecise that "definition [was] more a matter of personal usage than of judicial certainty," and it was still possible even "to accept the new constitution of parliamentary supremacy while clinging to the old constitution of fixed restraints."[51]

In this fluid and unsettled situation, it is scarcely satisfactory to dismiss the American view as "an archaism." As Reid explains, the fact that "the seventeenth-century constitution of customary rights would never be reestablished as the constitution of Great Britain does not prove that the eighteenth-century constitution of parliamentary supremacy had been established in the North American colonies." Rather, Reid

---

Revolution in the Law (New York: New York University Press, 1981), 60. This literature is explored in more detail in Jack P. Greene, "From the Perspective of Law: Context and Legitimacy in the Origins of the American Revolution. A Review Essay," *South Atlantic Quarterly* 85 (1986), 56–77.

[51] John P. Reid, *In a Defiant Stance: The Conditions of Law in Massachusetts Bay, the Irish Comparison, and the Coming of the American Revolution* (University Park, Pa.: Pennsylvania State University Press, 1977), 70; Reid, *In Defiance of the Law*, 25, 33, 36, 205; Reid, "The Ordeal by Law of Thomas Hutchinson," *New York University Law Review* 49 (1974): 602; Black, "Constitution of Empire," 1210–11; Thomas C. Grey, "Origin of the Unwritten Constitution: Fundamental Law in American Revolutionary Thought," *Stanford Law Review* 30 (1978): 858.

and Black both argue that the colonies operated under the aegis not of the British constitution but of an emerging imperial constitution that rested on solid legal foundations, the most important of which was the doctrine of usage.[52]

The primary "source of authority underlying both the seventeenth-century English constitution, and the contemporary American constitution[s] that colonial whigs were defending against the eighteenth-century British Constitution," writes Reid, "was custom." In this argument, Reid is seconding a point made in 1750 by Thomas Rutherforth: that the "content of a nation's constitution" was largely "a question of fact, to be determined by considering the history and customs of a people." To a very important extent, the American case ultimately rested on the contention, first asserted during the Stamp Act crisis, that both "interference in local affairs by Parliament through legislation" and "direct parliamentary taxation" were "contrary to the principles of the contemporary" colonial constitutions, as those "constitution[s] had been established by long custom and as" that custom "was currently sanctioned by accepted usage."[53]

As historians have long recognized, evidence for these claims is by no means insubstantial. During the eighteenth century, as Black notes and as has been argued at length in this volume, Britain's various overseas dominions had been "much, if not equally, blessed by the extension of the benefits of government by consent." In theory, the Crown's prerogative remained extensive in the colonies. Through a combination

---

[52] John P. Reid, "The Apparatus of Constitutional Advocacy and the American Revolution: A Review of Five Books," *New York University Law Review* 42 (1967): 194; Reid, "In the First Line of Defense: The Colonial Charters, the Stamp Act Debate, and the Coming of the American Revolution," ibid., 51 (1976): 177, 208–9, 211; Black, "Constitution of Empire," 1203.

[53] Reid, *In Defiance of the Law*, 79–80, 160; Reid, "In an Inherited Way: English Constitutional Rights, the Stamp Act Debates, and the Coming of the American Revolution," *Southern California Law Review* 49 (1976): 1127; Reid, "In Accordance with Usage: The Authority of Custom, the Stamp Act Debate, and the Coming of the American Revolution," *Fordham Law Review* 45 (1976): 341;'Grey, "Origins of the Unwritten Constitution," 863.

of statutes and custom, however, the assemblies in most colonies had managed largely to neutralize royal power. To an extraordinary degree, in fact, royal government in the colonies had come more and more to mean "government by the elected representatives of the people."[54]

The corollary to this diminution of royal power was the failure of Parliament to take an expansive role in colonial affairs. Precisely because Parliament thus played only a limited, "essentially conciliar" role in colonial matters, the fact "that the prerogative was at its height in the colonies reinforced the sense of" the colonies "as the king's dominions." As a result, Black observes, the "reduction of the king's power by English law, as well as by the ingenuity and effort of the colonial assemblies [,]... irresistibly [suggested] the reduction in law of all external power" – that of Parliament as well as that of the king – and thereby gave legitimacy to the American claim that rights established through custom "were beyond modification by Parliament" or the king, either one. As far as the colonists were concerned, then, "the supremacy of Parliament," as Reid puts it, "had not yet been established as part of their customary constitution[s] and, now that the Stamp Act [had] exposed the danger[s] of parliamentary supremacy, it would never be established," at least not among those colonies that left the empire in 1776.[55]

Most historians, including some earlier legal historians, have treated the disparity between the actualities of colonial self-government and metropolitan theory as a distinction between "fact and law" or, in the case of the present writer, between fact and theory. But, as the work of Black, Reid, and Grey makes clear, such distinctions seriously underestimate the legal force of custom in English law. The supposed "tension between fact and law," Black states, was actually a "tension within law." In English jurisprudence, as Reid explains,

---

[54] Black, "Constitution of Empire," 1193, 1198, 1200, 1203; Reid, "Ordeal by Law of Thomas Hutchinson," 599; Reid, "In Accordance with Usage," 366.
[55] Reid, *In Defiance of the Law*, 162, 169; Reid, "In Accordance with Usage," 357, 364; Black, "Constitution of Empire," 1202.

custom obtained "the force of law by a combination of time and precedent. Whatever had been done from time immemorial in a community was legal; whatever had been abstained from was illegal." "Historical fact was the source of constitutional custom," and, according to contemporary English practice well into the late eighteenth century, "rights established by custom and proven by time were legal rights" that, as Grey notes, were "judicially enforceable, even against the highest legislative and executive organs of government."[56]

The colonists, Grey observes, did not condemn British policies as "merely ... unjust or untraditional or even 'unconstitutional' in the extra-legal sense of that term." They denounced them "as *illegal* – and *the law*" they invoked "was the unwritten fundamental law of reasonable custom and customary reason that made up the British constitution." Historians who have treated "custom as a source of or authority for 'law' that in fact" was "not law, or" was "something less than law" have thus been wrong. As Black insists, colonial "gains made over the years in the direction of self-determination" through usage were "gains made in and by law," and the "reduction of the king's power and the increase in the representative dimension of the imperial constitution" were developments "in law [as well] as in fact."[57]

These legal historians thus underline the validity of the colonial argument that there was more than one constitution in the early modern British Empire. Although by the 1760s the British constitution had become the constitution of parliamentary supremacy, the emerging imperial constitution, like the separate constitutions of Britain's many overseas dominions, remained a customary constitution. As Rutherforth noted in 1750, usage that had "obtained in any civil society [from] ... time immemorial ... may be presumed to have obtained

[56] Black, "Constitution of Empire," 1202; Reid, *In Defiance of the Law*, 81, 160, 165; Reid, "In Accordance with Usage," 356–7; Reid, "Irrelevance of the Declaration," 61; Grey, "Origins of the Unwritten Constitution," 850.

[57] Grey, "Origins of the Unwritten Constitution," 850, 853–4, 890; Reid, "In Accordance with Usage," 344; Black, "Constitution of Empire," 1203, 1210.

with its consent." And just as, in Rutherforth's words, "whatever is consented to by a civil society, becomes a law of such society," so it was a hallowed English constitutional principle that nothing could become law without such consent.[58]

This principle lay at the heart of the familiar idea of a constitutional contract between the ruled and their rulers. According to that idea, neither party could change the contract without the consent of the other. No political and constitutional changes, in short, could take effect without the consent of all concerned parties as indicated either by longstanding acceptance through usage or by a formal legislative enactment by a representative body empowered to give such consent. Because historians have tended to trace the colonists' use of this argument to the writings of John Locke and various other natural law theorists, they have mostly failed to appreciate, as Reid writes, that it had also been "a central dogma in English and British constitutional law since time immemorial." Contract theory did not therefore rest only on philosophical grounds but, like the doctrine of usage, was also deeply rooted in "customary [English] jurisprudence" and had firm legal standing.[59]

Recognition of the legal status of the doctrines of consent and contract tends to give still further legal weight to the colonial argument that "parliament and the ministry in London, not they, [had] defied the ancient law" and attempted to violate their "old rights" by altering their "customary constitution[s]." At least before 1774, they admitted that it was legal for Parliament to regulate colonial trade because, as a quid pro quo for protection, they had through usage "'chearfully' consented" to such regulations. But they vehemently argued that it was illegal for Parliament to tax the colonies or otherwise interfere in unaccustomed ways with

---

[58] Grey, "Origins of the Unwritten Constitution," 863–4; Reid, "Irrelevance of the Declaration," 65.
[59] Reid, "Irrelevance of the Declaration," 72; Reid, "'In Our Contracted Sphere': The Constitutional Contract, the Stamp Act Crisis, and the Coming of the American Revolution," *Columbia Law Review* 76 (1976): 22.

their internal affairs because they had never given their consent to such exertions of parliamentary power. Through both formal parliamentary enactments in the wake of the Glorious Revolution and usage during succeeding decades, British people in Britain had obviously consented to the doctrine of parliamentary supremacy. In the colonies, however, neither the people at large through custom nor their representatives in the several colonial legislatures had given such consent. For Parliament to attempt to bind the colonies without that consent was nothing less than "a unilateral breach of an agreement that could properly be changed only by bilateral negotiation."[60]

However strong their case in law, the colonial claim that the imperial constitution was one of "principled limitation" by which they were guaranteed "government by consent" found little support in Britain. There, constitutional theory was running in an entirely different direction, one, in Black's words, that "in theory involved the obliteration of every trace of principled limitation from law and its relegation to the precarious plane of practice." Once metropolitan officials had subjected the colonial claim to the test of this new theory, any hope of winning a favorable hearing for that claim in London was "pretty much lost."[61]

But their refusal to take these claims seriously does not mean that metropolitan officials were "right about the law." As these legal historians have so cogently stressed, constitutional arrangements within the British Empire were far from precise, and each side could marshal effective legal arguments on behalf of its position. Nor, as Reid emphasizes, was there within the empire any "tribunal to which [such] a constitutional dispute could be taken for resolution except parliament itself – the very institution against which the colonists were

[60] Reid, "Irrelevance of the Declaration," 83; Reid, "In Our Contracted Sphere," 31, 40; Reid, "In a Defensive Rage: The Uses of the Mob, the Justification in Law, and the Coming of the American Revolution," *New York University Law Review* 49 (1974): 1087; Black, "Constitution of Empire," 1202–3.

[61] Reid, "In Accordance with Usage," 344; Black, "Constitution of Empire," 1203, 1210.

contending." In this unsettled situation, questions "of sovereignty and legitimacy" were by no means as clear as they were said to be in London and as so many later historians have assumed. The legal question of "whether usage was … the authority for the [imperial] constitution," the primary issue "dividing American Whigs from their fellow subjects in Great Britain" during the 1760s and 1770s, was still very much open to debate.[62]

The picture of the prerevolutionary constitutional debate that emerges from this legal history literature is thus one in which the quarrel was not over a right and a wrong interpretation of the constitution but a "struggle … between different levels of government," each of which had a legitimate constitutional case. By no means yet a modern unitary state, the early modern British Empire was directed by a "multicentric" rather than a "unicentric … authority." Imperial institutions in the colonies had little coercive power and depended for their effectiveness on the consent of local populations. Authority within the empire was dispersed into the hands of authoritative, powerful, and "largely autonomous local institutions." Not dependent for their effectiveness "on the support or the acquiescence of a central authority" and highly "resistant to centralized control," these institutions were regarded, both by those who composed them and those whom they served, as largely "independent recipients of constitutional power and authority." In this "diffuse and decentralized" political entity, local institutions invariably determined the nature of law and the constitution as much as did authorities at the center.[63]

Thus, in regard to extended polities in the era before the development of the modern consolidated state in the wake of

[62] Reid, "In a Defensive Rage," 1063; Reid, *In a Defiant Stance*, 162; Reid, "A Lawyer Acquitted: John Adams and the Boston Massacre Trials," *American Journal of Legal History* 18 (1974): 191; Reid, "In Accordance with Usage," 344.

[63] Reid, *In a Defiant Stance*, 2, 161; Reid, "In a Defensive Rage," 1091; Hendrik B. Hartog, "Losing the World of the Massachusetts Whig," in Hartog, ed., *Law in the American Revolution*, 146–7, 152–3, 160.

the French Revolution, it should not be assumed that the perspective of the center is the correct or even the dominant one. In a polity like the early modern British Empire where local power and traditions are strong in the peripheries and the authority and ideology of the center are weak, local institutions and customs may be at least as important in determining existing legal and constitutional arrangements as those of the center, and the perspective of the center is likely to be partisan. In the particular case of the British Empire at the time of the American Revolution, the antiquity of the notion of a customary imperial constitution of principled limitation, the strength of local institutions, the comparative recency of the doctrine of parliamentary supremacy, and the weakness of metropolitan authority in the colonies combined to make the perspective of the center a "tory perspective." Perhaps even more important, the failure of the metropolis to establish the legitimacy of its perspective in the colonies renders it invalid when applied to legal and constitutional arrangements within the empire as a whole.[64]

When Thomas Jefferson and his colleagues in the Second Continental Congress produced the Declaration of Independence in the summer of 1776, they made extensive use of natural rights theory, and in that way the Declaration represented something of a departure from the impressive political tracts and state papers they had been producing over the previous twelve years. Natural rights theory had not been absent from that literature, but it had never been more than complementary to their principal argument, which rested on law. Specifically, that argument, following logically from the colonists' own heritage of legal and constitutional thought over the previous century and a half, was largely founded on the English jurisprudential conception of government as limited government and of the British constitution as a constitution in which law set boundaries on the discretion or will of monarchs, judges, and legislators – a conception that, even after the rise of the doctrine of parliamentary supremacy, still had much vitality in Britain itself. Indeed, much of this literature was the work of colonial lawyers. Richard Bland, James Otis, Daniel Dulany, John Dickinson, James Wilson, Thomas Jefferson, John Adams, Alexander Hamilton, Charles Carroll of Carrollton, James Iredell – these were only the most prominent lawyers who contributed to the colonial case. Even more impressively, lay leaders, merchants, printers, and planters, including Stephen Hopkins, Benjamin Franklin, Samuel Adams, William Hicks, and William Henry Drayton, displayed a deep familiarity with the common culture of legal and constitutional thought that made the entire English-speaking world a single discursive community.

As the controversies of the 1760s and 1770s dramatically underline, that world did not always agree on the definition of crucial concepts, but it did possess a common vocabulary. Throughout those controversies, colonial spokesmen demonstrated extraordinary learning in legal and constitutional matters, conducting their case like a common-law litigation in the court of Anglophone public opinion. Displaying a tough law-mindedness, they had no doubt that the law, as they knew it from their metropolitan heritage and their own experience, could be marshaled in their favor and, for that reason, never hesitated to make law the foundation for their view of the constitutional organization of the empire.

EPILOGUE: LEGACY

For a century and a half before the American Revolution, metropolitans and colonials had wrestled with the difficult question of how, in the extended polity of the British overseas empire, to allocate authority in such a way as to preserve the British rights of colonists in the distant polities in America while providing a measure of central direction for the empire as a whole. Either explicitly or implicitly, this essentially legal and constitutional question was at the heart of the tensions that beset relations between colonies and Crown before and after 1763. When people on both sides of the Atlantic for the first time confronted it in a sustained and systematic way, between 1764 and 1776, they developed radically divergent views that ultimately led to the secession of thirteen of the North American colonies from the empire.

As James Madison later noted, for most colonial leaders, "the fundamental principle of the Revolution was, that the Colonies were coordinate members with each other and with Great Britain, of an empire united by a common executive sovereign, but not united by any common legislative sovereign." Maintaining that legislative authority was distributed broadly and equally among the several corporate entities that composed the empire, the colonists insisted both that the legislative power of "each American Parliament" was as "complete" as that of the British Parliament and that "the royal prerogative was in force in each Colony by virtue of its acknowledging the King for its executive magistrate, as it was in Great Britain by virtue of a like acknowledgement there." More than any other development, Madison correctly observed, "a denial of these principles by Great Britain, and the assertion of them by America, produced the Revolution."[1]

But separation from Britain by no means resolved this ancient question. To the contrary, it made it even more difficult by linking it inextricably with the equally vexing problem of how to forge a viable political and constitutional union out of thirteen distinct polities that had previously been tied together only by their common relationship to the British Empire through the emerging imperial constitution. To be sure, some colonial leaders had been considering a continental union since the Albany Congress in 1754. On several occasions during the prerevolutionary debates, some analysts had proposed establishing "a general legislature … for the whole British empire in America, composed of delegates from each colony" to which "the several provincial legislatures would be necessarily subordinated." But the first general American constitution began to grow up around the institution of the Continental Congress beginning with the first meeting of that body in the fall of 1774. Like the metropolitan, colonial, and imperial constitutions of the empire, it was, in the beginning, very largely a customary constitution.[2]

Whether a more formal constitutional union could be achieved and what form it should take were two of the most important constitutional questions confronting American resistance leaders throughout the early years of war and independence. Far from being an inevitable development, the

[1] Madison, "Notes on the Resolutions," 1799–1800, in Gaillard Hunt, ed., *The Writings of James Madison*, 9 vols. (New York: G. P. Putnams, 1900–1910), 6:373.
[2] See F. L. to *Pennsylvania Journal*, March 13, 1766, in Edmund S. Morgan, ed., *Prologue to Revolution: Sources and Documents on the Stamp Act Crisis, 1764–1766* (Chapel Hill: University of Nortrh Carolina Press, 1959), 91.

fabrication of such a union was highly problematic. From very early on, however, it had been apparent that the permanent establishment of such a union and the perpetuation of the new United States would be heavily dependent on the resolution of the old problem of the allocation of authority in an extended polity composed of many distinct corporate entities.

Military exigencies prevented more than a cursory discussion of this problem during the initial years of the union. "In the interval between the commencement of the Revolution and the final ratification of" the Articles of Confederation in 1781, observed Madison in 1800, "the nature and extent of the Union was determined by the circumstances of the crisis, rather than by any accurate delineation of the general authority." The states retained full jurisdiction over their internal affairs, but throughout the early war, power flowed into the central government. Considering itself "as vested with full power *to preserve the republic from harm*," Congress, as Alexander Hamilton later noted, performed "many of the highest acts of sovereignty, which were always chearfully submitted to [by the states] – the declaration of independence, the declaration of war, the levying an army, creating a navy, emitting money, making alliances with foreign powers." To an important degree, the Articles of Confederation represented an attempt to codify this situation by investing Congress with broad general powers and leaving the several states in charge of all matters of local concern.[3]

But the Articles provided no mechanism by which Congress could force the states to comply with its authority, and as the war dragged on, power tended to drain away from the Congress to the state governments. Moreover, as the war wound down and the necessity for united action against an external power correspondingly diminished in 1781–2, this process was accelerated. In the early modern British Empire, the peripheries had found themselves on the defensive against

---

[3] Madison, "Notes on the Resolutions," 6; 375; Hamilton to James Duane, [Sept. 3, 1780], in Harolde C. Syrett and Jacob E. Cooke, eds., *The Papers of Alexander Hamilton*, 26 vols. (New York: Columbia University Press, 1961–79), 2: 401.

the aggressive power of the center; under the Articles, it was precisely the opposite: The center found itself without sufficient authority to preserve the general interests of the United States against the power of the several states.[4]

Such an arrangement was, perhaps, the logical outcome of colonial constitutional arguments between 1764 and 1776. From the mid-1760s through 1787, "the emergence of political community itself as the locus of authority" had been, as Peter Onuf has put it, "the central theme of American constitutionalism." "While independence was accompanied by the formal inversion of 'sovereignty' above – in the king-in-parliament – to below – in the community at large – the relation of the [colonial] assembly [or, after 1776, the state legislature] to [the] community," Onuf points out, "was not essentially altered." Through the Revolution and beyond, those legislatures "continued to defend and guarantee local rights" as well as to exert broad authority over all matters of local concern.[5]

Winning independence in 1783 thus effectively secured for Americans the original goal of the Revolution – local control over local affairs – but this achievement had not been accompanied by an effort even explicitly to confront, much less resolve, "the underlying theoretical and practical problem of how to combine" the individual states "into an effective union." The Revolution, in short, had left the "organization of power in the United States" in a thoroughly ambiguous state. The effort to resolve this ambiguity, to solve the ancient problem of how, in an extended polity, to distribute authority between the center and the peripheries, would be the primary concern of American constitutional thought during the 1780s and during the national debate over the nature and structure of the new federal union promulgated in 1787–8.[6]

[4] Peter S. Onuf, *The Origins of the Federal Republic: Jurisdictional Controversies in the United States, 1775–1787* (Philadelphia: University of Pennsylvania Press, 1983), 201.
[5] Peter S. Onuf, ed., *Maryland and the Empire: The Antilon – First Citizens Letters* (Baltimore: Johns Hopkins University Press, 1974), 38–9.
[6] Onuf, *Origins of the Federal Republic*, 154, 158.

INDEX

Made in the USA
Coppell, TX
01 June 2020